Elements of Quality Online Education:

Into the Mainstream

Edited by *John Bourne & Janet C. Moore*

THE SLOAN CONSORTIUM
A Consortium of Institutions and Organizations
Committed to Quality Online Education

Volume 5 in the Sloan-C Series

Cover designs by Leighton Ige, Olin College.

Copyright ©2004 by Sloan-C™

All rights reserved. Published 2004

Printed in the United States of America

0 9 8 7 6 5 4 3 2 1

International Standard Book Number 0-9677741-6-0

Elements of Quality Online Education:

Into the Mainstream, Volume 5 in the Sloan-C Series

This is the fifth volume in the annual Sloan-C series of case studies on quality education online. In 1999, 2000, 2001, 2002, and 2003, the Sloan Foundation selected expert contributors to report on work in progress and to collaborate on research of importance to asynchronous learning networks. Each volume publishes contributions in the form of documented, peer-reviewed scholarly studies of learning and cost effectiveness, access, and faculty and student satisfaction.

Other titles available in this series:

Elements of Quality Online Education: Practice and Direction
Volume 4 ISBN 0-9677741-5-2
Elements of Quality Online Education
Volume 3 ISBN 0-9677741-2-8
Online Education: Learning Effectiveness, Faculty Satisfaction, and Cost Effectiveness
Volume 2 ISBN 0-9677741-1-X
Online Education: Learning Effectiveness and Faculty Satisfaction
Volume 1 ISBN 0-9677741-0-1

This book was made possible by a grant from the Alfred P. Sloan Foundation.

SCOLE
Sloan Center for OnLine Education
at Olin and Babson Colleges

Sloan-C has its administrative home at the Sloan Center for OnLine Education (SCOLE) at Olin and Babson Colleges. SCOLE has been established as a center that spans the two campuses of Olin College and Babson College. SCOLE's purpose is to support the activities of the Sloan Consortium, a consortium of higher-education providers sharing the common bonds of understanding, supporting and delivering education via asynchronous learning networks (ALNs). With the mission of providing learning to anyone anywhere, SCOLE seeks to provide new levels of learning capability to people seeking higher and continuing education. For more information about Sloan-C, visit www.sloan-c.org.

For more information about Olin and Babson Colleges, visit www.olin.edu and www.babson.edu.

Elements of Quality Online Education: Into the Mainstream

Volume 5 in the Sloan-C Series

Contents

INTRODUCTION

Frank Mayadas
President, Sloan-C

John Bourne
Executive Director, Sloan-C

Janet C. Moore
Chief Learning Officer, Sloan-C

Sponsored by the Alfred P. Sloan Foundation, and hosted by the University of Massachusetts Lowell, the fifth annual Sloan-C summer research workshop met at the Babson College Center for Executive Education in Needham, Massachusetts. Each year, the three-day workshop brings together education leaders from schools and organizations with diverse perspectives and a common goal of making quality education accessible in a wide range of disciplines. In 2003, representatives attended from:

- The Alfred P. Sloan Foundation
- American Distance Education Consortium
- Babson College
- Brigham Young University
- The City University of New York
- Drexel University
- Eastern Connecticut State University
- Empire State College
- Franklin W. Olin College of Engineering
- Hunter College
- Institute for Healthcare Improvement
- Kent State University
- Liberty Mutual
- Maricopa Community Colleges
- Microsoft - Education Solutions Group
- The National Labor College (George Meany Center for Labor Studies)
- New England College of Finance
- New Jersey Institute of Technology
- Pace University
- Pennsylvania State University
- Rensselaer Polytechnic Institute
- Rochester Institute of Technology
- Saint Joseph's College of Maine
- Skidmore College
- The Sloan Consortium
- Southern Regional Education Board
- State University of New York
- Stevens Institute of Technology
- University of Calgary
- University of Central Florida
- University of Hawaii
- University of Illinois
- University of Maryland University College
- University of Massachusetts Lowell

The summer research workshop convened shortly after the release of *Sizing the Opportunity* [i], a Sloan-C national survey of higher education leaders. The report discovered that leaders believe the quality, scale and breadth of online learning will continue its growth and transformative effects, resulting, within the next three years, in online learning outcomes that surpass learning outcomes in other modes. With these expectations in mind, the summer research workshop participants reviewed each others' work in progress on effective methods, needs, and the art of the possible.

The workshop brought forward many issues facing the online education community. These issues include defining a common language, combining online and traditional education, achieving scale, managing costs and sharing resources, identifying best practices and understanding new roles. The workshop papers that make up this volume address major challenges with respect to student satisfaction, learning effectiveness, assessment and evaluation, and blended learning.

In the ten years since the inception of the Sloan Consortium and the tenth anniversary of the Web browser, the field of online learning has entered the mainstream of higher education, making online learning a core ingredient of tomorrow's educational paradigms. In fact, now that digital natives are coming of age, on-ground and online education can no longer stand apart. The blending of the two delivery modes is continuous and unstoppable. Moreover, increasing demands for wide choice suggest that the blended agenda presses rapidly into new realms of inquiry. Thus, the title of this collection, the fifth volume in the Sloan-C series on quality is *Elements of Quality Online Education: Into the Mainstream.*

Student Satisfaction

In this volume, the studies on Student Satisfaction recognize that significant populations remain underserved. Yet asynchronous learning networks (ALNs) are widening access by easing some of the constraints of place-based, synchronous delivery, so that more students can achieve satisfaction and success.

- In "Promoting Student Support and Satisfaction in Online Learning," Meg Benke, Tana Bishop, Claudine SchWeber, Carol Scarafiotti, and Melody Thompson call for rethinking institutional processes and practices that have been designed for traditional learners in traditional classrooms, providing an array of model support services.

- In "Critical Factors in Student Satisfaction and Success: Facilitating Student Role Adjustment in Online Communities of Inquiry," Randy Garrison and Martha Cleveland-Innes define the relationships between student satisfaction and student success, noting that asynchronous learning networks (ALNs) offer opportunities to develop higher order learning in ways not possible before now. Explaining the significant ways that online students must adjust their traditional roles, they examine the implications for facilitating success and satisfaction.

- In "Enhancing Student Satisfaction through Faculty Development: The Importance of Teaching Presence," Peter Shea describes SUNY's ongoing study of student and faculty satisfaction, showing how research and best practices inform longitudinal assessments to continuously improve teaching, cognitive and social presence.

Learning Effectiveness

The studies on Learning Effectiveness share an emphasis on the ways that ALN exceeds the "no significant difference" minimum standard for learning outcomes.

- In "Learning Online: A Review of Current Research on Issues of Interface, Teaching Presence, and Learner Characteristics," Karen Swan presents new research insights and identifies areas for exploring how ALN can reach beyond the "as good as" benchmark, identifying specific ways online learning excels.

- In "The Psychology of E-Learning," Zheng Yan summarizes multidisciplinary psychological approaches to the study of online learning and learners, calling for greater collaboration among practitioners.

- In "Using Adaptive Hypermedia to Match Web Presentation to Learning Styles," Michael Danchak explains how the Kolb learning cycle incorporates learning and teaching preferences, enabling people to expand their own cognitive styles as they proceed through a range of learning activities built into course design.

- In "ALN Research: What We Know and What We Need to Know about Contextual Influences," Starr Roxanne Hiltz, J. Ben Arbaugh, Raquel Benbunan Fich, and Peter Shea examine the variables that affect quality in online learning—technology, organizational setting, the instructor, and the student—and call for empirical research that is multi-course, multi-disciplinary, multi-institutional, multi-cultural and multi-national to guide the development, design, and scalability of online learning.

Blended Environments

The studies on blending, combining face-to-face and online methods for learning, offer rich possibilities for what many see as the best of both learning modes.

- In "Three ALN Modalities: An Institutional Perspective," Charles Dziuban, Joel Hartman, Patsy Moskal, Steven Sorg, and Barbara Truman describe the growth of online learning at the University of Central Florida (UCF). So pervasive have web-enhanced courses become that UCF students view them as commonplace, and so the special designation "E" course will disappear from UCF's 2004 course schedule.

- In "Using ALN in a Blended Environment," John Harwood and Gary Miller describe transformative effects on The Pennsylvania State University, including pedagogy that is active, inquiry-based, resource-centered, and collaborative, serving community, service and internship learning.

- In "Model-Driven Design," Stephen Laster shares Babson College's systematic approach to implementing blended learning. The highly orchestrated design shows how to develop and deliver curricula that teach complex concepts and skills with multi-disciplinary input, with continuous refinement, and with technologies and traditional educational activities that achieve clear learning outcomes.

Assessment

The studies on assessment go to the core of the Sloan-C quality framework and its emphasis on continuous quality improvement by tracking progress towards goals.

- In "Assessment: Challenges and Opportunities in Online Learning," Anthony Picciano identifies questions helpful for assessing online programs and courses from internal and external perspectives.

- In "More Art than Science: The Postsecondary Assessment Movement Today," Barbara Wright provides a useful distinction between assessment and evaluation and shows that meaningful quality assessment measure what matters-- the demonstration of higher order thinking.

- In "Achieving Scale and Quality in Online Education through Transformative Assessment," Jacqueline Moloney, Anthony Picciano and Steve Tello explain how the University of

Massachusetts Lowell (UML) inaugurated assessment measures in its rapidly growing online programs. Using the Sloan-C quality elements in its assessment framework, UML sees the positive, transformative effects of assessment throughout an institution that is focusing on "how to improve the quality of learning while expanding the program and the return on investment to the campus."

- In "Assessment: Online Learning a Faculty Perspective," Anthony Picciano shows how assessment activities in a course on educational leadership led to faculty planning to ensure that student interaction remains high, encouraging community building and promoting social presence through pedagogy.

The studies in this volume suggest many ways that higher education envisions the future. In times of "profound, rapid, and discontinuous change" [ii], what does it take to solve the challenges of online, blended and face-to-face education in higher education? Certainly, as the summer research workshops demonstrate, a clear case is made for collaboration among institutions. Further, online collaboration can greatly exceed what is traditionally accomplished through ad hoc exchanges in face-to-face conferences and workshops. Thus, each year, Sloan-C expands the summer research workshop to online research workshops so that people can develop thinking and make collaboration really work.

In the now burgeoning online learning community, we have opportunities to use what has been learned about collaborative work (asynchronous and synchronous) to address challenges in higher education. Although we might tend to work in silos of inquiry, today's information infrastructures can make cross-world collaboration as easy as institutional small-group collaborations. When knowledge is organized, ordered, and used by everyone participating continuously, such interaction can advance the field much more rapidly than traditional communications media.

As a consortium of researchers, educators, administrators, and corporate groups, Sloan-C seeks to advance the field of online education for no less than the good of humanity, constructing new knowledge upon which legacies will be built. The commonplace creation of "swift knowledge" is within reach. With your support, higher education will become "an ordinary part of everyday life."

Sloan-C is a consortium of accredited colleges and universities and organizations dedicated to improving the quality, scale and breadth of online education continuously, so that education will become a part of everyday life, accessible and affordable for anyone, anywhere, at any time, in a wide variety of disciplines.

You are welcome to join Sloan-C: http://www.sloan-c.org

---

[i] *Sizing the Opportunity: The Quality and Extent of Online Education in the United States, 2002 and 2003* is available at http://www.sloan-c.org/resources/survey.asp.

[ii] *Preparing for the Revolution: Information Technology and the Future of the Research University.* National Research Council. National Academies of Sciences, November 2002.

Student Satisfaction and Student Success

PROMOTING STUDENT SUPPORT AND SATISFACTION IN ONLINE LEARNING

Meg Benke
Empire State College, State University of New York

Tana Bishop
University of Maryland University College

Melody Thompson
Pennsylvania State University

Carol Scarafiotti
Rio Salado College

Claudine SchWeber
University of Maryland University College

- The five pillars of learning effectiveness, cost effectiveness, access, faculty satisfaction and student satisfaction are interrelated and interdependent. Activities designed to strengthen one pillar affect the other pillars.

- High levels of student satisfaction result from convenience of access, course/program quality; administrative, instructional, and technical support; opportunities for personal interaction, and more.

- Most institutions have only now begun to deal with the challenges presented in providing the kind of access required by law as well as conscience.

- Multiple methods for orientation should be used, just in time, for students when they need them.

- "What education strives to satisfy is not the student, but the student's lifelong need for knowledge and skills."

I. THE CONTEXT FOR PROVIDING SUPPORT

Discussions of student satisfaction and decisions related to providing support services must take place in the overall context of online learning. The context developed by the Sloan Consortium is reflected in the image of five pillars of high-quality online education: learning effectiveness, cost effectiveness, access, faculty satisfaction, and student satisfaction. These pillars work together, and are dependent on each other for the strength of the enterprise as a whole. As a result, activities designed to "build up" one pillar must be planned, implemented, and evaluated thoughtfully and thoroughly in terms of their effects not only on that pillar, but on each of the other pillars and on the overall organizational structure as well.

Student satisfaction can influence and be influenced by the other four pillars in many ways. Following are just several examples of how the promotion of student support and satisfaction relates directly to the other elements of quality, and why planning and implementation needs to take these relationships into account.

A. Learning effectiveness and student satisfaction

These two pillars can interact in a variety of ways. In some cases, these two goals seem to be in conflict. Some online faculty have reported having students who resent rigorous courses with the high expectations for learning, who seem to want nothing more than an easy and/or entertaining path to course credits and, ultimately, certificates or degrees [1]. On the other hand, students who experience positive learning outcomes report higher levels of satisfaction with their educational experiences than do other students.

Spanghel [2] argues that this dichotomy should challenge institutions to invest resources in robust but "failure-preventive course and teaching designs … that ensure that learning occurs efficiently, that it lasts and that it leaves the learner with the desire to continue to question, study, and learn" (p. 4). He further emphasizes the relationship between satisfaction and learning outcomes in stating that:

> Although traditional assessment has often viewed standardized cognitive tests as more reliable gauges of student learning than other evidence, a good metric for appraising how students' (or employers', or parents', etc.) needs and expectations for educational services are being met can provide as valid and useful an assessment tool as a paper-and-pencil achievement test (pp.4–5).

B. Cost-effectiveness and student satisfaction

High levels of student satisfaction result from a number of factors: convenience of access, course/program quality; administrative, instructional, and technical support; opportunities for personal interaction, and more. Assessments of cost-effectiveness are based on the question, "Is the outcome worth the cost?" The linkage between cost and quality services and programs is critical. Bishop [3] found that most cost-effective studies focus on efficient ways to improve the learning and support services provided to both students and faculty. The studies typically examined ways in which higher education institutions might be able to increase access, improve curriculum, and extend additional and more convenient services. At the same time, the institutions needed to consider cost since dollars are finite and there are many competing demands for resources.

Each activity, each structure, each system implemented to promote student satisfaction bears some kind of resource cost, yet each may not contribute equally to either student satisfaction or organizational goals. As McGrath and colleagues [4] point out, "Many institutions offer student services based on administrators' perceptions of students' needs," (p. 97) which in turn are based on experience with the 18–22 year old traditional students. In an environment of limited resources, prioritizing the systems and services that contribute to student satisfaction becomes imperative since the decision to expend resources in one area often limits the ability to do so in another area. Poor choices in resource allocation will lower overall cost effectiveness.

Careful assessment of needs, planning, monitoring, and research and evaluation are necessary to ensure that resources are invested in services that students studying at a distance want, need, and, perhaps most important, will use. Only in this way can institutions be sure that the resources invested in promoting student support and satisfaction offer a return on investment or value on investment that contributes to the maintenance and/or expansion of their online programming. Such benefits may be the more obvious returns—such as more new enrollments and higher retention rates—or provide less easily measured, but still important values to the organization, such higher overall technological proficiency among faculty and positive public relations for the institution or program [5].

C. Access and student satisfaction

The access point for online educational programs is a computer and the Internet. Many students report high levels of satisfaction with this entryway to educational opportunities and resources. For some, the independence of online programming from geographic location has meant that they could participate in programs that otherwise would have been literally beyond their reach. For others, especially multiple-role adults, independence from time limitations has meant that they could finally fit educational activities into their already-full lives.

Yet we know that online education does not increase access for all students [6, 7]. Some potential students, because they have no access to a computer or Internet service, or because their technology platform is inadequate, are effectively shut out of online programs. Others, such as some resident students at traditional institutions, may feel themselves to be unwillingly caught up in the transformation of familiar ways of learning to unfamiliar and seemingly difficult-to-negotiate approaches, especially when institutions do not operate from a consistent technology base. For such students, the requirement that they gain access to their educational programs via a computer may decrease satisfaction with their educational experience. Moreover, students with disabilities may have limited or no access to online education; instead they are presented with barriers. Most institutions have only now begun to deal with the challenges presented in providing the kind of access required by law as well as conscience. Challenges include assuring that disabled students obtain the essence of the course, not a different course and that accommodations are made toward that end. The electronic nature of online communication means that audio components need to have transcriptions; texts and media need audio components or other assistive technology, and so on if students with such disabilities are in the course. Accommodations are required by Title II of the Americans with Disabilities Act [8, 9] Section 508 Amendment to the 1973 Workforce Rehabilitation Act and comparable state legislation. This also means that course designers and faculty need to learn how to effectively use the new tools. An example is available at the University of Maryland University College [10]. Thus, to increase both access and satisfaction, institutions need to continually assess the height of the "technology bar" that determines access and ensure that technology transformations are accompanied by appropriate student training and support.

D. Faculty satisfaction and student satisfaction

The experience of faculty members and students online are often treated as separate phenomena, yet anecdotal and more formal evidence suggests that faculty members see a close relationship between factors in faculty satisfaction and student satisfaction. It makes intuitive sense that higher levels of faculty satisfaction would be expressed through higher levels of commitment to teaching which would then result in more satisfied students. Specific factors that faculty report as contributing to a satisfying teaching experience include increased access to/by students, more and more convenient opportunities for high-quality interaction with students, and time and place flexibility for teaching. Related factors that contribute to student satisfaction are more immediate access to their instructors, increased opportunities for interaction with them, and quick turn- around time for feedback [11].

This similarity in reported factors is on the one hand encouraging since it indicates agreement on the part of both groups as to elements necessary to make the online teaching and learning experience satisfying. However, applying the factors can become a burden to faculty members under certain conditions, and thereby seriously compromise their satisfaction. For example, for many faculty members, maximizing the power and flexibility of instructional technology in their teaching means learning new skills, which can be both time consuming and psychologically challenging, particularly if institutional support is lacking. The frequent student assumption that "increased access" means constant, rather than periodic, availability leads to the faculty perception that "you're always on; there's no 'break time' while you have students out there taking the courses." [12] Since faculty in traditional institutions need that 'break time' in chunks sufficient to carry out their other responsibilities, particularly research, expectations of universal availability detract from their satisfaction.

As with the relationships with other pillars, a balance needs to be struck and maintained. Institutions need to ensure that student satisfaction is not achieved at the expense of faculty satisfaction, since a committed faculty will be a major determinant in the ultimate success of online higher education. Achieving this balance may mean increased institutional support for online faculty, establishment of realistic limits for both student expectations and faculty performance, and continuous assessment and evaluation of both student and faculty satisfaction.

We now know that student satisfaction, learning effectiveness, access, cost-effectiveness, and faculty satisfaction are interrelated [13], and perhaps inextricably linked areas of the learning environment. While research often is undertaken for a specific purpose, such as determining the factors that relate to student satisfaction, such an examination can lead to linkages. With well-established standards and guidelines in place and an array of best practices in the five core areas of quality online education, the research agenda is inching forward. That is, we now have an opportunity to connect research strands that will further our understanding and help improve the effectiveness and efficiency of online education. In this paper, we present an array of support services models and explore some of the interaction emergent in the research as it relates to student support and satisfaction.

II. PROVIDING APPROPRIATE STUDENT SUPPORT

Student support is a foundation for success in all five of the pillar areas. Providing effective online services often requires new ways of thinking about support and business processes. Many online learning programs have evolved from correspondence, study centers, video or other open learning programs designed primarily for adults. Consequently, the provision of student services focused on an adult student needs' perspective, rather than adapting campus-based services or relying on faculty as primary support providers. Effectively assessing the learner's needs and approaches to the use of services may increase effectiveness and use of services. The British Open University and distance learning institutions in Germany originally provided services through Study Centers and local tutors with student support services available by phone and correspondence packets on study skills, time management, test skills, etc. [14]. These have evolved to Web services and tutors, with the goal of providing comprehensive and user-friendly technical and registration services as a base [15].

Understanding the needs of individual learners in the institution's student population is critical. Community Colleges, such as Rio Salado, have examined student support needs from a generational perspective and how this might impact the services they provide. Differences among the Boomer, GenX, and Millennial students are more pronounced in the digital learning environment. While online learners need convenient student support services, satisfaction with such services may vary according to the student's generation as well as with the particular student's goals. Marc Prensky [16] characterizes "Digital Natives" as mainly "Baby Boomers who are moderately comfortable with digital tools" and "Digital Natives" as those Geers and Millennials who grew up with computers and/or with the Internet and can easily use digital tools "to experience knowledge." Thus, the preferences of these "digital immigrants" and "digital natives" who have differing views of the technology supported world should be considered when providing online student support services.

A "digital immigrant" may prefer a convenient but more high-touch type of support experience such as advising over the telephone combined with access to a web portal. On the other hand, a "digital native's" perception of a satisfactory advising service may include push/pull web design where a student can easily chart his/her progress toward a degree online and be provided with just-in-time reminders. Since "nontraditional" [17] students are the fastest-growing student population today, currently representing around 75% of the total undergraduate student body, and are increasingly gravitating toward online programs because they match their lifestyle needs, it is increasingly important to provide efficient and effective student services that meet the requirements of this unique student population.

As all types of institutions have developed online programs, student development programs and services on campuses have been adapted to serve online learners, sometimes with specialized online staff and sometimes using existing services of campus-based offices. Institutions find that students in traditional classroom settings want access to electronic support services. Bishop and SchWeber [18] note that the offering of online courses and services at the University of Maryland University College has resulted in a "spillover effect." That is, all students, regardless of their preferred course delivery method, want to have the option of using electronic services such as admissions, registration, advising, and library.

Distance education methods are now merging with student development approaches used with on-campus students [19] For example, Scheer and Lockee [20] examined the possible application of their wellness model to promote life management for distance learning students. This approach is one that focuses on balancing interdependent areas of a learner's life. The researchers conducted a needs' assessment of students in three online Master's programs to determine the potential use of services from a campus wellness program depending upon self-reported success in online programs. The results of this research were used to create an online Wellness Resource Center at Virginia Polytechnic Institute [21]. The areas of highest interest and potential for use were the Links to Wellness Inventories, Salary information on Careers, Exercise and Health Meal Options, Relaxation Options and ways to meet other learners face-to-face.

Providing support services that meet individual learner's needs is a critical element in overall student satisfaction. In the online environment, this often requires some rethinking of internal processes and practices that typically have been designed for traditional learners in traditional classrooms. Regardless of the particular student populations our institutions serve, it is clear that their needs require continuous review and consideration. Along with the rapidly changing technology of the 21st century, educational institutions must stay committed to finding ways in which they can continuously improve processes and services to those they serve.

III. INCREASING STUDENT SATISFACTION

The interrelatedness of the pillars shows that it is important to use a comprehensive approach to what happens in the interaction between the faculty member and the students within the online class and in the supports that surround the learning environment. In this section of the paper, we present some of the emergent best practices that integrate various elements of the quality online framework.

A. Student orientation and first-year experiences

An assumption in promoting access, student satisfaction, faculty satisfaction, learning effectiveness and cost-effectiveness is that the goal is to find the best match between the learner and the institution's program offerings. This match will be enhanced by an orientation and first year program that assists the students in becoming an effective online learner. As orientation services are provided at a distance, the type of learner should be considered. Is the student working totally at a distance or taking courses and using services from a variety of formats?

Student orientation programs in the online environment encompass a wide range. Some provide very basic information about how to use the software, while others include a quiz that students take to help them understand how they can be a successful online learner. The recommended approach is one that offers a more comprehensive orientation services model to ensure that new students have a positive experience. Moore [22] summarized current practices in orientation. "Some online programs require orientation; some simply offer it; some charge for it; some discount it; some grade it and some don't offer online orientation. Some programs encourage or require in-person orientation ...." (p.19).

Orientation programs that go beyond the basics promote ways for learners to get to know faculty and to interact with other students. Feeling connected to faculty and other learners promotes active learning and more effective learning through social interaction in classrooms [23] or in online programs [8, 24]. Retention and assessment practices that promote engagement in term-long or year-long programs typically are referred to as "the first-year experience." Some colleges focus on ways to choose high-enrollment first year classes and target student success factor enhancements. Pace University runs a student orientation course for credit. Faculty at many colleges include student success documents or references within their courses. If faculty have readily available resource materials and information that they can provide students, they can dedicate more of their focus to the learning environment itself.

Rio Salado College uses a "periodic experience audit" as one way to find out how they can better serve students. They invite a selection of distance students to use the computers in the administration office and show how they navigate the services and courses. Program administrators report gaining significant information on ways to improve their programmatic design and methods. Other schools have visited students in their homes to examine how services are used.

Some general principles about learner orientation include the following were gathered from a 2003 Sloan online seminar on student satisfaction led by Meg Benke.

- It is of primary importance that transactional services should all be handled efficiently and seamlessly for the online learner. Worries about getting books or having to visit a campus hundreds of miles away to take a placement test will cloud students' ability to focus on new learning.
- Multiple methods for orientation should be used, just in time, for students when they need them. For example, the same study skill resources can be made available during an orientation seminar,

as a CD-ROM to be used when needed, or embedded within a course.

- Different institutions with different students will have diverse responses. Generational models might show that younger learner don't want coached instruction, they may prefer hands-on or other independent approaches. Baby Boomers often want coached instruction.

As an example, Empire State College has a student ambassador program where current or graduate students serve as informal advisors and orientation leaders by telephone and online. In addition, the College has a first-year experience program that is credit-based. It has evolved from a voluntary self-paced orientation to a required mentor led, independent study and group study. First year students work with mentor to pick among the following two-credit options for the first term enrolled:

- Mentor led educational planning independent study or seminar—goals setting, time management, distance learning study skills, what is an educated person, focused research into chosen area of study, writing and math, information and library resources.
- Information Literacy
- Assessing Learning
- Effective Academic Writing
- Exploring the Disciplines
- Independent Learning Strategies
- Introduction to guided independent study
- Planning and finalizing your degree.

While a costly model involving extensive faculty resources in mentoring, the online educational planning and orientation program does make sure that students understand the educational process and are prepared to be effective learners. A variety of approaches using different media applications are referenced on the Sloan-C Best Practices on the resource web site.

B. Academic Advising and Tutorial Services

Academic Advising is a two-way function that is critical to student success and satisfaction. The success of this function relies upon the student to provide accurate and current information about, himself/herself along with academic goals and program of study. Student satisfaction also corresponds to the ability for the advisor and student to obtain, track, distribute, and use the information provided. With the growth of online education, the academic advising function is more complex for advisors and students. At one time, students typically enrolled in only one institution to complete all their course work; now they have the ability to select course work from institutions around the globe. This has changed the nature of advising since many students are used to Internet time and expect their home institution to efficiently assist them with transfer course equivalency issues.

The Internet Goes to College [25] study reports that 86% of college students compared to 59% of the general population have gone online, that 49% of students first began using the Internet before they arrived at college, and that college Internet users are" twice as likely to use instant messaging on any given day compared to the average Internet user" (p. 2). Likewise, this ubiquitous use of the Internet by today's college students foretells of more demand upon institutions to provide students with easy online access to information such as what courses from other institutions apply to their educational goals. Students who can monitor information sent from other institutions become empowered and take more ownership of the advising process.

A few basic principles of online academic advising include:

- Information about the student including assessment data, career goals, academic plans, and transfer course equivalency data must be stored in secure, sharable electronic files that are easily updated and available to advisors, other staff members who assist in the advising function and the student being advised.

- The academic advising function should be designed to scale thus allowing the advisor to establish a satisfactory online relationship with large numbers of advisees.

- The academic advising function must enable students to easily monitor, online, their academic progress toward completion of degree and certificate requirement and other education goals. Typical degree audit systems have been developed from the advisor perspective and often not student friendly especially for the student desiring a self-service approach.

Students who are sophisticated online consumers expect academic advising functions to contain features that are customized as well as personalized, thus allowing students to get the information in ways convenient to them

C. Academic advising in a partnership model

Western Governors University (WGU) provides a view of futuristic academic advising in their mentored guidance approach [26]. WGU, designed as a non-teaching institution that provides pathways to degrees through partnerships with other colleges, universities, corporation and training organizations, utilizes an online catalog containing 1200 courses from 45 partnering institutions to help prepare students for competency assessments. Courses are mapped to specific degree competencies so that with mentor guidance a student can know which competency a course covers. The student and mentor develop an Academic Action Plan that includes a projected graduation date and all items that must be completed including such things as courses, other learning opportunities, planned assessments. The student and assigned mentor communicate by email or phone at least every two weeks about student progress.

D. One stop, student focused advising

Rio Salado College, a community college serving over 20,000 online students each year adopted a one-stop model of academic advising. This model is based upon the use of a sophisticated electronic student database that provides students and advisors with online access to all the information needed to monitor student progress toward an academic goal. This includes information such as student check sheets, data about the arrival of transcripts from other institutions, class schedules, and program admittance status. Through the electronic student file, students can easily monitor their progress at times convenient to them. Also each student with an academic goal is assigned an online advisor who communicates directly with the student.

E. Pre-advising

Some online colleges are helping students to do some self-assessment before they commit to an actual program. Capella University's "Two Minute Advisor" [27] helps potential students match their educational and personal goals with courses and programs through an online automated program. Students answer a series of questions students and are provided with immediate feedback on possible types of programs and other services that meet their needs. Pace University has embedded initial assessments in courses.

F. Service standards

Managing students' expectations with online services can help promote student satisfaction as illustrated by Canada's Athabasca University. The University has established and posted their service standards for academic advising, Expect the Best Service Standards, on their website [28]. The information, which includes the service and service delivery time (the standard) as well as the contact, so that students anywhere know what to expect.

G. Student tutorial services

Pew's 2002 study [29], finds today's college students to be heavy users of the Internet who see it as a "functional tool ... that has greatly changed the way they interact with others and with information as they go about their studies." For example, 62% of students in this study "use the email to set up appointments with their professors and 68% "subscribe to one or more academic-oriented mailing lists that relate to their studies." It stands to reason that these students' expect tutorial services that are conveniently accessible, and thus the pillars access and learning effectiveness must interact to produce student satisfaction. Nonetheless, providers of tutorial services must also factor cost effectiveness and faculty satisfaction into their decision making about tutorial services. Some issues to consider as providers establish and /or update tutorial services are:

- **Access** — Can students easily find information about tutorial services on the web site? Can students make appointments for tutoring online on line as well as by phone? Are students provided with choice in the way in which tutoring services are delivered? Do delivery methodologies include phone, Internet, FAX, virtual study groups, as well as in person? Can tutoring services be made available 24/7? What is the breadth of subjects available through online tutorial services?
- **Learning effectiveness** — What is needed to make online tutoring as effective as face-to-face tutoring? Are tutors skilled in the pedagogy of tutoring online? Do online tutors have access to the necessary tools such as white boards? Can they share files with students?
- **Faculty involvement** — What role will faculty assume in promoting online tutoring services to students? Are they willing to integrate tutoring information into their online courses to provide "just in time" assistance for difficult concepts?
- **Cost effectiveness** — Can the institution justify developing and maintaining a comprehensive online tutorial service? Is outsourcing to an online tutorial service a cost effective way of providing convenient online tutorial services? Who should pay for the cost of such services—the institution, the student, both?

IV. STUDENT SATISFACTION AND FACULTY SATISFACTION INTERSECT

The nature of teaching and learning creates a symbiotic relationship between students and faculty, in which these parties interact so closely that "faculty satisfaction cannot sustain itself independently of student outcomes" [30]. Student satisfaction is one of the key outcomes measures by which faculty are assessed and the quality of programs evaluated [31] (Middle States Commission on Higher Education 2002). An interesting finding from emergent studies is the more direct linkage between what satisfies students and what satisfies faculty. That link is *interaction*.

Two recent studies have shown that student satisfaction is highly correlated with interaction. Carswell and

Fleming [31] and Abdul-Hamid [32] examined course evaluations in the UMUC Graduate School and UMUC-wide, respectively. The Graduate School study examined data from 19,500 students over four semesters, and the all-UMUC study investigated the course evaluations of 29,425 students in fall 2002. Carswell and Fleming found two interaction variables ("support and guidance" and "stimulate interest") to be among the key predictors of student satisfaction. The UMUC Graduate School defined interaction by these two variables. Abdul-Hamid found significant correlations between "student-to-student interaction" and "student-to-faculty interaction" and "recommend faculty." In that study, the term "interaction" was used without any particular specification. That is, the UMUC course evaluations used the term "interaction" broadly. Regardless of how precisely one defines "interaction," students responded positively to the notion of regular communication among students and between student and faculty. Abdul-Hamid's findings showed low student withdrawal rates correlated with courses in which there was a high level of interaction. That is, when students perceived a high level of interaction in a course, this resulted in fewer course withdrawals. This would suggest that a faculty member can influence student persistence through interaction.

The findings from these student satisfaction studies fit with some other research about faculty satisfaction in the online environment. For example, Hartman and Truman-Davis [33] surveyed faculty teaching online courses in fall 1999 to investigate factors that provide faculty satisfaction in the online environment. They found a high correlation between faculty satisfaction and the quantity and quality of interactions, a correlation that was "statistically significant ...for the amount of interaction ..." (p. 121). This is supported by other research, such as that conducted by Fredericksen, et al. [34], who found that interaction between students was the most influential factor affecting instructors.

A pilot study conducted by one faculty member at UMUC (2001–2002) indicated that faculty can take action to influence student satisfaction. Along with other factors, Chen [35] increased interaction, defined broadly as noted above in Abdul-Hamid [32], in his spring 2002 class after working with a team studying instructor best practices in fall 2001. By implementing strategies that applied the best practices principles, he found a "significant increase on average scores and learning" (p. 2) when comparing pre- and post-test data. This pilot is now being extended to a larger group of UMUC faculty to try and improve the learning experience and ultimately student persistence in the online environment.

V. BUILDING COMMUNITY AND PROMOTING INTERACTION AND SOCIALIZATION IN THE FIELD

Student development models promote the importance of learners being part of a community. While online learners may have deliberately not chosen a campus-based experience, attending a college is more than participating in courses. Some of the most effective means to promote community have been through discussion groups in the major, (particularly well developed at Excelsior College, for example.) Other colleges have built traditions such as phone or online conferences with guest speakers to promote intellectual and social connections, connections with alumni and virtual or site-based graduations.

Research has not been extensive on the value of community promotion to students either inside or outside of the online class environment. SUNY research investigating student satisfaction with courses shows that students value the connection with their peers, but this did not correlate with either student satisfaction or reported student learning [8]. As educators, we may need to be more specific clear about the expectations for social interaction. Some of it is just social, some of it is directed at learning objectives, and both have value. This also has impact on faculty relationships and their role in promoting student satisfaction.

VI. EVALUATING STUDENT SERVICES AND SATISFACTION

We face a particular challenge in working online with understanding the relationship between learner satisfaction and learner expectations. Sener and Humbert [36] showed how the consumer perspective sometimes is misinterpreted to mean that the customer is always right. They appropriately point out that there are a variety of stakeholders. Student satisfaction should be interpreted as a blend of meeting the student's needs, meeting unexpressed needs, faculty and programmatic expectations and societal needs.

Spangehl [2] concurs, noting widespread misunderstanding of what it means to satisfy student needs. He suggests that this confusion has led to superficial assessments and a resultant suspicion on the part of faculty members as to the value of satisfaction measures, particularly compared to measures of cognitive achievement. He believes that worthwhile measures of satisfaction are both possible and valuable when reflected in questions such as "How did taking Freshman Composition help you acquire the skills and knowledge you needed to succeed?" rather than those focusing on abstract feelings about the course. "What education strives to satisfy is not the student, but the student's lifelong need for knowledge and skills" (p. 5).

Tucker [37] points out several challenges to assessing student satisfaction and the extent to which students' needs have been met. He note that higher education's students are "polymorphous," that the needs of different students often conflict with each other, and that the long- and short-term needs of individual students often conflict, making evaluations of satisfaction challenging and suggesting the need for varied, multi-point approaches. Recognizing this challenge, the Pennsylvania State University World Campus monitors student satisfaction at the end of each course and also when students finish their programs. While some of the elements of satisfaction measured are common to both survey instruments, others are designed to assess students' attitudes reflective of the different stages of their educational experiences.

Orzoff [38] stresses the multifaceted nature of the student experience and the importance of evaluating the different elements of that experience as they relate to each other. Viewing the student as a **learner** (in relation to the educational experience), a **consumer** (in relation to the business experience), and an **end-user** (in relation to the technology experience), he offers a matrix approach to evaluation that matches performance measures of needs and goals, satisfaction, processes, and outcomes for each of these three aspects of the student's identity. Following is an example of an evaluation report that integrates all of these measures onto a "dashboard" for monitoring success [38]:

The "Dashboard"

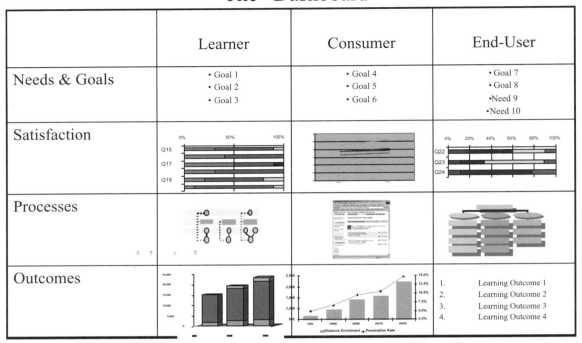

Figure 1. Matrix approach to student services (figure used with permission of the author)

Evaluations of student services should be interpreted in the context of the evaluations of other effectiveness pillars and an institution's unique strategic goals. Important questions to be asked are "What assessment approaches provide actionable data?" and "What performance standards can be developed and shared across higher education to provide the basis for both informed student decision making and continuous quality improvement in the area of student support?"

VII. REFERENCES

1. **Martin, W. Allen.** Being There is What Matters. *Academe*, 1999 September/October. Available from: http://www.uttyler.edu/amartin/dised_599.htm (accessed 2003).

2. **Spangehl, S.** Aligning Assessment, Academic Quality and Accreditation. Assessment and Accountability Forum, Summer 2000. Available from:

   http://www.intered.com/public/v10n2_spangehl.pdf (accessed June 2003).

3. **Bishop, T.** Linking Cost Effectiveness with Institutional Goals: Best Practices in Online Education, In *Elements of Quality Online Education: Practice and Direction, Volume 4 in the Sloan-C Series*, edited by J. Bourne and J.C. Moore, 75–86. Needham, MA: Sloan-C, 2003.

4. **McGrath, J., Middleton, H., and Crissman, T.** World Campus: Setting standards in Student Services. In *Elements of Quality Online Education, Volume 3 in the Sloan-C Series,* edited by J. Bourne and J.C. Moore, 83–100. Needham, MA: Sloan-C, 2002.

5. **Estabrook, L.** Rethinking Cost-Benefit Models of Distance Learning. In *Elements of Quality Online Education, Volume 3 in the Sloan-C Series*, edited by J. Bourne and J.C. Moore, 71–80. Needham, MA: Sloan-C, 2002.

6. **Bates, A.** *Cultural and Ethical Issues in International Distance Education.* Presentation at the Engaging Partnerships: Collaboration and Partnership in Distance Education UBC/CREAD conference, Vancouver, Canada, September 21–23, 1999.

   Available from: http://bates.cstudies.ubc.ca/pdf/CREAD.pdf.

7. **Tait, A.** The Convergence of Distance and Conventional Education. Some Implications for Policy. In *The Convergence of Distance and Traditional Education*, eds. A. Tait and R. Mills, 141–160. New York: Routledge, 1999.

8. **Title II of the Americans with Disabilities Act.** 1990. http://www.ada.gov.

9. **Section 508 Amendment to the 1973 Workforce Rehabilitation Act.** 1998. http://www.section508.gov.

10. **University of Maryland.** http://www.umuc.edu/odell/cade.

11. **Shea, P., Swan, K., Fredericksen, E., Pickett, A.** Student Satisfaction and Reported Learning in the SUNY Learning Network. In *Elements of Quality Online Education Volume 3 in the Sloan-C Series*, edited by J. Bourne and J.C. Moore, 145–155. Needham, MA: Sloan-C, 2002.

12. **Thompson, M. M.** Faculty Satisfaction in Penn State's World Campus. In *Online Education, Volume 2: Learning Effectiveness, Faculty Satisfaction, and Cost Effectiveness*, edited by J. Bourne and J.C. Moore, 129–144. Needham, MA: Sloan-C, 2001.

13. **Moore, J. C.** *Elements of Quality: The Sloan-C™ Framework*. Needham, MA: Sloan-C, 2002.

14. **Stewart, D., Keegan, D. and Holmberg, B.** *Distance Education: International Perspectives*. New York: Routledge, 1988.

15. **Moore, M.G. and Kearsley, G.** *Distance Education: A Systems View*. Belmont, CA: Wadsworth Publishing Company, 1996.

16. **Prensky, M.** Digital Natives, Digital Immigrants. *On the Horizon*. NBC University Press 9(5): October 2001.

17. **The National Center for Educational Statistics (NCES).** "The Condition of Education 2002." June 2002. http://nces.ed.gov/pubsearch/pubsinfo.asp?pubid=2002025 and at http://nces.ed.gov/programs/coe/glossary/n.asp. NCES identifies nontraditional students as those with at least one of the following characteristics: delayed enrollment, part-time attendance, full-time employment, financially independent from parents, responsible for dependents, single parent, and lacking a high school diploma.

18. **Bishop, T. and SchWeber, C.** Linking Quality and Cost. In *Online Education: Proceedings of the 2000 Sloan Summer Workshop on Asynchronous Learning Networks. Volume 2 in the Sloan-C Series*, edited by J. Bourne and J. C. Moore. Needham, MA: Sloan-C, 2001.

19. **Schwitzer, A.M., Ancis, J.R. and Brown, N.** Promoting Student Learning and Student Development at a Distance: Student Affairs Concepts and Practices for Televised Instruction and Other Forms of Distance Education. American College Personnel Association, Lanham, MD. 2001.

20. **Scheer, S.B. and Lockee, B.B.** Addressing the Wellness Needs of Online Distance Students. *Open Learning* 18(2):2003.

21. **Virginia Polytechnic Institute.** http://www.vto.vt.edu/owrc.

22. **Moore, J.C.** *Elements of Quality, Synthesis of the August 2002 Seminar*. Needham, MA: Sloan-C, 2003.

23. **Tinto, V.** *Leaving College: Rethinking the Causes and Cures of Student Attrition*. 2nd ed. Chicago: University of Chicago Press, 1993.

24. **Hiltz, R.S., Coppola, N. Rotter, and Turoff, M.** Measuring the Importance of Collaborative Learning for the Effectiveness of ALN: A Multi-Measure, Multi-Method Approach. *JALN* 4(2): September 2000.

25. **Jones, S.** The Internet Goes to College, Pew Internet and American Life Project. 2002. Available from http://www.pewinternet.org.

26. **Western Governors University.** http://www.wgu.edu/wgu/index.html.

27. **Capella University.** http://www.capella.edu/reborn.html/index.asp.

28. **Athabasca University.** http://www.athabascau.ca/misc/expect/academic.html.

29. **Hartman, J. and Truman-Davis, B.** Factors Related to the Satisfaction of Faculty Teaching Online Courses at the University of Central Florida. In *Online Education: Proceedings of the 2000 Sloan Summer Workshop on Asynchronous Learning Networks. Volume 2 in the Sloan-C Series*, edited by J. Bourne and J.C. Moore. Needham, MA: Sloan-C, 2001.

30. **Middle States Commission on Higher Education**. Distance Learning Programs: Interregional Programs for Electronically Offered Degrees and Certificate Programs, 2002. Available from: http://www.mache.org/distguide02.pdf.

31. **Carswell, A. and E. Fleming.** Student Faculty Evaluation Study Final Report. Adelphi, MD: University of Maryland University College, 2003 (in preparation for publication).

32. **Abdul-Hamid, H.** *Relationship Between Student's Course Evaluation and Grading: Pilot Study*, Confidential Document by the Institute for Research and Assessment in Higher Education/Office of Distance Education. 2003.

33. **Fredericksen, E., Pickett, A., Swan, K., Pelz, W., and Shea. P.** Factors Influencing Faculty Satisfaction in the SUNY Learning Network. Paper given at the Sloan Summer ALN workshop. Urbana, Illinois: August 1999.

34. **Maina, S., and Chen, J.** Best Online Instructional Practices: The Role of Interactive Components in Enhancing Success in Online Learning. UMUC: Institute for Research and Assessment in Higher Education, 2003.

35. **Sener, J. and Humbert, J**. Student Satisfaction with Online Learning: An Expanding Universe. In *Elements of Quality Online Education, Volume 3 in the Sloan-C Series*, edited by J. Bourne and J.C. Moore. Needham, MA: Sloan-C, 2003.

36. **Tucker, R.** *The Rhetoric of Quality*. Adult Assessment Forum, Summer 1997.

37. **Orzoff, J. H.** *Measuring the student experience*. Presentation at the Eduventures Education, Technology and Curriculum Summit. Columbia University, NYC: May 13–14, 2003.

VIII. ABOUT THE AUTHORS

Meg Benke has been with Empire State College since 1990, currently as Dean of the Center for Distance Learning, and connected with distance education since 1983. The Center for Distance Learning enrolls 17,000 distance learning enrollments every year and students can do complete degrees online. Empire State College offers many student services on the web such as the Writer's Complex (online writing center), student ambassadors, library career site and all services such as admissions, registration, and financial aid. Dr. Benke's work in education has focused on the connections between work, employers and education. Dr. Benke also teaches in the graduate and undergraduate programs in the areas of adult educational policy, human systems, leadership, human resource development, distance education and training and learning organizations. Dr. Benke studies outcomes for students in distance learning and the assessment of prior learning. Since coming to Empire State College, Dr. Benke has written and presented primarily in the areas of learner supports for distance learners and union/employer sponsored distance learning. She has convened a national teleconference on student services for adult students through the American College Personnel Association where she has also served as Vice President for Professional Development.

Tana Bishop is the Associate Dean for Administration in the Graduate School at University of Maryland University College. Prior to that, she was Assistant Director for the United Kingdom and Iceland with UMUC's European Division. She also worked in Japan as the Executive Director of the Navy Relief Society, a non-profit financial institution. Other professional experience included many years as an educator. She spent more than a decade living and working outside the United States. That international experience has influenced her interest in offering synchronous courses and degree programs to diverse student populations. Dr. Bishop holds bachelors and masters degrees in Japanese Studies and a Ph.D. in Education. Her areas of specialization include the economics of education, educational leadership, and international teaching and learning. She currently serves as President of the Maryland Association of Higher Education.

Carol Scarafiotti is the Dean of Instruction at Rio Salado College, a community college nationally recognized as a role model for innovation and excellence in eLearning. Having led the effort to create a system's approach to distance learning at Rio Salado College, she has first hand knowledge of what it takes sustain a distance learning program with over 220 unique fully online courses, with registration available every two weeks, along with 22,000 students enrolled annually. In 2002 she received the Sloan C Award for Excellence in Online Access. She is recognized for her collaborative approaches with faculty in achieving innovative instructional design and support systems and for her expertise in assessment of learning outcomes and development of adjunct faculty support services. She frequently speaks at conferences about issues related to the eLearning culture in higher education.

Melody M. Thompson is the Director of Quality and Planning for Penn State's World Campus. In that role, her primary responsibilities are World Campus organizational process improvement, policy development, and strategic planning. Her primary research interests are faculty satisfaction and the institutional policy environment for online learning. Dr. Thompson is also an Affiliate Assistant Professor of Education in the Adult Education Program, where she teaches graduate classes with a focus on the experience of women and minorities in adult education and on the history of the field. Before coming to the World Campus, she was the publications editor of The American Center for the Study of Distance Education (ACSDE) and the editor of DEOS (Distance Education Online Symposium). Dr. Thompson has written and lectured extensively in the fields of adult education and distance learning. She holds a B.A. in English from Bryn Mawr College and both an M.Ed. and D.Ed. in Adult Education from Penn State.

Claudine SchWeber is Collegiate Professor and Associate Provost for Distance Education and Lifelong Learning. Her involvement in distance communication began when she was a mediator and training director for the Council of Better Business Bureaus, where she examined and wrote about the use of technology for dispute resolution. Dr. SchWeber has been working in the distance education arena for almost a decade, and has published articles that deal with the "time" issue for faculty; the cost of online education, quality challenges. As a faculty member in both the UMUC Graduate School and Undergraduate Studies, she has the opportunity to apply some of what she has learned to her online classes. She has led workshops and presentations worldwide, including representing the US State Department. Several years ago she received a Fulbright to discuss and lead workshops in distance education(http://www.cies.org/specialists/ss_cschweber.htm). She speaks three languages and is a native of Paris, France. Her professional life is a testament to lifelong learning, having begun as a criminal justice professor and later a mediator and arbitrator.

CRITICAL FACTORS IN STUDENT SATISFACTION AND SUCCESS: FACILITATING STUDENT ROLE ADJUSTMENT IN ONLINE COMMUNITIES OF INQUIRY

D. Randy Garrison
University of Calgary

Martha Cleveland-Innes
Athabasca University

- Students are being asked to adapt to online learning as well as to higher expectations in terms of critical and self-directed learning.

- From the start students must understand expectations and feel they are welcome and belong to a community of learners.

- The growing complexity and the design of more sophisticated online learning experiences represent a significant challenge and role adjustment for students.

- Students make an adjustment from a more didactic traditional teacher centered face-to-face educational environment to one where they are expected to assume increased responsibility to generate answers.

- Facilitators must be aware of the culture emerging within the group and relationships developing, while acting to shape and direct both.

I. INTRODUCTION

Teaching and learning roles and responsibilities are evolving rapidly as asynchronous online learning communication technologies increasingly become a core element in higher education. We have moved beyond issues of access [1] with the focus shifting to engaging students in worthwhile and satisfying learning experiences. Students are being asked to adapt to online learning as well as to higher expectations in terms of critical and self-directed learning. They are being inundated with information that they are required to interpret and construct meaning. These challenges raise serious questions and issues in terms of student satisfaction and success. This is further compounded when face-to-face classroom experiences are blended with those of online learning. Considering the challenges, it is essential that students get off to a good start with an appreciation of new teaching and learning approaches, modes of communication, and higher expectations. We begin the paper with a discussion of several key concepts and issues.

II. THEORETICAL BACKGROUND

A. Student Satisfaction and Success

Appropriate role adjustment will provide a sense of belonging as well as the willingness and ability to participate and contribute. From the start students must understand expectations and feel they are welcome and belong to a community of learners. Without this, the ability to fully engage and be cognitively present is compromised, and concomitantly, learner satisfaction and success will be jeopardized. In the case of poor adjustment, personal and performance satisfaction will be negatively affected. We see the requirement for satisfaction socially, cognitively and instructionally. These elements of a community of inquiry exist in the dimensions of role identity.

It is interesting to note that most students enroll in online learning for reasons of flexibility and convenience [2]. Considering the importance of time and place independence, satisfaction in terms of access will initially be a "hygienic" factor (i.e., minimal condition), but will only be sustained through a satisfying and successful learning experience. Certainly from a learning perspective, Shea, Swan, Frederickson and Pickett [3] found that satisfaction and learning was significantly correlated with interaction, feedback and clear expectations. Swan [4] found that students "who rated their level of activity as high also reported significantly higher levels of course satisfaction and significantly higher levels of perceived learning" (pp. 315–316). On the other hand, students may be successful but not satisfied with the learning experience. Rivera and Rice [5] found that while "overall student performance did not suffer" in an online course, lack of support "affected the students' level of satisfaction." Moreover, other studies suggest that satisfaction may well be associated with interaction with the teacher and a feeling of community [5]. So, we should recognize that long-term satisfaction and success go beyond access and do not necessarily go hand-in-hand.

Even at that, relying only on student satisfaction or success may well limit the options and potential of online learning and hide the unique properties of ALN. As important as it may be, student satisfaction only has larger and lasting value if it is combined with academic success. Sener and Humbert [2] ask a crucial question: "What is optimal student satisfaction." Their answer:

> At first glance this may seem like an easy question to answer: the more satisfied the students, the better. In reality, however, to some extent there is a fundamental contradiction between maximizing student satisfaction and providing the best possible learning experience. (p. 7)

The point is that students don't always know what is best for them educationally. Therefore, both satisfaction and success must be addressed in a way that will extend beyond the narrow perspective and impression of the student or the grade obtained in the course. Issues of cognitive, social and teaching presence (i.e., community of inquiry) must be juxtaposed with student assessment of satisfaction and success. The challenge of providing students with what they need and not just what they want, argues for participation in a community of learners and the need for role adjustment. Active participation in a critical community of inquiry is not a common experience for most undergraduate students.

B. Online Communities of Inquiry

Considering that satisfaction and success are linked to interaction and learning, attention must be directed to the teaching and learning transaction. In fact, it has been argued that critical thinking and higher learning outcomes are effectively facilitated through discourse in communities of inquiry [6, 7]. As we move beyond access issues we are beginning to recognize that asynchronous online learning has the properties and potential to support higher-order learning activities and outcomes. Collaboration and independence together represent the distinctive properties of online learning and provide the opportunity for both discourse and reflection [8]. Satisfaction and success are dependent upon the integration of these capabilities and the realization of quality learning environments and outcomes.

Learning communities for educational purposes consist of three core elements – social, cognitive and teaching presence [9]. Satisfaction and success result when all three elements are integrated harmoniously in a way that supports critical discourse and reflection. Experience has shown that when one or two of these elements are ignored, the quality and sustainability of the learning experience is threatened. For example, if the discussion is not well managed and allowed to fragment, students will stop participating. Social presence that only provides a sense of connection without purpose leads neither to satisfaction or success. Social and cognitive presence must be integrated through teaching presence to ensure intended goals are realized efficiently and effectively. This integration of the external and internal, the collaborative and the reflective, is the key to higher-order learning and reflects the key properties of online learning [8].

The creation of communities of inquiry online requires re-conceptualizing approaches to teaching and learning, which in turn represents a redefining of roles for the student and teacher. Role adjustment and empowerment in online learning is directly supported by a sense of community and mastery of specific skills [10]. Davie and Wells [10] argue that a sense of community provides the support to work together and challenge one another. In support of this argument, Rovai [11] found a "positive significant relationship between sense of community and cognitive learning" (p. 328). Mastery of specific skills such as communicating with text and analyzing masses of information is also an important element in empowerment. Successful adjustment to the role of online learner empowers students to engage in critical discourse and achieve higher learning outcomes. Role adjustment leading to empowerment is essential if students are to be responsible and meaningfully engaged.

C. Role Adjustment

Asynchronous learning networks represent new possibilities and a significant shift in the learning experience and outcomes. These networks represent a qualitative shift in the multi-dimensional nature of online communication and interaction as well as in the demands placed on students in terms of expected learning outcomes in coping with the knowledge age. This growing complexity and the design of more sophisticated online learning experiences represent a significant challenge and role adjustment for students.

To understand this role adjustment [12] is to appreciate the properties and changing dynamics of asynchronous learning networks. This role adjustment must be understood in the context of the learning community. Role adjustment is a continual shifting of expectations and requirements among individuals interacting within a community. Learning communities are essential for students to have the opportunity to test appropriate behaviors and successfully acquire new roles. Through adjustment to the new role comes community, made up of individuals comfortable participating within the community. Through focused interaction within the community comes the critical evaluation and synthesis of ideas. Thus, online communities of inquiry are crucial to successful higher-order learning outcomes. If the goal is higher-order learning, it is not a simple transfer of the traditional classroom role to that of online learner.

Understanding expectations, new skills and guidance is required to help students adjust. Initially the focus is on "role taking" (observation and practice); "role making" emerges as students gain increased control and make role-related decisions on their own. This latter state is reflective of students taking responsibility to construct meaning and confirm understanding in the quest to reach higher levels of learning. Thus, adjustments and the balance among social, cognitive and teaching presences is dynamic and will evolve as learning progresses. This development, however, is not inevitable and requires a teaching presence in design, facilitation and direct involvement. Through instructor support comes adjustment to the online community of inquiry, and through adjustment comes satisfaction and success. It is clear that the instructor plays an important role in student satisfaction. Shea et al. [3] reported the highest correlation between satisfaction and the quality of interaction with the instructor.

Role adjustment is further complicated with blended learning designs that are gaining favor in higher education as blending provides the opportunity to combine the best elements of face-to-face and online learning. Blended learning represents significant rethinking and a shift in design. It is not sufficient to simply add a chat room or even discussion board onto a classroom based approach. A key element of blended learning and student satisfaction is interaction. Blended learning generally provides greater flexibility and a wider range of educational options. Considering the potential synergies, there is every reason to expect blended learning to be both satisfying and successful from the student perspective. The complexity of blended learning and the diversity of designs also bring challenges, particularly in evaluating its success [2].

III. ROLE ADJUSTMENT STUDY

The transition to online learning of students in six graduate courses at Athabasca University was studied by means of a questionnaire administered online. The courses were delivered fully online with a combination of print and electronic materials supplemented with online conferencing. The questionnaire consisted of three sections. The instrument consisted of 28 Lickert-type questions derived from the community of inquiry model. The instrument was pilot tested and validated through factor analytic procedures [13]. The second section asked students to describe their adjustment to online learning from the perspectives of learning activities and outcomes, of the learning community, and of the course design and facilitation. A final section gathered various demographic data, which are not reported here.

The questionnaire was administered during the first and last two weeks of classes. The overall return rate was 47 percent. Data reported here focuses only on first time online learners. The sample consisted of 22 respondents.

A. Pre/Post Comparison

Table 1 reports the mean differences and significant levels for each of the items. It should be noted that items 1–9 are on cognitive presence; 10–19 social presence; and 20–28 on teaching presence. Responses indicated a positive adjustment from pre to post test across all items in comparison to experienced online learners. That is, after having experienced online learning and adjusting to this learning experience, they rated themselves more closely to experienced online learners.

Table 1: Pre and post-test differences

Compared to *experienced online learners*, how would you rate your online learning experiences with the following?

Activity Items	Mean Difference	Significance
1. Synthesize ideas	-.1579	.268
2. Apply ideas or concepts	-.1667	.269
3. Stimulate your curiosity	-.1953	.429
4. Confirm understanding of concepts	-.4211*	.016
5. Know how to participate	-.4737**	.008
6. Identify relevant new information	-.2632*	.021
7. Understand the issues being presented	-.2778	.172
8. Understand expectations	-.3684*	.049
9. Take responsibility	.1667	.187
10. Express your emotions	-.2778	.205
11. Being open & disclose your personality	-.0526	.790
12. Responding to others' comments	-.2632	.310
13. Sustain discussion	-.3158	.187
14. Feeling part of the class community	-.1053	.607
15. Feeling comfortable engaging in discussion	-.4737*	.035
16. Ask questions	-.2632	.172
17. Engage in exchange of ideas	-.4737*	.035
18. Generate tentative solutions	-.2222	.163
19. Refer to others by name	-.3684*	.015
20. Accepting teacher assessment	-.1875	.333
21. Accepting teacher feedback	-.1250	.432
22. Teaching assistance in reaching consensus	-.1111	.495
23. Direct teaching intervention	-.2353	.216
24. Teacher interaction	-.3333	.187
25. The organization of the class	-.5263**	.008
26. Adjust to the climate	-.5556**	.008
27. Teaching methods	-.5789**	.007
28. Adjust to the context	-.3889	.090

*$p =/< .05$; **$p =/< ..01$

The items with the greatest change in the initial perception of online learning for cognitive presence were 'knowing how to participate,' 'confirming understanding' and 'identify relevant new information.' In terms of social presence the items indicating the greatest change in perception of online learning were 'refer to others by name,' 'feeling comfortable engaging in discussion,' and 'engaging in an exchange of ideas.' The items for teaching presence that showed the greatest change in perception of online learning were 'organization of the class,' 'adjusting the climate/context,' and 'teaching methods.'

From these data, the greatest change or adjustment for both social and cognitive presence is associated with interaction, exchanging ideas, and confirming understanding. In terms of teaching presence, the most significant adjustments were associated with teaching methods, class management, and climate. Therefore, the greatest concern and adjustment would appear to be associated with learning or cognitive issues. The social presence issues related to emotions and feelings did not show a significant change.

B. Open Responses

Three open-ended questions asked students to describe their adjustment cognitively, socially and from a teaching perspective. From a cognitive or learning perspective, the greatest adjustment for first time students was associated with interaction. While this is consistent with the quantitative findings, a more specific issue is raised around the nature of the communication. This is the challenge of composing written communication that would not be misinterpreted. Adjustment was also challenged by increased interaction with fellow students, which concomitantly meant less teaching presence. In short, students reported having to assume primary responsibility for achieving learning outcomes.

From the perspective of social presence, students expressed concern about the ability to get to know fellow students and feeling part of a learning community. This adjustment was attributed first to the communication medium as well as learning to use the medium to get to know fellow students. At first it was difficult to remember who was who. There was also reluctance on the part of some students to be personally open and a concern to not offend. As one student stated; "Personal information is not a factor in a face-to-face environment and is only offered once you feel comfortable [with] your class members. On-line learning reverses the process."

From a teaching presence perspective, it was very clear that the students had difficulty adjusting to the role of the teacher as facilitator. They expressed a desire to have the teacher more visible and present. This was particularly true in terms of delayed teacher feedback and availability to answer questions. It would appear that students had to make an adjustment from a more didactic traditional teacher centered face-to-face educational environment to one where they were expected to assume increased responsibility to generate answers. This is consistent with the findings of Swan [4] where "interaction with instructors seemed to have a much larger effect on satisfaction and perceived learning than did interaction with peers" (pp. 322–323).

IV. DISCUSSION

The results of this study strongly suggest that there is a significant adjustment to online learning for the first time online student. The fundamental adjustment for the first time online student was associated with interacting online and having to communicate via the written word. Students were initially very uncertain how to interact online and of the expectations. This was compounded by interacting with fellow students and learning how to initiate and sustain an educational exchange. It would appear that teacher presence in the form of facilitating interaction and a sense of community is a crucial role in the adjustment, satisfaction and success of online learning.

From the limited findings of this study, role adjustment would appear to be most directly associated with issues of interaction (see Figure 1). However, before exploring the connection to satisfaction and success, it is important to note that interaction in an online learning context is shaped by the properties of the medium. These are the properties of connectivity, asynchronicity, and communication [8, 14]. Interaction is a complex dynamic shaped by these properties as well as the participants in the transaction. Students were challenged to connect to other students in the learning community, to cope with the asynchronicity and lack of immediate teacher feedback, and to communicate in a text-based medium.

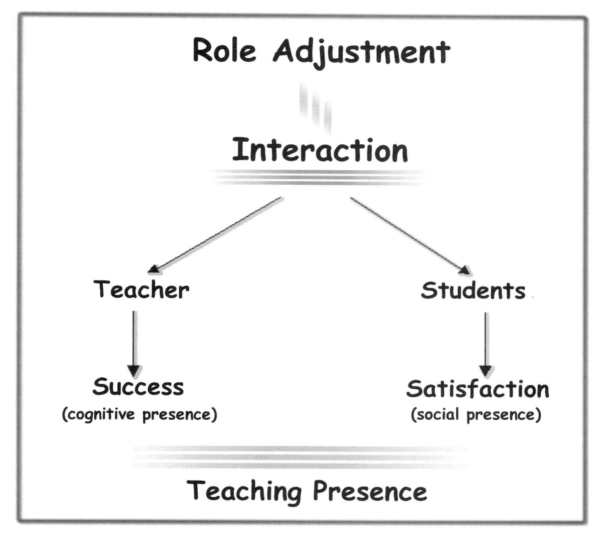

Figure 1: Linking role adjustment, satisfaction and success

While much of the role adjustment was associated with interaction, there appeared to be differential effects with regard to interacting with the teacher or fellow students. It would seem that much of the adjustment with regard to the teacher interaction related to feedback and answering questions (i.e., cognitive presence). On the other hand, much of the concern with regard to students was getting to know the other students and gaining a sense of community. Certainly these were the dominant concerns but they are in no way mutually exclusive—there is considerable overlap. What brings the two together is, of course, teaching presence. Only through teaching presence can the full integration of cognitive and social elements be realized and a community of inquiry be created online.

Thus, it is interesting to speculate on the differences between satisfaction and success in a highly interactive online learning experience. One explanation that is an over-simplification but with some merit is that satisfaction with the learning experience is more heavily shaped by how students connect with each other. On the other hand, success from a learning perspective is much more strongly influenced by the teacher. Certainly there is some evidence for this in this study. Again, however, the danger is to view satisfaction and success in a dualistic manner. They certainly influence each other but not necessarily in a simple linear relationship.

V. PRACTICAL IMPLICATIONS

Implications for effective practice and a successful and satisfying online educational experience focus on engaging learners in meaningful discourse through asynchronous written communication. Most students do not have the communication skills to engage in critical discourse online. Thus teachers will need to model and facilitate interaction and meaningful discourse. Without help, the first time online learner and others will likely not have experienced purposeful discussion online. Teaching presence is essential at the start of a course as students face a major shift in approach. They need to be afforded responsibility and control but not be abandoned. There are specific conditions that have to be established and maintained to create if cognitive presence that will result in higher learning outcomes. Students need to understand and experience the right balance of independence and interaction or reflection and collaboration.

In this study, cognitive presence was strong. What was less well established was social presence and clear expectations about how students were to properly relate to each other. It was also clear that students expected greater teaching presence. Facilitators should consider the level of role adjustment a student needs to make in each of the three presences. Some students will need support and encouragement to project themselves within the community. Others need support to be cognitively present and require guidance in synthesizing, applying and evaluating information. In terms of both cognitive and social presence, perhaps smaller groups of students need to be considered to allow students to get to know each other better as well as to encourage increased cognitive engagement. Consideration needs to be given to teaming students, providing private coaching, and assigning student moderators.

Teaching presence must be strong as students become engaged in the activities of the course. Community is established through authentic and worthwhile activities, clear role assignments, stimulating questioning, focused and inclusive interaction, timely responses to requests, and group projects. Engagement in a community of learners should encourage students to provide teaching presence as well. Students themselves are a valuable resource that should be valued and utilized. At the same time, this does not mitigate the essential role of the facilitator. Certainly, the facilitator has a responsibility to provide clear expectations, tasks, feedback, evaluation of progress, and summarize discussions before moving the community on in a timely manner. Attending to issues of role adjustment can empower students and facilitate higher learning. For example, students still focused on reiterating what is presented to them in course material can be encouraged through carefully designed questions to think more critically. Students engaged minimally in conferences that fall behind in assignments can be invited to take a more active role in the community.

Finally, the facilitator must check on the functionality of the community as a whole. All the issues related to group dynamics and group development are at play in a community of inquiry. Groups evolve and roles change. Facilitators must be aware of the culture emerging within the group and relationships developing, while acting to shape and direct both. The bottom line is that the role of facilitator in an online community of inquiry has expanded expectations, expectations that include managing a community and ensuring individuals in that community are playing an appropriate role. Beyond content expertise, facilitators are responsible to provide cognitive, social and teaching presence within the community.

VI. CONCLUSION

In conclusion, the Sloan-C series and others have provided strong evidence that online learning is as good as face-to-face instruction. The challenge is now to demonstrate how online learning can be better than traditional classroom lectures. The quality of higher education is not enhanced with the current trend to larger lectures. One very promising approach to this situation is the potential of combining the strengths of face-to-face and online learning.

Blended learning is not a simple recipe or solution to a variety of problems in higher education. The reality is that blended learning necessitates questioning and rethinking the educational experience and fusing the advantages of face-to-face and asynchronous communication in ways that meet the specific needs of each course, program and institution. Blended designs are flexible, and virtually no two blended learning designs will be identical. Blended learning is a viable means for introducing asynchronous online learning in campus based universities with little risk and minimal resistance. Moreover, it will provide the opportunity to study and understand the possibilities and properties of asynchronous online learning networks. However, blending does bring added challenges in terms of role adjustments and introduces new factors for satisfaction and success.

Finally, future research must focus on the features of text-based communication and how they merge with the asynchronous and collaborative properties of online learning. While we understand the superficial characteristics of written communication, we have little practical knowledge of its influence on facilitating higher-order learning and the design of successful and satisfying learning outcomes. A recent survey of online learning found that encouraging critical thinking was of the highest priority needing support [15]. That is, only 22% stated that they were successful facilitating critical thinking online. Few had the understanding and ability to use online learning to support complex, higher-order learning. This study and previous research would suggest that interaction (i.e., engaging students) is the key to successfully facilitating higher-order learning and should be the focus of future research in this area.

VII. REFERENCES

1. **Garrison, D. R.** Theoretical Challenges for Distance Education in the 21st Century: A Shift from Structural to Transactional Issues. *International Review of Research in Open and Distance Learning* 1(1): 1–17, 2000.

2. **Sener, J. and J. Humbert.** Student Satisfaction with Online Llearning: An Expanding Universe. In Bourne, J. and Moore, J.C. (Eds.), *Elements of Quality Online Education: Practice and Direction, Vol. 4 in the Sloan-C Series*, 245–260. Needham, MA: Sloan-C, 2003.

3. **Shea, P., K. Swan, E. Frederickson and A. Pickett.** Student Satisfaction and Reported Learning in the SUNY Learning Network. In Bourne, J. and Moore, J.C. (Eds.), *Elements of Quality Online Education, Volume 3 in the Sloan-C Series*, 145–155. Needham, MA: Sloan-C, 2002.

4. **Swan, K.** Virtual Interaction: Design Factors Affecting Student Satisfaction and Perceived Learning in Ssynchronous Online Courses. *Distance Education* 22(2): 306–331, 2001.

5. **Rivera, Julio, C. & Margaret, L. Rice.** A Comparison of Student Outcomes & Satisfaction Between Traditional & Web Based Course Offerings. *Online Journal of Distance Learning Administration*, Volume V (III). State University of West Georgia, Distance Education Center, 2002. Retrieved April 24, 2003: http://www.westga.edu/~distance/ojdla/fall53/rivera53.html.

6. **Garrison, D. R. and W. Archer.** *A Transactional Perspective on Teaching-Learning: A Framework for Adult and Higher Education*. Oxford, UK: Pergamon, 2000.

7. **Hudson, B.** Critical Dialogue Online: Personas, Covenants, and Candlepower. In Rudestam, K. E. and Schoenholtz-Read, J. (Eds.), *Handbook of Online Learning: Innovations in Higher Education and Corporate Training*, 53–90. Thousand Oaks: Sage Publications, 2002.

8. **Garrison, D. R.** Cognitive Presence for Effective Asynchronous Online Learning: The Role of Reflective Inquiry, Self-Direction and Metacognition. In Bourne, J. and Moore, J.C. (Eds.), *Elements of Quality Online Education: Practice and Direction, Vol. 4 in the Sloan-C Series*, 47–58. Needham, MA: Sloan-C, 2003.

9. **Garrison, D. R. and T. Anderson.** E-Learning in the 21st Century: A Framework for Research and Practice. London: Routledge/Falmer, 2003.

10. **Davie, L. E. and R. Wells**. Empowering the Learner through Computer-Mediated Communication. *The American Journal of Distance Education* 5(1): 15–23, 1991.

11. **Rovai, A. P.** Sense of Community, Perceived Cognitive Learning, and Persistence in Asynchronous Learning Networks. *The Internet and Higher Education* 5(4): 319–332, 2002.

12. **Cleveland-Innes, M. and D. R. Garrison.** Becoming a Member of an Online Community: Role Identity Acquisition for Online Learners. Submitted to the *Journal of Distance Education*, unpublished.

13. **Garrison, D. R., M. Cleveland-Innes and T. Fung.** Student Role Adjustment in Online Communities of Inquiry: Model and Instrument Validation. *Journal of Asynchronous Learning Networks* 8(2): April 2004.

14. **Garrison, D. R., T. Anderson and W. Archer** Critical Inquiry in a Text-Based Environment: Computer Conferencing in Higher Education. *The Internet and Higher Education* 2(2–3): 87–105, 1999.

15. *Technology and Student Success in Higher Education: A Research Study on Faculty Perceptions of Technology and Student Success*, Summary Report. Ryerson, Toronto: McGraw-Hill, 2003.

VIII. ABOUT THE AUTHORS

Dr. D. Randy Garrison is the Director of the Learning Commons at the University of Calgary. He is also a full professor in the Faculty of Education. He served as Dean, Faculty of Extension at the University of Alberta from 1996 to 2001. Garrison has published extensively on teaching and learning in distance, higher, and adult education contexts. Contact: D. Randy Garrison, University of Calgary, Biological Sciences Building, Room 530L, Calgary, Alberta, Canada, T2N 1N4. Tel: (403) 220-6764; FAX: (403) 282-0730; Email: garrison@ucalgary.ca

Dr. Martha Cleveland-Innes has served as a practitioner, researcher and facilitator of learning for more than two decades in the field of adult, higher and continuing education. She is currently a faculty member in the Centre for Distance Education at Athabasca University. Her research interests are social factors in student approaches to learning, student role adjustment in online environments, affective learning outcomes in distance education and learning in the workplace. Contact: Martha Cleveland-Innes, Athabasca University, Centre for Distance Education, Athabasca, Alberta, Canada, T9S 3A3. Tel: (780) 675-6180; FAX: (403) 238-7762; Email: martic@athabascau.ca

ENHANCING STUDENT SATISFACTION THROUGH FACULTY DEVELOPMENT: THE IMPORTANCE OF TEACHING PRESENCE

Peter J. Shea, Alexandra M. Pickett, and William E. Pelz
State University of New York
SUNY Learning Network

- Teaching presence has three components: instructional design and organization; facilitating discourse, and direct instruction.

- Instructional design and organization include: setting curriculum, designing methods, establishing time parameters, utilizing the medium effectively, and establishing netiquette.

- Facilitating discourse includes: identifying areas of agreement and disagreement, seeking to reach consensus and understanding, encouraging, acknowledging, and reinforcing student contributions, setting the climate for learning, drawing in participants and prompting discussion, and assessing the efficacy of the process.

- Direct instruction includes: presenting content and questions, focusing the discussion on specific issues, summarizing discussion, confirming understanding, diagnosing misperceptions, injecting knowledge from diverse sources, and responding to technical concern.

- We need greater understanding of how best to leverage online student-student interaction to achieve optimal learning outcomes.

I. INTRODUCTION

The SUNY Learning Network (SLN) is the online instructional program developed for the sixty-four colleges and approximately 400,000 students of the State University of New York. The major goals of the SUNY Learning Network are to increase access to SUNY's diverse, high-quality instructional programs and to ensure the quality of online instruction for learners in New York State and beyond.

The SUNY Learning Network has seen tremendous growth since its inception in 1995. The annual growth in courses, from eight in 1995–1996 to approximately 3000 in 2002–2003, and annual growth in enrollment, from 119 in 1995–1996 to over 53,000 in 2002–2003, with courses offered at all undergraduate and graduate levels from fifty-six of our institutions, indicates that the project has met, and in many ways exceeded, original projections. Significant growth also brings significant challenges and in many ways this paper is about our efforts to confront issues of quality in large scale learning environments design. While we continue to address these challenges we take pride in the recognition past efforts have received. The program has been recognized by EDUCAUSE as the 2001 award winner for Systemic Improvement in Teaching and Learning in addition to two Sloan Consortium awards, for Excellence in Faculty Development (2001) and for Excellence in ALN Programming (2002). In 2003, William Pelz, lead-trainer for the SUNY Learning Network was recognized with the Sloan-C Award for Excellence in Online Teaching.

II. HELPING FACULTY CREATE AND SUSTAIN QUALITY ONLINE TEACHING AND LEARNING

Previously [1] we described the faculty development process and identified elements of support for the creation of "teaching presence" that are embedded in SLN training. We also explained how faculty learn about and enact these in the online courses they teach to create and sustain cognitive presence. It was our intention to attend to both the general principles of good practice in higher education articulated by Chickering & Gamson [3] and to how they are identified and enacted in online, asynchronous environments. We used the Anderson et al. [4] framework to discover whether the faculty development efforts result in effective pedagogy, and the correlation of aspects of the framework with measures of student satisfaction, and learning.

How can a faculty development process help faculty to learn to be effective online instructors, i.e., to engage in behaviors that are likely to result in high levels of learning, and student satisfaction? Clearly, to achieve this goal we need to focus on the elements put forth by Bransford et al. [2], and the trainings need to emphasize the importance of learning-centered, knowledge-centered, assessment-centered, and community-centered environments. Additionally, because SLN is a higher education learning environment, we need to emphasize the importance of the specific principles of good practice in undergraduate education outlined by Chickering & Gamson [3]. Finally, because the goals of the trainings are to help faculty understand the nature of online, asynchronous learning we need to emphasize many of the indicators of social presence outlined by Rourke et al. [10] and teaching presence outlined by Anderson et al. [4] that lead to better *online* learning. Our goals in designing a workshop around teaching presence included providing opportunities to understand all of the components of this concept, to consider how faculty were or were not engaging in teaching presence behaviors, and to improve current practices through reflection and course revision.

In previous studies of teaching presence [1] we discussed faculty development in great detail, especially as it relates to teaching presence, and we examined how faculty learn about these concepts and practices through SLN trainings. In the present study we briefly review recent revisions to our faculty development process meant to foster greater understanding of teaching presence. We also present results from our most recent faculty survey indicating progress in this area.

A. Helping Faculty Create and Sustain Teaching Presence

Anderson et al. [4] define teaching presence as "the design, facilitation, and direction of cognitive and social processes for the realization of personally meaningful and educationally worthwhile learning outcomes." Teaching presence in this model has three components: 1) Instructional Design and Organization, 2) Facilitating Discourse and 3) Direct Instruction.

A recent faculty development cycle included a session devoted to the topic of teaching presence. Questions that participants addressed included:

What is teaching presence, why is it important?

How do we measure or identify teaching presence in an online course?

What are some design features that can enhance teaching presence?

How can we improve teaching presence through online classroom management?

What tools does the SLN Course Management System (CMS) provide to facilitate teaching presence?

Through this workshop and by leveraging elements of the SLN CMS, new faculty gradually learn from trainers, instructional designers, and experienced online faculty how to effectively design online learning, engage in productive dialogue, and to implement direct instruction online. In the course of the workshop, faculty consider to what degree they are engaging in teaching presence behaviors and how they might improve there current practices. (For more details about the SLN faculty development program as it relates to teaching presence, see Shea et al. [1].)

We will provide a brief summary of each of teaching presence below and the survey questions meant to elicit students' responses regarding these components of teaching presence.

1. Instructional Design and Organization.

Under the category, "Instructional Design and Organization" the authors include:

setting curriculum

designing methods

establishing time parameters

utilizing the medium effectively

establishing netiquette

Survey items meant to elicit faculty perceptions of teaching presence were written in consultation with Terry Anderson, principle author of the paper from which this construct was drawn. Items were written as statements and faculty were asked to express their level of agreement based on a five-point Likert-type scale. The questions were meant to elicit faculty perceptions of their own behaviors as well as their affects on student understanding and learning in the course. The statements that related to instructional design and organization included the following:

a. Setting the Curriculum

Overall, I clearly communicated important course goals (for example, I provided documentation on course learning objectives).

Overall, my students clearly understood the goals and objectives for this course without confusion or questions.

Overall, I clearly communicated important course topics (for example, I provided a clear and accurate course overview).

Overall, my students clearly and accurately understood the topics in this course without confusion or questions.

b. Designing Methods:

Overall, I provided clear instructions on how to participate in course learning activities (for example, I provided clear instructions on how to complete course assignments successfully).

Overall, my students easily followed my instructions on how to participate in course learning activities without confusion or questions.

c. Establishing Time Parameters

Overall, I clearly communicated important due dates/time frames for learning activities that helped my students keep pace with the course (for example, I provided a clear, comprehensive, and accurate course schedule, due dates, etc.).

Overall, my students were able to easily follow and keep pace with the important due dates/time frames for learning activities in my course without confusion.

d. Utilizing the medium effectively

Overall, I helped my online students take advantage of the online environment to assist their learning (for example, I provided clear instructions on how to participate in online discussion forums).

Overall, my online students participated in the learning activities I designed in my course according to my instructions and to my satisfaction without confusion.

e. Establishing Netiquette

Overall, I helped my online students to understand and practice the kinds of behaviors acceptable in online learning environments (for example, I provided documentation on "netiquette," i.e., polite forms of online interaction).

Overall, my online students interacted acceptably with me and with others in the class.

2. Facilitating Discourse

Another component of teaching presence in the Anderson et al. [4] model is *facilitating discourse*. The task of facilitating discourse is necessary to maintain learner engagement and refers to "focused and sustained deliberation that marks learning in a community of inquiry" [4].

The authors provide indicators of the act of facilitating discourse, which include:

identifying areas of agreement and disagreement
seeking to reach consensus and understanding
encouraging, acknowledging, and reinforcing student contributions
setting the climate for learning
drawing in participants and prompting discussion
assessing the efficacy of the process

Inasmuch as the construct of teaching presence is meant to account for activities and behaviors of both instructors *and* students we decided to write parallel questions for this part of the survey. In a robust learning environment, one characterized by sustained productive discourse we would hope to find both faculty and students engaging in teaching presence. In fact Anderson and colleagues [4] explain that they chose the term "teaching presence" rather than "teacher presence" for this reason. Items meant to elicit faculty perceptions of this aspect of teaching presence include:

a. Identifying areas of agreement/disagreement

Overall, **I** identified areas of agreement and disagreement on course topics that assisted students to learn.

Overall, **students** in this course were helpful in identifying areas of agreement and disagreement on course topics that assisted their fellow students to learn.

b. Seeking to reach consensus

Overall, **I** guided the class towards agreement/understanding about course topics that assisted my online students to learn.

Overall, **students** in this course were helpful in guiding the class towards agreement/understanding about course topics that assisted their fellow students to learn.

c. Reinforce student contributions

Overall, **I** acknowledged student participation in the course (for example, I replied promptly in a positive, encouraging manner to student submissions).

Overall, **students** in this course acknowledged student participation in the course (for example, students replied in a positive, encouraging manner to other student submissions).

d. Setting climate for learning

Overall, **I** encouraged students to explore concepts in the course (for example, I encouraged "thinking out loud" or the exploration of new ideas).

Overall, **students** in this course encouraged their classmates to explore concepts in the course (for example, students encouraged each other to "think out loud" or to explore new ideas).

e. Drawing in participants, prompting discussion

Overall, **I** helped to keep students engaged and participating in productive dialog.

Overall, **students** in this course helped to keep each other engaged and participating in productive dialog.

f. Assessing the efficacy of the process

Overall, **I** helped keep students on task in a way that assisted them to learn.

Overall, **students** in this course helped keep each other on task in a way that assisted them to learn.

Overall the **quality** of interaction I had with my students was very high in this online course.

Overall the **quality** of interaction between my students was very high in this online course.

3. Direct Instruction

Anderson et al. [3] also include indicators of direct instruction in their framework for the analysis of teaching presence. These indicators include:

presenting content and questions

focusing the discussion on specific issues

summarizing discussion

confirming understanding

diagnosing misperceptions

injecting knowledge from diverse sources

responding to technical concern

This aspect of the model equates with Chickering & Gamson's [3] concerns about interaction and for prompt, assistive feedback, again with emphasis on the needs of *online* learners. Attention to direct instruction is also essential for sustaining the knowledge-centered learning environment emphasized by Bransford et al. [2]. Questions meant to elicit faculty perceptions of direct instruction included the following:

g. Present content/Questions

Overall, **I** presented content or questions in my online course that helped students to learn.

Overall, **students** in this course presented content or questions that helped each other to learn.

h. Focus the discussion on specific issues

Overall, **I** helped to focus discussion on relevant issues in my online course in a way that assisted students to learn.

Overall, **students** in this course helped to focus discussion on relevant issues in a way that assisted each other to learn.

i. Confirm understanding

Overall, **I** provided explanatory feedback that assisted students to learn (for example, I responded helpfully to discussion comments or course assignments).

Overall, **students** in this course provided explanatory feedback that assisted each other to learn (for example, students responded helpfully to discussion comments or course assignments from each other).

j. Diagnose misconceptions

Overall, **I** helped students to revise their thinking (for example—I corrected misunderstandings) in a ways that helped students to learn.

Overall, **students** in this course helped each other to revise their thinking (for example—corrected misunderstandings) in ways that assisted learning.

k. Inject knowledge from diverse sources

Overall, **I** provided useful information from a variety of sources that assisted students to learn (for example, I provided references to articles, textbooks, personal experiences, or links to relevant external websites).

Overall, **students** in this course provided useful information from a variety of sources that assisted each other to learn (for example references to articles, textbooks, personal experiences, or links to relevant external websites).

Regarding the final indicator of direct instruction, responding to technical concerns, it should be noted that faculty in SLN are specifically instructed not to respond to student technical difficulties, as this diverts instructor resources away from their primary role, facilitating learning. It is the role of the SLN Help Desk to address all technical issues and faculty are advised to refer all such questions to the Help Desk to avoid students becoming dependent of instructors for technical support.

III. FACULTY AND STUDENT PERCEPTIONS OF "TEACHING PRESENCE"

As part of the cycle of course design and faculty development we engage in regular efforts to evaluate online teaching and learning in SLN. Each semester we conduct surveys of participating faculty and students through an integrated, web-based data collection process. In the Spring 2003 semester, we implemented a follow-up questionnaire on faculty perception of teaching presence. To create the survey, we framed questions around teaching-presence indicators identified by Anderson et al. [4].

In this most recent survey (Spring 2003) we received responses from 366 faculty about 60% of faculty teaching for that period.

Faculty are asked, via email and through messages posted online, to complete the web-based survey by SLN administration. Follow up communications are sent to non-respondents two weeks and four weeks after the initial request. While the survey is completely voluntary, the format of the instrument requires that all questions be answered before the survey may be submitted successfully, so for these surveys, faculty responded to all items. Participants are instructed that the results of their individual survey will not be revealed and that it is a voluntary activity.

A. Faculty Training and Teaching Presence

In the Fall 2002 faculty development cycle, instructors teaching in the SUNY Learning Network engaged in day-long sessions on the topic of teaching presence. Instructors also received follow-up support from their assigned instructional designers to assist with implementing ideas from the workshop in their online courses. Once again questions that participants addressed included:

What is teaching presence, why is it important?

How do we measure or identify teaching presence in an online course?

What are some design features that can enhance teaching presence?

How can we improve teaching presence through online classroom management?

What tools does the SLN Course Management System (CMS) provide to facilitate teaching presence?

After engaging in the teaching presence workshop, faculty had opportunities to revise their courses and then taught again in the following semester. At the conclusion of the semester, faculty were asked to evaluate their course by answering questions on a Teaching Presence Survey. What follows are summaries of faculty responses to the questions asked on the Teaching Presence Survey as well as student perceptions about the same question, and those responses that correlated highly with measures of student satisfaction and reported learning. Questions are organized by the components of teaching presence identified by Anderson et al. [4]. Survey items were followed by a five point Likert-type scale that asked faculty to express their level of agreement or disagreement to statements eliciting responses related to teaching presence. Frequencies of response are presented for each question followed by the correlation between the responses for that item and student satisfaction and reported learning.

IV. RESULTS

A. Instructional Design and Organization

Overall, faculty rating for questions about instructional design and organization were quite high. Approximately 93% of faculty respondents expressed agreement about statements reflecting good practices in instructional design and organization as defined in the survey. This compares with approximately 85% of students respondents who expressed agreement about their instructors in this category. In attempting to determine how relevant this group of indicators are to student satisfaction and reported learning we correlated these variables. On average, students who reported high levels of instructional design and organization in their courses also tended to report high levels of satisfaction and learning ($r = .64$ for satisfaction and $r = .60$ for reported learning). This correlation replicates the findings from our preliminary study of teaching presence [1].

Table 1. Average correlation for variable related to instructional design and organization

	Satisfaction	Reported Learning
Correlation	.64	.60
Significance	.000	.000

While faculty tended to rate their courses very highly on measures of instructional design and organization, they were not as enthusiastic regarding students ability to follow the design and organization. This can be seen most plainly in survey results at "strong-agreement" end of the Likert scale. For example:

Setting the Curriculum	% of faculty who strongly agreed
Overall, I clearly communicated important course goals…	54%
Overall, my students clearly understood the goals and objectives for this course…	29%
Overall, I clearly communicated important course topics…	55%

Overall, my students clearly and accurately understood the topics... 26%

Designing Methods:
Overall, **I** provided clear instructions on how to participate in course learning activities... 43%
Overall, my students easily followed my instructions on how to participate in course learning... 21%

Establishing Time Parameters
Overall, **I** clearly communicated important due dates/time frames for learning activities... 66%
Overall, my students were able to easily follow important due dates/time frames... 34%

In general it appears that faculty in these courses felt strongly that they established good instructional design but were less resolute about benefits to students. This may be a familiar result for those who feel they sometimes labor in vain to provide good instruction online or in the classroom. Still, these are clearly results that require additional investigation.

B. Facilitating Discourse

Relative to results for Instructional Design and Organization results for indicators that reflect effective discourse facilitation were somewhat lower. For this category faculty were asked to rate both themselves and their students. This dual scoring system reflects the belief that, in a learner-centered classroom we would hope and expect to see students facilitating some of the discourse supportive of their learning.

On average, approximately 82% of faculty respondents agreed or strongly agreed with statements indicating that they helped facilitate productive discourse and approximately 75% agreed or strongly agreed with statements indicating that their students helped facilitate productive discourse. This compares with approximately 75% of student respondents who agreed or strongly agreed with statements indicating that their instructor helped facilitate productive discourse and the approximately 69% who agreed or strongly agreed with statements indicating that their classmates helped facilitate productive discourse.

Results of instructors self assessments for facilitating discourse follow:

Identifying areas of agreement/disagreement   Agree/Strongly Agree
Overall, **I** identified areas of agreement and disagreement on course topics... 71%
Overall, **students** in this course were helpful in identifying areas of agreement 74%
and disagreement...

Seeking to reach consensus
Overall, **I** guided the class towards agreement/understanding about course topics 76%
that assisted my online students to learn.
Overall, **students** in this course were helpful in guiding the class towards 77%
agreement/understanding about course topics that assisted their fellow students to learn.

Reinforce student contributions
Overall, **I** acknowledged student participation in the course (for example, 95%

I replied promptly in a positive, encouraging manner to student submissions).

Overall, **students** in this course acknowledged student participation in the course   88%
(for example, students replied in a positive, encouraging manner to other student submissions).

Setting climate for learning

Overall, **I** encouraged students to explore concepts in the course (for example,   83%
I encouraged "thinking out loud" or the exploration of new ideas).

Overall, **students** in this course encouraged their classmates to explore concepts   69%
in the course (for example, students encouraged each other to "think out loud" or the explore new ideas).

Drawing in participants, prompting discussion

Overall, **I** helped to keep students engaged and participating in productive dialog.   76%

Overall, **students** in this course helped to keep each other engaged and participating   76%
in productive dialog.

Assessing the efficacy of the process

Overall, **I** helped keep students on task in a way that assisted them to learn   92%

Overall, **students** in this course helped keep each other on task in a way that assisted   67%
them to learn.

Overall the **quality** of interaction I had with my students was very high in this online course.   83%

Overall the **quality** of interaction between my students was very high in this online course.   71%

Overall, students who reported effective discourse facilitation on the part of their instructor also tended to report high levels of satisfaction and learning (r = .64 for satisfaction and r = .58 for reported learning).

Table 2. Average correlation for variables related to facilitating discourse on the part of the instructor:

	Satisfaction	Reported Learning
Correlation	.61	.58
Significance	.000	.000

While students rated their classmates almost as high as their instructor on effective discourse facilitation, the correlation between their rating of their classmates discourse facilitation and their satisfaction and reported learning were not as high. (r = .41 for satisfaction and r = .43 for reported learning).

Table 3. Average correlation for variables related to facilitating discourse on the part of students:

	Satisfaction	Reported Learning
Correlation	.41	.43
Significance	.000	.000

C. Direct Instruction

Regarding direct instruction approximately 89% of faculty respondents agreed with statements indicating that they had provided helpful direct instruction and approximately 71% agreed with statements indicating that their students had done so. This compares with the approximately 78% of student respondents who agreed with statements indicating that the instructor provided helpful direct instruction and the approximately 65% who agreed with statements indicating that their classmates did so. Again in a learner-centered environment we would hope and expect to see some students providing some direct instruction. Students who reported that their instructor and other students provided higher levels of direct instruction also tended to report higher levels of satisfaction and reported learning.

Results of instructor's self-assessments in this area follow:

Present content/Questions

Overall, **I** presented content or questions in my online course that helped students to learn.	96%
Overall, **students** in this course presented content or questions that helped each other to learn.	74%

Focus the discussion on specific issues

Overall, **I** helped to focus discussion on relevant issues in my online course in a way that assisted students to learn.	89%
Overall, **students** in this course helped to focus discussion on relevant issues in a way that assisted each other to learn.	74%

Confirm understanding

Overall, **I** provided explanatory feedback that assisted students to learn (for example, I responded helpfully to discussion comments or course assignments).	94%
Overall, **students** in this course provided explanatory feedback that assisted each other to learn (for example, students responded helpfully to discussion comments or course assignments from each other).	73%

Diagnose misconceptions

Overall, **I** helped students to revise their thinking (for example, I corrected misunderstandings) in a ways that helped students to learn.	89%
Overall, **students** in this course helped each other to revise their thinking (for example, corrected misunderstandings) in ways that assisted learning.	69%

Inject knowledge from diverse sources

Overall, **I** provided useful information from a variety of sources that assisted students to learn (for example, I provided references to articles, textbooks, personal experiences, or links to relevant external websites).	82%
Overall, **students** in this course provided useful information from a variety of sources that assisted each other to learn (for example, references to articles, textbooks, personal experiences, or links to relevant external websites).	71%

Again, recall from our previous study that student rating of their experience in online courses is strongly related to their perceptions of teaching presence in the courses. This hold true for both students' general reports of satisfaction and for their overall reports of learning. So, for example, on average, students who reported effective direct instruction on the part of their instructor also tended to report high levels of satisfaction and learning (r = .63 for satisfaction and r = .61 for reported learning).

Table 4. Average correlation for variables related to direct instruction on the part of the instructor:

	Satisfaction	Reported Learning
Correlation	.63	.61
Significance	.000	.000

Again, while students rated their classmates relatively high on effective discourse facilitation, the correlation between their ratings of their classmates and their satisfaction and reported learning were not as high (r = .40 for satisfaction and r = .43 for reported learning) when compared to the correlation with the instructor.

Table 5. Average correlation for variables related to direct instruction on the part of student:

	Satisfaction	Reported Learning
Correlation	.40	.43
Significance	.000	.000

These results highlight both the importance of teaching presence (correlations between the different categories and student satisfaction and learning are quite high) and the essential place that faculty occupy in online learning. Students look to faculty to play the central role in their online courses, much as they do in the traditional classroom—when students perceive that faculty are "failing" to play this role, they tend to report lower levels of satisfaction and learning. It appears that though students do report that their classmates can and do engage in forms of teaching presence, this perception is correlated at lower levels than with faculty expressions of teaching presence.

D. Differences in Perception

One result that may be important relative to teaching presence in online learning is the discrepancy between faculty and student perceptions of different aspects of this construct. A comparison of faculty and student responses appears below. Included are items in which there was a greater than 10% point difference in perceptions.

E. Results—Instructional Design and Organization

% of respondents who felt: Agree or Strongly Agree

I clearly communicated course goals.   (95% overall)

My instructor clearly communicated course goals.   (87% overall)

I provided clear instructions on how to participate in   (96% overall)
course learning activities.

My instructor provided clear instructions on how to participate in   (85% overall)

course learning activities.

I established "netiquette".	(93% overall)
My instructor established "netiquette".	(80% overall)
Overall I acknowledged student participation in the course.	(95% overall)
My instructor acknowledged my participation in this course.	(79% overall)
Overall students acknowledged fellow student participation in the course.	(89% overall)
Overall other students acknowledged my participation in this course.	(78% overall)
Overall I kept students on task in ways that assisted them to learn.	(93% overall)
Overall my instructor kept students on task in ways that assisted them to learn.	(76% overall)
Overall the quality of interaction between me and my students was very high.	(83% overall)
Overall the quality of interaction between me and my instructor was very high.	(72% overall)

The discrepancies between faculty and student perceptions of teaching presence can, in part, be attributed to a natural inclination—faculty were asked to self assess, while students were asked to assess the performance of another, i.e. their instructors. It might be expected that faculty would rate their own performance relatively highly, while students might be more critical of the performance. However, these discrepancies are telling and may be useful in future faculty development efforts. They represent areas where faculty may need to be more cognizant of their behaviors to meet student expectations.

Given the relatively strong correlations between student reports of learning and satisfaction and their perception of these indicators of teaching presence, we have made efforts to support SLN faculty to understand this concept better. We feel that increasing faculty awareness of teaching presence can be reasonably expected to result in higher levels of student satisfaction and learning. To test the relationship between increased understanding of teaching presence and student reports of the levels of teaching presence in their courses we identified 954 students whose instructors had participated in the teaching presence workshop described above in the faculty development cycle immediately preceding the Spring 2003 semester.

F. Results Relative to the Workshop on Teaching Presence

While discrepancies exist between student and faculty perceptions of different aspects of teaching presence, one result was relatively clear – students of faculty who had engaged in teaching presence were more satisfied and reported higher levels of learning than those students whose instructors had not attended the training. An analysis of survey results indicate that students in courses taught by faculty who attended the teaching presence workshops rated their instructors and courses higher on all of the measure of teaching presence and significantly higher on the following measures of teaching presence relative to students whose instructors had not attended the training:

1. Utilizing the medium effectively

Overall, **the instructor** for this course helped me take advantage of the online environment to assist my learning (for example, provided clear instructions on how to participate in online discussion forums).

Table 6

	N	Mean	Std. Dev.
Prof. attended training	954	4.24	.91

Prof. did not attend training	5109	4.15	.93
t-test for Equality of Means	t	df	Sig. (2-tailed)
Utilized Medium	2.729	6061	.006

2. Establishing Netiquette

Overall, **the instructor** for this course helped student to understand and practice the kinds of behaviors acceptable in online learning environments (for example, provided documentation on "netiquette" i.e., polite forms of online interaction).

Table 7

	N	Mean	Std. Dev.
Prof. attended training	954	4.21	.86
Prof. did not attend training	5109	4.09	.94
t-test for Equality of Means	t	df	Sig. (2-tailed)
Netiquette	3.510	6061	.000

3. Identifying areas of agreement/disagreement

Overall, **the instructor** for this course was helpful in identifying areas of agreement and disagreement on course topics in ways that assisted me to learn.

Table 8

	N	Mean	Std. Dev.
Prof. attended training	954	4.01	.97
Prof. did not attend training	5109	3.90	.99
t-test for Equality of Means	t	df	Sig. (2-tailed)
Inst. id Agreement/ Disagreement	2.928	6061	.003

4. Seeking to reach consensus

Overall, **the instructor** for this course was helpful in guiding the class towards agreement/understanding about course topics in a way that assisted me to learn.

Table 9

	N	Mean	Std. Dev.
Prof. attended training	954	3.97	.96

Prof. did not attend training	5109	3.90	1.01
t-test for Equality of Means	t	df	Sig. (2-tailed)
Inst. Reach Consensus	2.114	6061	.035

5. Drawing in participants, prompting discussion

Overall, **the instructor** for this course helped to keep students engaged and participating in productive dialog.

Table 10

	N	Mean	Std. Dev.
Prof. attended training	954	3.95	1.02
Prof. did not attend training	5109	3.85	1.07
t-test for Equality of Means	t	df	Sig. (2-tailed)
Inst. Helped Keep Class Engaged	2.623	6061	.009

Overall, **other participants** in this course helped to keep students engaged and participating in productive dialog.

Table 11

	N	Mean	Std. Dev.
Prof. attended training	954	3.90	.86
Prof. did not attend training	5109	3.84	.91
t-test for Equality of Means	t	df	Sig. (2-tailed)
Stud. Helped Keep Class Engaged	1.976	6061	.048

6. Assessing the efficacy of the process

Overall, **the instructor** for this course helped keep the participants on task in a way that assisted me to learn.

Table 12

	N	Mean	Std. Dev.
Prof. attended training	954	4.02	.96

	N	Mean	
Prof. did not attend training	5109	3.95	.99
t-test for Equality of Means	t	df	Sig. (2-tailed)
Inst. Kept Class on Task	1.908	6061	.054

Overall, **other participants** in this course helped keep us on task in a way that assisted me to learn.

Table 13

	N	Mean	Std. Dev.
Prof. attended training	954	3.74	.89
Prof. did not attend training	5109	3.70	.91
t-test for Equality of Means	t	df	Sig. (2-tailed)
Inst. Focused the Discussion...	1.976	6061	.048

7. Focus the discussion on specific issues

Overall, **the instructor** for this course helped to focus discussion on relevant issues in a way that assisted me to learn.

Table 14

	N	Mean	Std. Dev.
Prof. attended training	954	4.12	.89
Prof. did not attend training	5109	4.04	.97
t-test for Equality of Means	t	df	Sig. (2-tailed)
Inst. Focused the Discussion...	2.256	6061	.024

Overall, **other participants** in this course helped to focus discussion on relevant issues in a way that assisted me to learn.

Table 15

	N	Mean	Std. Dev.
Prof. attended training	954	3.86	.87
Prof. did not attend training	5109	3.80	.89
t-test for Equality of	t	df	Sig. (2-tailed)

	t	df	Sig. (2-tailed)
Means			
Stud. Focused the Discussion	1.905	6061	.054

8. Confirm understanding

Overall, **other participants** in this course provided explanatory feedback that assisted me to learn (for example, responded helpfully to discussion comments or course assignments).

Table 16

	N	Mean	Std. Dev.
Prof. attended training	954	3.86	.85
Prof. did not attend training	5109	3.78	.91
t-test for Equality of Means	t	df	Sig. (2-tailed)
Stud. Provided Feedback	2.628	6061	.009

9. Inject knowledge from diverse sources

Overall, **the instructor** for this course provided useful information from a variety of sources that assisted me to learn (for example, references to articles, textbooks, personal experiences, or links to relevant external websites).

Table 17

	N	Mean	Std. Dev.
Prof. attended training	954	4.11	1.00
Prof. did not attend training	5109	4.04	.99
t-test for Equality of Means	t	df	Sig. (2-tailed)
Inst. Injected Info from Diverse Sources	1.958	6061	.050

10. Student Satisfaction

In addition students whose instructors had attended the teaching presence workshop reported significantly higher levels of satisfaction with their courses then their peers whose instructors had not attended.

Table 18

	N	Mean	Std. Dev.
Prof. attended training	954	4.13	.99
Prof. did not attend	5109	4.05	1.02

	t	df	Sig. (2-tailed)
training			
t-test for Equality of Means	t	df	Sig. (2-tailed)
Course Satisfaction	2.206	6061	.027

11. Reported Learning

The same result was found regarding reported learning in their online courses compared to similar courses they had taken in the classroom, i.e. students of instructors who had participated in teaching presence workshop were more likely to report that their learning was higher online than in the classroom.

Table 19

	N	Mean	Std. Dev.
Prof. attended training	954	3.35	1.12
Prof. did not attend training	5109	3.25	1.14
t-test for Equality of Means	t	df	Sig. (2-tailed)
Reported Learning Compared	2.371	6061	.018

Given the strong correlation identified between levels of teaching presence and student satisfaction and learning it is quite possible that an increased awareness of these concepts on the part of the faculty had a positive impact on the students' experience of the course, their learning in the course and their reported satisfaction and learning relative to their peers without this advantage. These results should be viewed cautiously however due to lack of randomization in the design of the study.

V. CONCLUSIONS

Overall, results of the survey of faculty perceptions of teaching presence were quite encouraging. In general, faculty rate their performance as quite high on measures of these important online instructional behaviors. They also rate their students' contributions highly. There were two areas in which discrepancies were identified. Faculty ratings of their enactment of teaching presence differed from the benefits they reported. So, while faculty felt strongly about their performance on several measures, they rated students associated behaviors less positively. For example, faculty strongly agreed with statements reflecting their provision of clear instructions, yet were less enthusiastic in their rating of students' abilities to follow these instructions. Also of interest are the discrepancies between faculty perceptions of their own teaching presence and students ratings of the faculty. Faculty rated themselves higher than students did on many measures. Inasmuch as there is a high correlation between all categories of teaching presence and student satisfaction and reported learning, it is important that we communicate these perceived differences to faculty. Closing these gaps will help us to avoid lower levels of satisfaction and learning on the parts of online students.

Differences identified between instructors who have engaged in the teaching presence training and those who had not yet participated are also encouraging. We believe that it is reasonable to expect that opportunities to reflect on how to enhance instructional design and organization, facilitation of discourse, and direct instruction may have resulted in higher levels of teaching presence and, we suggest higher levels of student satisfaction and reported learning. Ongoing analysis of the data will be conducted to determine whether these faculty differ significantly on other relevant variables when compared to faculty who did not attend the training. This information would lend further support to the conclusion that teaching-presence training may have influenced the positive findings.

We will continue the process of revising training based on these results. At this point we have additional evidence to suggest that greater emphasis be placed on training those measures of teaching presence for which we either did not find any significant differences in student ratings, and/or on those teaching-presence measures that were rated, on average, somewhat lower than others. Again, these appear to be measures that presume greater emphasis on productive student-to-student interaction. Greater focus on well designed cooperative and collaborative instructional approaches may have a positive impact.

In summary we continue to believe that an emphasis on multiple perspectives represents a step forward in the development of effective online learning environments. Attention to the principles espoused by Bransford et al. [2], Chickering & Gamson [3], as well as Garrison et al. [9] and Anderson et al. [4] may be the best approach to ensuring high quality in the development of future online learning forums. We will continue to facilitate understanding of this emerging model (Figure 1) with the SLN community as we seek to improve the experience of students and faculty in the SUNY Learning Network.

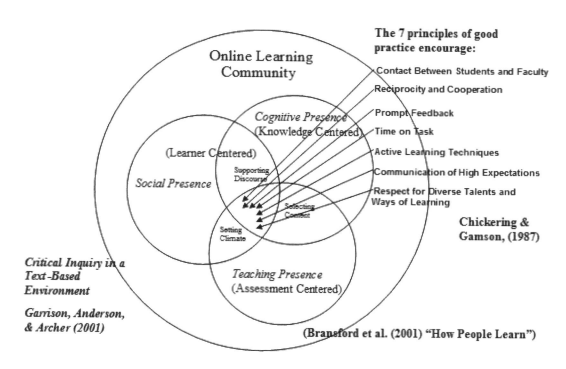

Figure 1. A conceptual framework for high quality, higher education, online learning environments.

VI. REFERENCES

1. **Shea, P., Fredericksen, E., Pickett, A., and Pelz, W.** A Preliminary Investigation of Teaching Presence in the SUNY Learning Network. In *Elements of Quality Online Education: Practice and Direction, Volume 4 in the Sloan-C Series*, eds. J. Bourne and J.C. Moore. Needham, MA: Sloan-C, 2003.
2. **Bransford, J., Brown, A., Cocking, R., Donovan, M., and Pellegrino, J. W.** *How People Learn.* National Academy Press, 2000.
3. **Chickering, A. W., and Gamson, A. F.** *Seven Principles for Good Practice in Undergraduate Education.* Racine, WI: The Johnson Foundation, Inc/Wingspread, 1987.
4. **Anderson, T., Rourke, L., Garrison, D. R., and Archer W.** Assessing Teaching Presence in a Computer Conferencing Context. *Journal of Asynchronous Learning Networks* 5(2): September 2001.
5. **Shea, P., Fredericksen, E., Pickett, A., and Pelz, W.** Measures of Learning Effectiveness in the SUNY Learning Network. In *Online Education: Learning Effectiveness, Faculty Satisfaction, and Cost Effectiveness*, eds. J. Bourne and J.C. Moore. Needham, MA: Sloan-C, 2001.
6. **Shea, P., Pelz, W., Fredericksen, E., and Pickett, A.** Online teaching as a catalyst for Classroom-based Instructional Transformation. In *Elements of Quality Online Education, Volume 3 in the Sloan-C Series*, eds. J. Bourne and J.C. Moore. Needham, MA: Sloan-C, 2002.
7. **Shea, P., Swan, K., Fredericksen, E., and Pickett, A.** Student Satisfaction and Reported Learning in the SUNY Learning Network. In *Elements of Quality Online Education, Volume 3 in the Sloan-C Series*, eds. J. Bourne and J.C. Moore. Needham, MA: Sloan-C, 2002.
8. **Kuh, G.** The National Survey of Student Engagement: Conceptual Framework and Overview of Psychometric Properties 2001. http://www.indiana.edu/~nsse/acrobat/framework-2001.pdf.
9. **Garrison, D. R., Anderson, T, and Archer, W.** Critical Inquiry in a Text Based Environment: Computer Conferencing in Higher Education. *The Internet and Higher Education* 2(2-3): 1-19, 2000.
10. **Rourke, L., Anderson, T., Garrison, D. R., and Archer, W.** Assessing Social Presence in Asynchronous Text-based Computer Conferencing. *Journal of Distance Education* 14.2: 1999. http://cade.athabascau.ca/vol14.2/rourke_et_al.html.
11. **Sheehan, K.** Email Survey Response Rates: A Review. *Journal of Computer Mediated Communication* 6(2): 2001.
12. **Twigg, C.** Expanding Access to Learning: The Role of Virtual Universities. Troy, NY: Center for Academic Transformation, 2003.
13. **Johnson, D., Johnson, R., and Stanne, M.** Methods of Cooperative Learning: What Can We Prove Works? Minneapolis, MN: University of Minnesota Cooperative Learning Center, 2001.

VII. AUTHOR BIOGRAPHIES

Peter Shea is the Director of the SUNY Learning Network, the State University of New York's multiple-award winning online education system. He is also Director of the SUNY Teaching, Learning, and Technology Program and coordinates SUNY's participation in the MERLOT Project (Multimedia Educational Resource for Learning and Online Teaching) a national consortium for the collection and peer review of online teaching and learning materials. Dr. Shea is also a visiting assisting professor in the Department of Educational Theory and Practice at the University at Albany, where he has taught at the graduate level both online and in the classroom. He is the author of many articles and several book chapters on the topic of online learning and co-author of the recent book, *The Successful Distance Learning Student*.

Alexandra M. Pickett is the Assistant Director of the SUNY Learning Network (SLN), the asynchronous learning network for the State University of New York under the offices of the Provost and Advanced

Learning and Information Services. A pioneer in instructional design and faculty development for asynchronous web-based teaching and learning environments, Ms. Pickett has, since 1994, led the development of the instructional design methods, support services, and resources used by SLN to support the development and delivery of full web online courses by SUNY campuses and faculty. She has spent the past eight years conceptualizing and implementing scaleable, replicable, and sustainable institutionalized faculty development and course design and delivery processes that in the 2002–2003 academic year will result in the delivery of 2,500+ courses with 50,000+ student enrollments. One of the original SLN design team members, she co-designed the course management software and authored the 4-stage faculty development process and 7-step course design process used by the network. Her comprehensive approach to faculty development includes an online faculty resource and information gateway, an online conference for all faculty with the opportunity to observe a wide variety of online courses, a series of workshops for new faculty, instructional design sessions for returning faculty looking to improve their courses, a developer's handbook, a course template, a faculty HelpDesk, online mechanisms for faculty evaluation of SLN services, and an assigned instructional design partner. In 2001 SLN was honored to receive the Sloan Consortium Award for Excellence in ALN Faculty Development for 2001 and the Educause award for Systematic Progress in Teaching and Learning for 2001. Today, working with 56 of the 64 SUNY institutions, she has directly supported or coordinated the development of more than 1,500 SUNY faculty and their web-delivered courses. Her research interests are in faculty satisfaction and the effective instructional design of online courses, and student satisfaction and perceived learning. She has co-authored a number of studies on these topics and has published and presented the results both nationally and internationally.

Visit http://SLN.suny.edu/developer and http://SLN.suny.edu/conference

Bill Pelz is Professor of Psychology at Herkimer County Community College. Bill joined the faculty of HCCC in August of 1968, the second year the college was in operation. During his 34 year tenure at HCCC he has served as Chair of the Humanities and Social Science Division and Director of Distance Learning, but has always returned to his first love—teaching. In 1994 he was presented with the SUNY Chancellor's Award for Excellence in Teaching—a most cherished prize. Bill was also recognized in 2003 with the Sloan-C Award for Excellence in ALN Teaching. Bill has published an odd assortment of scholarly and academic articles, most recently focused on the area of student and faculty satisfaction with asynchronous teaching and learning. His current research interest is in isolating the pedagogical factors which influence student achievement in virtual learning environments.

Bill has developed and taught a total of eight asynchronous credit courses and four asynchronous non-credit courses. Since 1999 his teaching load has been entirely online. In addition to teaching full-time on the Internet, Bill is also the Coordinator of the HCCC Internet Academy, the HCCC Campus Instructional Design Specialist, and the Lead Trainer for the SUNY Learning Network, having trained in excess of 1000 SUNY faculty during the past three years. He currently represents The State University of New York in the discipline of Psychology on the national Merlot Project, which is assembling a collection of high quality web-based learning objects for use in higher education. Bill is a vocal advocate for Asynchronous Learning Networks (ALNs), and has developed and taught an asynchronous course called "Online Pedagogy: Creating a Successful Asynchronous Course" for the SUNY Teaching, Learning and Technology Cooperative.

Special thanks to Martha Pedersen for her assistance in preparing this paper.

Learning Effectiveness

LEARNING ONLINE: A REVIEW OF CURRENT RESEARCH ON ISSUES OF INTERFACE, TEACHING PRESENCE AND LEARNER CHARACTERISTICS

Karen Swan
Research Center for Educational Technology, Kent State University

- By striving to make online learning "as good as face-to-face," we may be overlooking, even sacrificing, its distinct potential.

- Careful course design may take over some aspects of teaching presence from course instructors and help lessen the well documented burdens of online teaching.

- Terry Anderson and colleagues identified:
  - Five indicators of teaching presence in the design and organization category (setting curriculum, designing methods, establishing time parameters, utilizing the medium effectively, and establishing netiquette),
  - Six indicators for facilitating discourse (identifying areas of agreement and disagreement, seeking to reach consensus and understanding, encouraging, acknowledging, and reinforcing student contributions, setting the climate for learning, drawing in participants and prompting discussion, and assessing the efficacy of the process), and
  - Seven indicators for direct instruction (presenting content and questions, focusing the discussion on specific issues, summarizing discussion, confirming understanding, diagnosing misperceptions, injecting knowledge from diverse sources, and responding to technical concerns).

I. INTRODUCTION

This section explores learning effectiveness in asynchronous learning networks. Effectiveness in online learning has traditionally been defined in terms of face-to-face learning. The benchmark for quality has been that online learning is "at least equivalent to learning through an institution's other delivery modes, in particular, through its traditional, face-to-face, classroom-based instruction" [1]. Measures of learning have typically included general performance measures, such as exam and project scores and/or course grades [2, 3, 4, 5, 6], and teacher [7, 8, 9] and student perceptions of learning [10, 11, 12, 13].

More recently, however, authors have noted that by striving to make online learning "as good as face-to-face," we may be overlooking, even sacrificing, its distinct potential [14, 15]. Thus, some researchers have focused on aspects of online learning they view as unique, such as personalization [14], support for reflective inquiry [16], interactivity [17, 18], and support for collaboration [19, 20]. Indeed, more recent studies that do compare online learning to learning in traditional environments have begun to focus on the how the unique qualities of asynchronous environments work to support or constrain learning relative to traditional classroom environments [21].

Research on online learning has also begun to focus more on specific facets of online learning and the complex interactions among them. The papers in this section are good examples of this trend. In this introduction to them, I explore recent research on learning effectiveness in three areas that seem particularly promising, research that has caught my eye and my imagination in the past year. These include studies of interface issues, investigations of teaching presence, and research on learner characteristics. All three topics seem to have important implications for effective practice as it relates to learning within online environments. Perhaps more importantly, all three seem intricately connected in complex ways whose unraveling might have much more important practical import.

II. ISSUES OF INTERFACE

Quite a long time ago in digital years, Michael Moore [17] identified three kinds of interactivity that affected learning online — interaction with content, interaction with instructors, and interaction among peers. Not long after, Hillman, Willis, and Gunawardena [22] noted that new and emergent technologies had, at least temporarily, created a fourth type of interaction, learner-interface interaction, which they defined as the interaction that takes place between a student and the technology used to mediate a particular distance education process. Interactions with interfaces thus refers to the use learners must make of specific technologies, platforms, applications, and course templates to interact with course content, instructors and classmates (Figure 1). Ten years later, interfaces no longer represent the kinds of barriers to interaction they once did, but it is becoming increasingly clear that interactions with interfaces significantly afford and/or constrain the quality and quantity of the other three interactions [23].

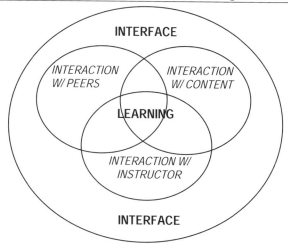

Figure 1: Interaction with Interface Conceptualized. Swan, 2003

A particularly compelling example of the influence of interface on online learning can be found in Jim Hewitt's studies of patterns of development in online discussions [24, 25]. Hewitt explored patterns of interactivity in 673 multi-message threads found in the online discussions of 92 graduate students enrolled in five asynchronous online courses [24]. For example, there were 344 four message threads in the discussions Hewitt sampled. In a four message thread, there are six possible patterns (Figure 2; numbers indicate sequence in time, indentations indicate responses to a previous posting). One might expect a reasonably equal distribution of these patterns across the sample, yet he found nearly three times as many instances of the elongated pattern (F) as any of the others, and few instances of both the truncated pattern (A) and the sequence that was out of temporal order. He found similar frequencies of patterns in the other (longer and shorter) threads in the sample.

Hewitt attributed these disparities to students' habits of participation in online discussions, habits he maintains are encouraged by the design of discussion interfaces to flag unread notes. Indeed, when he investigated user logs, he found that most students (97.6%) read messages before they posted messages, read only messages flagged as unread (82%), and tended to respond to messages that were less than 48 hours old (80%). In a follow-up study [25], Hewitt found that these patterns of interaction could be replicated using a Monte Carlo simulation based on nothing more that typical rates of reading and posting messages and a rule which stated that only messages flagged as unread would be responded to.

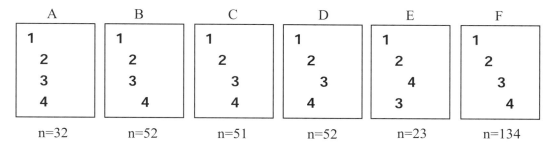

Figure 2: Frequencies of Patterns of Interaction in Four Message Threads. Adapted from Hewitt, 2003

Hewitt [24, 25] concluded that patterns of interactivity in online discussion were clearly influenced by interfaces that flag messages as unread and only display a single message at a time to favor elongated threads and discussions he characterizes as growing like forest fires, at the edges. The problem with this, he observes, is that potentially interesting and important threads are unintentionally abandoned, and that unintentional changes in topic supplant central themes, resulting in disjointedness and discussions that are often peripheral to course content. He suggests experimenting with differing interfaces and/or discussion assignments to support more meaningful learning. His results demonstrate the powerful mediating effects of interface design on learning through online course discussions.

Another interesting focus in research on the effects of interface design on student learning involves the growing use of a variety of media to deliver course content. Researchers, designers and practitioners of online learning are beginning to ask what combinations of text, pictures, animations, audio and video best support student learning. Richard Mayer [26] has been studying these issues for the past fifteen years in experimental studies of students' understanding and transfer of scientific explanations. In over 20 separate investigations, Mayer and his colleagues meticulously tested what combinations of multimedia resulted in the greatest transfer of learning.

For example, Mayer [26] randomly assigned students to interact with two versions of a computer-based explanation of the phenomenon of lightning, one in which animations depicting lightening generation were accompanied by textual explanations and one in which the same animations were accompanied by narrations explaining them. Student performances on tests of their ability to transfer their understanding were compared between groups and significant differences favoring animation with narration were found. Mayer made similar comparisons of the effects of differing combinations of media and variations in the sequencing and organization of multimedia presentations on such topics as human respiration, automotive braking, airplane lift and plant growth on transfer of learning, and replicated his results multiple times in all cases. Findings from this work are summarized in Table 1 which shows both findings from this work (research effect) and suggests practical applications of the findings (design principle).

	RESEARCH EFFECT	**DESIGN PRINCIPLE** When designing multimedia, . . .
MODALITY	better transfer from animation and narration than from animation and text	. . . Present explanations of animations in spoken form.
CONTIGUITY	better transfer when narration and animation are presented simultaneously rather than sequentially	. . . Present narration and animation simultaneously.
MULTIMEDIA	better transfer from animation and narration rather than from narration alone	. . . Provide narration for animations.
PERSONALIZATION	better transfer when narration is conversational rather than formal	. . . Present narration in a conversational style.
COHERENCE	better transfer when irrelevant video, narration, and/or sounds are excluded	. . . Avoid extraneous video and audio.
REDUNDANCY	better transfer from animation and narration than from animation, narration and on-screen text	. . . Do not add text to presentations involving animations with narration.
PRETRAINING	better transfer when explanations of system components precedes rather than follows a narrated animation	. . . Begin explanations with concise descriptions of system components.
SIGNALING	better transfer when different parts of a narration are signaled	. . . Include signaling that identifies the organization of the presentation.
PACING	better transfer when the pace of presentation is learner controlled	. . . Allow the learner to have control over the pace of the presentation.

Table 1: Effects and Principles of Multimedia Design. Adapted from Mayer, 2001

Chi-Hui Lin [27] did a similar experimental study of the effects of differing multimedia presentations on student learning, but with an added twist. Lin categorized subjects' epistemological beliefs as either mature or naïve on four dimensions — First Time Learning, Omniscient Authority, Quick Learning, and Simple Learning, and then compared their learning of mathematical concepts from online instructional materials that included either static graphics, animations or video representations. Results of a two-way ANOVA with performance as the dependent variable showed a main effect for graphical representation — students given the animations outperformed students shown video, but no effect for epistemological beliefs, and no interactions between representations and epistemology. However, when attitudes towards learning were used as the dependent measure, a main effect for epistemological beliefs (students with mature Quick Learning beliefs, those who believe that learning takes time, outperformed students with naïve Quick Learning beliefs) and very interesting interactions between graphical representations and epistemological beliefs were revealed. Lin found that among students interacting with instructional materials containing animations, those with mature Omniscient Authority beliefs (those who believed that learning results from the work of the learner) had better attitudes toward learning than students with naïve Omniscient Authority beliefs (those who believed that learning results from the work of a teacher). The opposite was true among students interacting with instructional materials containing video illustrations. A similar interaction was found on the Simple Learning dimension. Lin's work provides an intriguing glimpse into interactions between interface design and learner characteristics, and suggests that this may be a rewarding area for future research.

Other research on the effects of interaction with online interfaces involves the design of particular interfaces. For example, Chang, Sung and Chiou [28] investigated the efficacy of a hierarchical hyper-concept map (HHCM) interface as compared with a simple hierarchical navigation system and a linear course presentation for supporting junior high students learning of computer concepts. The hierarchical concept map organization provided students with a navigable representation of the structure of each unit of study as well as a hierarchical representation of the units (simple hierarchical navigation). The linear presentation provided no meta-indexing of the instructional materials. Chang, et al. also tested and categorized students as field dependent/independent to see whether this might affect the effects of the various treatments. Using analysis of covariance, with GPA as the covariate to partial out the effects of general aptitude, the researchers tested the effects of interface and field dependence/independence on two dependent measures, a test of computer hardware achievement (CHAT) and logs of time students spent using the online materials. Although field independent students significantly outscored field dependent students on performance measures, no interaction between field dependence/ independence and interface designs was found. In addition, the HHCM group scored significantly better than the linear group on performance measures, and took significantly less time reading the materials than students in both the linear group and the hierarchical navigation group. The authors argue that the results suggest that students learned faster and slightly better from the HHCM interface.

Another study of a particular interface design was conducted by Gutl and Pivec [29] to explore the efficacy of a Virtual Tutor (VT) application for scaffolding the problem solving of undergraduate computer science students. The VT combined capabilities for multimedia representation with an expert system to provide problem solving support for students learning computer programming. The authors compared the problem solutions of students randomly assigned to work either using the VT or using traditional print resources. Although the sample size was too small for statistical comparisons (n=21), they report that all the VT students (n=11) provided correct solutions to a transfer problem, whereas two of the students working with print materials provided incorrect solutions and two provided incomplete solutions. In addition, students working with the print materials experienced time problems, while students working with the VT did not. The authors argue that the results show that students solved problems better and faster using the Virtual Tutor. Because both this study and the Chang, et al. study reported above explore design concepts as well as particular implementations, their results may suggest ways in which interfaces can be designed to better support student learning. It is worth noting that the interfaces advocated in both studies exploit the unique capabilities of online computing environments.

Two studies that explored both interface and teaching presence issues also deserve mention. Both studies compared instructor-provided feedback on assignments with web-based model comparison types of feedback and both argue for the superiority of instructor-provided feedback. Riccomini [30] investigated pre-service education students' application of behavior-analysis and instructional-analysis skills on criterion tasks after receiving either instructor-delivered corrective feedback on a similar task or being directed to a web-based exemplary model that students could then compare with their own solutions to the task. Riccomini used an experimental, counter-balanced design in which students were randomly assigned to groups who received one type of feedback for one of the tasks and the other type of feedback on the other. He found that students receiving instructor delivered corrective feedback significantly outscored students using web-based model comparison feedback on both tasks.

Researchers at Michigan State University [31] made a similar comparison of instructor-delivered and web-based assignment feedback. This is an interesting study because it examines learning from real-world, web-based applications. The Michigan State physics department created a program to generate individualized homework assignments. In response, former students created a web application that generated answers with explanations to those problems. This study compared the performances of students using this third party site for help with their homework with those of students who took advantage of an instructor supported discussion site where they could get help on their homework from graduate assistants (GAs). The researchers further distinguished between students who posted to the instructor supported discussion, and students who just read those discussions. Using correlational analyses, they examined the relationships between the use of each of the online homework support sites and students' grades on homework, quizzes, and midterm and final exams, with the effects of aptitude (operationalized as composite ACT scores) partialled out. They found positive correlations between posting to the sanctioned site and grades on homework, midterm, and final exams, and between visiting the sanctioned site and grades on midterm and final exams. Interestingly, there was a negative correlation between just visiting the sanctioned site and homework grades. On the other hand, there was a positive correlation between using the third party site and homework scores, but negative correlations between using that site and grades on quizzes, midterms, and final exams. The results of this and the previous study indicate that web-based explanations of homework may not support conceptual learning without instructor interaction (teaching presence), at least with undergraduate populations. The authors of both studies suggest that individualized interrogation of students' conceptual understandings and remediation of misconceptions were what led to greater learning in the instructor-supported conditions. They further note that the students in their studies may not have been able to make needed comparisons between their own work and the exemplars provided. Further research in this area could prove fruitful. In particular, considering the Virtual Tutor results, it might be interesting to make comparisons between instructor-supported feedback and expert system feedback.

Finally, researchers at the National Technical University of Athens (NTUA), Greece have developed a survey instrument that specifically looks at the effectiveness of interfaces for delivering instruction and supporting learning [32]. CADMOS-E is a stepwise evaluation method that uses pre- and post-course surveys and regression analysis to assess the learning effectiveness of a delivery system in terms of: quality of the learning resources, changes in preferred mode of study, computer-mediated interactions with peers and instructors, contribution of web-based learning resources to the acquisition of knowledge and skills, and time spent with the learning resources, while factoring in such learner characteristics as previous computer experience and learning styles. The researchers used CADMOS-E to evaluate the effectiveness of an online course in software engineering offered at NTUA, then redesigned the course based on their initial findings, and re-evaluated the redesigned course. In the first evaluation, the authors found that the greatest amount of the variance in learning effectiveness could be attributed to "contribution of the web-based resources to the acquisition of knowledge and skills" (28%), followed by "changes in preferred mode of study" (11%) and interaction with the instructor (9%). In the second evaluation, they found "contribution of the web-based resources to the acquisition of knowledge and skills" again to be the greatest contributor to the variance in learning effectiveness, this time accounting for 37.5% of the variance, followed by "changes in preferred mode of study" (15%) and "time spent with the learning resources" (4%). The authors attribute the increased importance of the "contribution of the web-based resources to the acquisition of knowledge and skills" in the second study to improvements made in course design as a result of the first evaluation. It is also interesting to note that that "interaction with the instructor" declined in importance in the second study to where it was no longer a predictor variable. These findings may suggest that careful course design may take over some aspects of teaching presence from course instructors and help lessen the well documented burdens of online teaching. In any case, the instrument and its application to the redesign of course materials and interfaces seems very promising and a direction that might well guide both research and practice in the future.

III. TEACHING PRESENCE

Anderson, Rourke, Garrison and Archer [33] coined the term "teaching presence" to refer to "the design, facilitation and direction of cognitive and social processes for the purpose of realizing [students'] personally meaningful and educationally worthwhile outcomes." Anderson, et al. conceive of teaching presence as composed of three categories of activities—course design and organization, facilitation of discourse, and direct instruction. While they ascribe much of this activity to the work of instructors, they recognize that it also can be accomplished otherwise, through interaction among students for example, or, as suggested above, through clever interface designs [29, 32]. Kashy, et al. [31] and Riccomini's [30] findings concerning the superiority of interactive instructor supported corrective feedback over static and general exemplars, however, suggest that we must be very careful in considering how teaching presence is mediated through course interfaces. At the very least, they suggest that interaction is a critical element in meaningful feedback.

Indeed, many scholars maintain that online learning can support greater interaction between teachers and students than is typically found in face-to-face environments and argue that for this reason they can also support more meaningful learning [34]. Gutl and Pivec's [29] work, in this vein, perhaps suggests ways in which course interfaces might be designed to extend teaching presence. The research of Bures and colleagues [35] on motivation and Davies [36] on intentionality likewise indicates how teaching presence can interact with learner characteristics to support or constrain learning, as does the work of Gunn and McSorran [37] on gender and Morse [38] on culture (see following section on learner characteristics). Clearly, current work on the effects of various aspects of online learning is uncovering a variety of evidence that points to complex interactions among such aspects. Central to this complexity, is the notion of teaching presence.

For example, an ongoing study at the SUNY Learning Network (SLN) provides substantial evidence of the focal relationship between teaching presence and student satisfaction with and perceived learning from online courses [39, 40]. Basing their studies directly on the categories and subcategories of teaching presence identified by Anderson, et al. [33], SLN researchers used end-of-term survey data from summer (n=1,150), and fall, 2003 (n=6,088) to explore correlations between students' perceptions of teaching presence and their satisfaction and perceived learning from online courses. The authors found significant correlations between all measures of teaching presence, both that the teaching presence of their instructors and, interestingly, that of their fellow students, and students' satisfaction with and perceived learning from online courses.

Specifically, Anderson, et al. [33] identified five indicators of teaching presence in the design and organization category (setting curriculum, designing methods, establishing time parameters, utilizing the medium effectively, and establishing netiquette), six indicators for facilitating discourse (identifying areas of agreement and disagreement, seeking to reach consensus and understanding, encouraging, acknowledging, and reinforcing student contributions, setting the climate for learning, drawing in participants and prompting discussion, and assessing the efficacy of the process), and seven indicators for direct instruction (presenting content and questions, focusing the discussion on specific issues, summarizing discussion, confirming understanding, diagnosing misperceptions, injecting knowledge from diverse sources, and responding to technical concerns). Shea et al. [39, 40] asked students to respond to questions concerned with each of these subcategories using a five-point Likert type scale ranging from disagree strongly to agree strongly, for example, "Overall, *the instructor* for this course provided clear instructions on how to participate in course learning activities (for example, provided clear instructions on how to complete course assignments successfully)." Questions concerning the facilitation of discourse and direct instruction were presented with respect to both the instructor and other students, for example, "Overall, *other participants* in this course helped to keep students engaged and participating in productive dialog." The researchers collapsed and averaged scores for each category of teaching presence then correlated these with students' reported satisfaction with and learning from their courses. The results of these analyses are given in Tables 2 and 3 below.

CATEGORY (of teaching presence)	SUMMER, 2002				SPRING, 2003			
	satisfaction		perceived learning		satisfaction		perceived learning	
	r	p	r	p	r	p	r	p
design and organization	.64	< .01	.59	< .01	.64	< .01	.60	< .01
facilitating discourse	.64	< .01	.58	< .01	.61	< .01	.58	< .01
direct instruction	.64	< .01	.61	< .01	.63	< .01	.61	< .01

Table 2: Correlations between Teaching Presence of Instructors and Student Satisfaction and Perceived Learning
Shea, Fredericksen, Pickett, and Pelz, 2003; Shea, Pickett and Pelz, 2003

CATEGORY (of teaching presence)	SUMMER, 2002				SPRING, 2003			
	satisfaction		perceived learning		satisfaction		perceived learning	
	r	p	r	p	r	p	r	p
facilitating discourse	.36	< .01	.37	< .01	.41	< .01	.43	< .01
direct instruction	.39	< .01	.39	< .01	.40	< .01	.43	< .01

Table 3: Correlations between Teaching Presence of Students and Student Satisfaction and Perceived Learning
Shea, Fredericksen, Pickett, and Pelz, 2003; Shea, Pickett and Pelz, 2003

As seen above, the results demonstrate a strong correlation between the teaching presence of instructors and student satisfaction and perceived learning. Perhaps even more interesting are the more moderate correlations found between the teaching presence of fellow classmates and student satisfaction and perceived learning. These findings indicate that teaching presence is indeed distributed across online interactions as indicated by Garrison, et al.'s [41] model. Although Shea et al.'s findings [39, 40] relate teaching presence to *perceived* learning only, the data used was derived from large and diverse population enrolled in courses at all academic levels in different topic areas, and offered through multiple institutions. The similarity of results across semesters also points to their robustness. Further investigation of the relationship between teaching presence and learning is clearly indicated, especially research linking teaching presence to actual performance data, and research investigating the complex interrelationships among interactions with instructors, peers, interfaces, and course content.

Two other recent articles concerned with teaching presence and online discussion also deserve mention for their intriguing refinements of the concept. In a case study of the development of an interpretive community in an online graduate course on gender and culture in children's literature, Kay Vandergrift [42] develops the concept of "restrained presence" and its importance in the development of community. Vandergrift describes restrained presence as the instructor's refraining from comment in discussion to let students find and voice their opinions. She writes, "A faculty role that balances restraint and presence seems to encourage students to make the online class their own." Amy Wu [43], in a theoretical article on the application of constructivist principles to support online discourse, seems to argue for a similar restrained instructor role as well as for the use of the principles of collaborative learning in the facilitation of course discussions. Specifically, she recommends structuring peer interaction around authentic tasks, applying questioning strategies, role assignment, interdependent assessment, and requiring student reflection on the discussion itself. In Wu's view, the role of the instructor in all of this is to facilitate student collaboration by providing appropriate structures, not to direct the discussion. Wu's notion of the collaborative structuring of online discussion brings to mind Hewitt's findings [24, 25] concerning interface issues and perhaps suggests some ways discussion interfaces might be designed to better support learning.

Vandergrift [42], Wu [43] and Shea, et al. [39, 40], as well as many others, recommend specific training in teaching presence for all online instructors. Such recommendation is clearly a good one. Research on the effects of such professional development on teaching presence and student learning would be very useful. Research further refining our understanding of teaching presence is also indicated. Further investigation of this interesting concept would surely increase our understanding of the seemingly symbiotic relationship between interactions with instructors, peers, and course interfaces and their mutual effects on the learning of course content.

IV. LEARNER CHARACTERISTICS

Distance educators have long been concerned with the effectiveness of online learning for all students. As more and more programs are put online, questions of whether or not asynchronous online learning might be differentially effective for different kinds of students have become more critical. Dziuban and Dziuban [44], for example, developed a measure of online learning style based on Long's work [45] in adolescent psychology, the Long-Dziuban Reactive Behavior Protocol, which classifies students along two dimensions: aggressive/passive and dependent/independent. The aggressive/passive dimension has to do with the energy students bring to the learning experience. Aggressive learners are very active, passive learners are not. The dependent/independent dimension has to do with control of learning and need for approval. Dependent learners have a greater need for approval than independent learners who tend to want to control their own learning. In an interesting study of attrition among online students at the University of Central Florida, the researchers found that students who dropped out of online classes were almost exclusively dependent. The findings suggest that success in online courses is, in an important sense, related to students' need, or lack thereof, for instructor approval. They thus have implications for research on teaching presence as well as for research on learner characteristics and learning effectiveness. Katrina Meyer [46] similarly reports that students with independent learning styles are more likely to succeed in online courses than students with dependent learning styles. She further maintains that visual learners are more successful online than aural and/or kinesthetic learners, and that students with high motivation, greater self-regulatory skills, greater self-efficacy concerning online learning and better computer skills are more likely to perform well in online courses than students without these characteristics. One wonders why learners with specific characteristics outperform others or persist when others don't. Learning effectiveness research should certainly explore this question and its corollary, how can we better support all kinds of learners online. This latter question again overlaps issues of interface and teaching presence.

While Aragon, Johnson and Shaik, N. [47] found no differences in the performance of online students as determined by three different learning style measures—Grasha and Reichmann's Student Learning Style Scale (SLSS) [48], Weinstein, Palmer, and Schulte's Learning and Study Strategies Inventory (LASSI) [49] and/or Kolb's Learning Style Inventory (LSI) [50], they did find significant differences in learning styles as determined by Kolb's LSI between traditional, face-to-face students and online learners. Online students were more likely to prefer reflective observation and abstract conceptualization, while face-to-face learners were more likely to prefer active experimentation. In an analogous comparison of the characteristics of online and face–to-face students enrolled in a community college in the Chicago area, Halsne and Gatta [51] found that the online learners had several distinguishing characteristics. They were predominately visual learners, whereas traditional students were primarily auditory or kinesthetic learners. Online learners spent, on average, an hour more per week on class work than did their traditional student counterparts. The results also indicated that online students were typically older, whiter, richer, and more likely to be women than their face-to-face counterparts. They were typically full-time, professional workers and part-time students, as compared with traditional students who were more likely to be full-time students with part-time, service-type jobs. While some of these differing characteristics in online and face-to-face populations clearly involve self-selection relative to accessibility needs, some may be related to performance, or perceived performance, needs. Learning style and media preference characteristics, for example, clearly might have implications for interface design. These certainly deserve further investigation.

Indeed, learner characteristics and their effects on learning in online environments is an important topic in online learning research. While findings in this area are preliminary, they are plainly intriguing. In the previous discussion of interface issues, findings linking success in online learning to field independence [28] and attitudes about online learning to epistemological beliefs [27] were reviewed. Another interesting study by Nachmias and Shany [52] found differences in both learning and attitudes towards learning among middle school students with differing thinking styles as defined by Sternberg's theory of mental self-government (global/local, internal/external, liberal/conservative) [53]. Subjects were 110 eighth and ninth graders enrolled in an online course on web searching. The researchers measured students' performance in terms of grades, successful web searches, completion of assignments, and use of asynchronous communication. Attitudes were assessed by survey responses concerning course satisfaction and attitudes toward the online learning process. T-test analyses revealed that students with liberal and/or internal thinking styles outperformed students with conservative and/or external thinking styles as measured by grades, successful web searches and completion of assignments. Students with liberal and/or internal thinking styles also were more positive about the online learning process. Correlations between performance and attitudinal variables were also found, as were some correlations between these and prior Internet experience. Interestingly, no correlations were found between any variables and gender. These findings may mirror those of Dziuban and Dziuban [44], Meyer [46], Chang, et al. [28] and Lin [27] with a much younger population, indicating perhaps their significance. They certainly deserve further investigation.

Bures, Aundsen and Abrami [35] investigated relationships between student motivation and student acceptance of learning via computer conferencing, operationalized as frequency of contributions to online discussions, satisfaction with computer conferencing, grades, and time spent online. Both trait (individual characteristics) and state (task-related) motivation variables were explored. Subjects were 167 undergraduate students in ten courses chosen at random from online offerings at multiple universities. The researchers found that students with a learning (vs. performance) orientation spent more time on online activities and got higher grades. Regression analyses revealed that trait motivation variables explained 23.5% of the variance in satisfaction with computer conferencing, while state motivation variables explained 16.7% of the variance, and that the introduction of state motivation variables improved the model. Similarly, trait motivation variables explained 7.9% of the variance in time spent on online activities, and that, while not significant predictors, state motivation variables improved the model. These results suggest not only that individual motivation can be an important factor in online learning, but that task specific states of motivation affect online learning. The authors conclude that course developers and instructors should encourage students to pursue mastery learning goals (learning orientation) and design activities that are personally relevant to students (state motivation). Again, the findings suggest that learner characteristics interact with interface and teaching presence issues to affect learning.

Similar conclusions were reached by Davies [36] who studied learner intentionality in online courses by communicating weekly via email with 20 undergraduate students enrolled in an online course. The author also interviewed all students face-to-face at the end of the semester. He found that the students he studied had two kinds of intent: learning and course completion. These correspond with learning orientation and performance orientation in the Bures, et al. [35] study. Davies found that learning intent was by far more energizing for students, but that course completion superceded learning when deadlines approached. He also found that the students he studied did not take online courses as seriously as face-to-face courses, often believing them to be easier and so sometimes put off studying for them. He concludes that online courses should not inadvertently promote course completion as a primary goal, nor should they be too easy. Rather he suggests promoting learning intent, possibly through asking students to reflect on their own learning. These findings and those of Bures, et al., [35] are supported by Duane Grady's [54] content analysis of online discussions. Grady used an interesting methodology that involved a semantic analysis program, Diction 5.0, to explore the use of terminology in online discussions. He found that the top performing students and the top performing teams in a graduate level course in economics consistently used language that was more enthusiastic, determined and committed than that of low performing students and teams, whose language expressed low accomplishment, low activity and hardship. Because motivation seems to play a significant, perhaps a particularly significant role in online learning, these finding clearly need further investigation as do related issues of interface design and teaching presence.

Of special interest in research on learner characteristics are issues of gender, ethnicity, culture and language, in particular, whether specific classes of people are disadvantaged by online environments, and if they are, how such disadvantages might be ameliorated. For example, as noted above [51], women are more likely than men to be online learners, but Blum [55] among others suggests they may be disadvantaged relative to male learners by a lack of technical skills, a corresponding lack of computer self-efficacy and male dominance of online discussions. An intriguing paper by Cathy Gunn and Mae McSporran [37] provides evidence, based on their research and the research and experience of several colleagues, which supports Blum's findings, but also indicates that women's lack of technical skills and computer self-efficacy may result in women working harder and getting better grades in online courses than men. Gunn and McSporran further report corollary findings indicating that online learning works particularly well for women and mature students, and less well for younger male students. The authors suggest that overconfidence may be a problem for younger males and that it might make sense to find ways to help younger males get assistance and keep up with their coursework. This suggestion parallels the work of Davies [36] on intentionality and may point to ways in which learner characteristics, interface design, and teaching presence interact to support or constrain learning, as well as ways of ameliorating such tendencies. It also may suggest reasons why research investigating gender differences in learning in online environments has reported very mixed results. It may be that gender really is not a factor but that underlying variables sometimes associated with gender are.

The increasing internationalization of online courses leads to questions concerning differences in the perception of online learning among students from differing cultures. Although very little research has been done in this area, Morse's [38] exploratory study in this area is based on a characterization of learners that may prove useful for both research and practice. Morse characterizes cultures, according to Hall [55], as falling along a continuum running from low to high context. In low context cultures, low levels of mutually understood information provide communication context, therefore, communication requires a large amount of explicit information to convey meaning. In high context cultures, high levels of mutually understood information provide context and listeners do not need to be given much background information. Western cultures tend to be low context. Western educational environments are correspondingly learning centered and emphasize the development of personal skills and attitudes as well as content learning. Eastern cultures tend to be high context. Eastern educational environments are correspondingly teaching centered and emphasize content and knowledge acquisition. Morse explored the effects of such differences on student perceptions of the advantages and disadvantages of online learning among students enrolled in an online graduate seminar. Subjects (n=24) were evenly split between low and high context backgrounds. Interestingly, students from both groups perceived similar disadvantages and ranked them similarly in importance. All students had difficulty reading computer material, found certain student postings too lengthy, and found following online discussions time consuming. On the other hand, while low context students reported the advantages of online learning to be personal convenience, time to reflect on others' opinions, and time to think about their own contributions, in that order, high context students found the ability to say what they thought as the greatest advantage in online learning, followed by the ability to think about their own contributions, and personal convenience. The author concludes that "the perceptions are based on learning patterns which are developed as part of a participants' ethnic/cultural development, and are potentially challenged by participation in an asynchronous communication network, which of itself is implicitly culturally based" (p. 51). She suggests that greater awareness of such differences might lead to better communication for all participants. The point is well-taken. Research in this area is clearly needed and it may be that, at least in this preliminary stage, distinguishing online learners by cultural background along a high/low continuum may be more useful than distinguishing them by native language.

V. SUMMARY AND DISCUSSION

In this paper, the effects of interface design, teaching presence, and learner characteristics on student learning in online courses were explored and found to be both significant and meaningful. In all three areas, empirical findings clearly demonstrate that course interfaces, teaching presence, and learner characteristics affected the quality of students' learning online.

The research reveals that a common feature of most discussion interfaces, the flagging of unread messages, profoundly affects the shape online discussions take [24, 25], and so, one would assume, the kinds of learning that takes place therein. It shows that particular media and combinations of media are more supportive of online learning than others [26, 27, 28], as are specific instructional sequences [26] and particular navigational interfaces [28]. It establishes the fact that interfaces matter [32], and suggests that they may matter a great deal to learning online. Indeed, my guess is that current research has exposed just the tip of the iceberg. The research also clearly demonstrates that teaching presence matters in online learning; in particular, it highlights the significance of interactions that scaffold student learning [30, 31] such as individualized corrective feedback and support for problem solving. The research further suggests that such scaffolding is shared across instructors, course designs, and learners themselves [27, 39, 40, 42, 43]. We need to better understand this distribution. Concepts like restrained presence and structured facilitation may help guide us in fruitful directions.

The research identifies specific learner characteristics (i.e. field independence [28], high motivation [35, 36, 37], high self-efficacy [46], mature epistemological beliefs [27]) and particular learning styles (i.e. visual [46], independent [44, 46], internal [53], liberal [53], intentional [35, 36, 54], self-regulated [46]) that are more supportive of learning online than are other learner characteristics and learning styles. Many of these are also supportive of face-to-face learning, but some are unique and some seem magnified in online learning. All can be improved through various means with varying degrees of success. Certain learner characteristics, however, such as gender and culture cannot be changed. Thus, whether these findings reflect something intrinsic to the online learning medium or simply current features of common interfaces and teaching practices is critically important. This brings us to a last, but by no means least, finding embedded across the results reviewed here. It is simply that these observed effects are interrelated in a web of complex relationships. Interfaces interact with teaching presence interacts with learner characteristics and more, in ways we are just beginning to explore, let alone understand. Unraveling these relationships and developing models of learning online will not only increase or understanding of learning online but of understanding of learning in general and so improve the practice of online teaching and learning.

Issues of interface, teaching presence, and learner characteristics, are certainly important ones for understanding and improving online learning. They also clearly overlap. Indeed, all three of these concepts are touched on in the papers which follow. In the first, Zheng Yang investigates e-learning as a psychological phenomenon. Drawing on the work of authors from his upcoming special issue of the *Journal of Educational Computing Research*, Yang argues for the application of a variety of psychological approaches and conceptual frameworks to the study of online learning. He also makes a case for more empirical and more interdisciplinary studies of the psychology of e-learning. In the second paper, Michael Danchak describes a very intriguing interface he is working on that differentially presents information to students based on their learning style as identified on Kolb's LSI [50]. He calls his interface the Adaptive ExplanAgent and has found initial tests of the concept encouraging. Danchak's research and development work provides a concrete example of how interfaces of the future might be designed to adapt teaching presence to learner characteristics. In the final paper in this section, Roxanne Hiltz, Ben Arbaugh, Raquel Benbunan-Fich, and Peter Shea provide a thorough conceptual review of the research on the influences of contextual factors, including interaction with interfaces, learner characteristic, and teaching presence, on learning in asynchronous environments, and offer thought provoking directions for future investigations.

VI. REFERENCES

1. **Moore, J. C.** *Elements of Quality: The Sloan-C Framework.* Needham, MA: Sloan-C, 2002.
2. **Johnson, S. D., Aragon, S. R., Shaik, N. and Palma-Rivas, N.** Comparative Analysis of Learner Satisfaction and Learning Outcomes in Online and Face-to-Face Learning Environments. *Journal of Interactive Learning Research* 11(1): 29–49, 2000.
3. **Maki, R. H., Maki, W. S., Patterson, M., and Whittaker, P. D.** Evaluation of a Web-Based Introductory Psychology Course. *Behavior Research Methods, Instruments, and Computers* 32: 230–239, 2000.
4. **Fallah, M. H. and Ubell, R.** Blind Scores in a Graduate Test: Conventional Compared with Web-Based Outcomes. *ALN Magazine* 4(2), 2000. http://www.sloan-c.org/publications/magazine/v4n2/fallah.asp.
5. **Freeman, M. A. and Capper, J. M.** Exploiting the Web for Education: An Anonymous Asynchronous Role Simulation. *Australian Journal of Educational Technology* 15(1): 95–116, 1999. http://www.ascilite.org.au/ajet/ajet15/freeman.html.
6. **Arbaugh, J. B.** Virtual Classroom Versus Physical Classroom: An Exploratory Study of Class Discussion Patterns and Student Learning in an Asynchronous Internet-Based MBA Course. *Journal of Management Education* 24(2): 213–233, 2000.
7. **Dobrin, J.** Who's Teaching Online? *ITPE News* 2(12): 6–7, 1999.
8. **Hoffman, K. M.** What are Faculty Saying? *eCollege.com,* May 1999.
9. **Hiltz, S. R.** Impacts of College-Level Courses Via Asynchronous Learning Networks: Some Preliminary Results. *Journal of Asynchronous Learning Networks* 1(2): 1997.
10. **Shea, P., Fredericksen, E., Pickett, A., Pelz, W. and Swan, K.** Measures of Learning Effectiveness in the SUNY Learning Network. In J. Bourne and J. C. Moore (Eds) *Online Education: Proceedings of the 2000 Sloan Summer Workshop on Asynchronous Learning Networks, Volume 2 in the Sloan-C Series.* Needham, MA: Sloan-C, 2001.
11. **Fulford, C. P., and Zhang, S.** Perceptions of Interaction: The Critical Predictor in Distance Education. *The American Journal of Distance Education* 7(3): 8–21, 1993.
12. **Picciano, A. G.** Developing an Asynchronous Course Model at a Large, Urban University. *Journal of Asynchronous Learning Networks* 2(1): 1998.
13. **Dziuban, C. and Moskal, P.** Emerging Research Issues in Distributed Learning. Orlando, FL: Paper delivered at the 7th Sloan-C International Conference on Asynchronous Learning Networks, 2001.

14. **Twigg, C.** *Innovations in Online Learning: Moving Beyond No Significant Difference.* The Pew Learning and Technology Program, 2000. http://www.center.rpi.edu/PewSym/mono4.html.

15. **McDonald, J.** Is "As Good as Face-to-Face" As Good as it Gets? *Journal of Asynchronous Learning Networks* 6(2): 10–23, 2002. http://www.sloan-c.org/publications/jaln/v6n2/v6n2_macdonald.asp.

16. **Garrison, D. R.** Cognitive Presence for Effective Asynchronous Online Learning: The Role of Reflective inquiry, Self-Direction and Metacognition. In J. Bourne and J. C. Moore (Eds) *Elements of Quality Online Education: Practice and Direction,* 47–58. Needham, MA: Sloan-C, 2003.

17. **Moore, M. G.** Three Types of Interaction. *American Journal of Distance Education* 3(2): 1–6, 1989.

18. **Swan, K.** Building Communities in Online Courses: The Importance of Interaction. *Education, Communication and Information* 2(1): 23–49, 2002.

19. **Scardamalia, M. and Bereiter, C.** Computer Support for Knowledge-Building Communities. In T. Koschmann (Ed.), *CSCL: Theory and Practice of an Emerging Paradigm.* Mahwah, NJ: Lawrence Erlbaum Associates, 1996.

20. **Benbunan-Fich, R. and Hiltz, S. R.** Impact of Asynchronous Learning Networks on Individual and Group Problem Solving: A Field Experiment. *Group Decision and Negotiation* 8: 409–426, 1999.

21. **Koory, M. A.** Differences in Learning Outcomes for the Online and F2F Versions of "An Introduction to Shakespeare." *Journal of Asynchronous Learning Networks* 7(2): 18–35, 2003. http://www.sloan-c.org/publications/jaln/v7n2/v7n2_koory.asp.

22. **Hillman, D. C., Willis, D. J. and Gunawardena, C. N.** Learner-Interface Interaction in Distance Education: An Extension of Contemporary Models and Strategies for Practitioners. *The American Journal of Distance Education* 8(2): 30–42, 1994.

23. **Swan, K.** Learning Effectiveness: What the Research Tells Us. In J. Bourne and J. C. Moore (Eds) *Elements of Quality Online Education: Practice and Direction,* 13–45. Needham, MA: Sloan-C, 2003.

24. **Hewitt, J.** How Habitual Online Practices Affect the Development of Asynchronous Discussion Threads. *Journal of Educational Computing Research* 28(1): 31–45, 2003.

25. **Hewitt, J.** Towards an Understanding of How Threads Die in Asynchronous Computer Conferences. Paper presented at the annual meeting of the American Educational Research Association, Chicago: 2003.

26. **Mayer, R. E.** *Multimedia Learning.* New York: Cambridge University Press, 2001.

27. **Lin, C-H.** Effects of Computer Graphics Types and Epistemological Beliefs on Students' Learning of Mathematical Concepts. *Journal of Educational Computing Research* 27(3): 265–274, 2002.

28. **Chang, K-E., Sung, Y-T and Chiou, S-K.** Use of Hierarchical Hyper-Concept Maps in Web-Based Courses. *Journal of Educational Computing Research* 27(4): 335–353, 2002.

29. **Gutl, C. and Pivec, M.** A Multimedia Knowledge Module Virtual Tutor Fosters Interactive Learning. *Journal of Interactive Learning Research* 14(2): 231–258, 2003.

30. **Riccomini, P.** The Comparative Effectiveness of Two Forms of Feedback: Web-Based Model Comparison and Instructor Delivered Feedback. *Journal of Educational Computing Research* 27(3): 231–228, 2002.

31. **Kashy, D. A., Albertelli, G. H., Bauer, W., Kashy, E. and Thoennessen, M.** Influence of Non-Moderated and Moderated Discussion Sites on Student Success. *Journal of Asynchronous Learning Networks* 7(1): 31–36, 2003. http://www.sloan-c.org/publications/jaln/v7n1/v7n1_kashy.asp.

32. **Psarmiligkos, Y. and Retalis, S.** Re-Evaluating the Effectiveness of a Web-Based Learning System: A Comparative Study. *Journal of Educational Multimedia and Hypermedia* 12(1): 5–20, 2003.

33. **Anderson, T., Rourke, L., Garrison, D. R., and Archer W.** Assessing Teaching Presence in a Computer Conferencing Context. *Journal of Asynchronous Learning Networks* 5(2): 2001.
http://www.sloan-c.org/publications/jaln/v5n2/index.asp.

34. **Lavooy, M. J. and Newlin, M. H.** Computer Mediated Communication: Online Instruction and Interactivity. *Journal of Interactive Learning Research* 14(2): 157–165, 2003.

35. **Bures, E. M., Aundsen, C. and Abrami, P. C.** Motivation to Learn Via Computer Conferencing: Exploring How Task-Specific Motivation and CC Expectations are Related to Student Acceptance of Learning Via CC. *Journal of Educational Computing Research* 27(3): 249–264, 2002.

36. **Davis, R. S.** Learner Intent and Online Courses. Paper presented at the annual meeting of the American Educational Research Association. Chicago: 2003.

37. **Gunn, C. and McSporran, M.** Dominant or Different? Gender Issues in Computer Supported Learning. *Journal of Asynchronous Learning Networks* 7(1): 14–30, 2003.

    http://www.sloan-c.org/publications/jaln/v7n1/v7n1_gunn.asp.

38. **Morse, K.** Does One Size Fit All? Exploring Asynchronous Learning in a Multicultural Environment. *Journal of Asynchronous Learning Networks* 7(1): 37–55, 2003.

    http://www.sloan-c.org/publications/jaln/v7n1/v7n1_morse.asp.

39. **Shea, P. J., Fredericksen, E. E., Pickett, A. M. and Pelz, W. E.** A Preliminary Investigation of "Teaching Presence" in the SUNY Learning Network. In J. Bourne and J. C. Moore (Eds) *Elements of Quality Online Education: Practice and Direction*, 279–312. Needham, MA: Sloan-C, 2003.

40. **Shea, P. J., Pickett, A. M. and Pelz, W. E.** A Follow-Up Investigation of "Teaching Presence" in the SUNY Learning Network. *Journal of Asynchronous Learning Networks* 7(2): 61–80, 2003.

    http://www.sloan-c.org/publications/jaln/v7n2/v7n2_shea.asp.

41. **Garrison, D. R., Anderson, T. and Archer, W.** Critical Inquiry in a Text-Based Environment: Computer Conferencing in Higher Education. *The Internet and Higher Education* 2(2–3): 87–105, 1999.

42. **Vandergrift, K. E.** The Anatomy of a Distance Education Course: A Case Study Analysis. *Journal of Asynchronous Learning Networks* 6(1): 76–90, 2002.

    http://www.sloan-c.org/publications/jaln/v6n1/v6n1_vandergrift.asp.

43. **Wu, A.** Supporting Electronic Discourse: Principles of Design from a Social Constructivist Perspective. *Journal of Interactive Learning Research* 14(2): 167–184, 2003.

44. **Dziuban, J. I., and Dziuban, C. D.** Reactive Behavior Patterns in the Classroom. *Journal of Staff, Program, and Organization Development* 15(2): 85–91, 1997/98.

45. **Long, W. A.** Adolescent Maturation: A Clinical Overview. *Postgraduate Medicine* 57(3): 54–60, 1985.

46. **Meyer, K. A.** The Web's Impact on Student Learning. *THE Journal*, May, 2003. http://www.thejournal.com/magazine/vault/A4401.cfm.

47. **Aragon, S. R., Johnson, S. D., and Shaik, N.** The Influence of Learning Style Preferences on Student Success in Online vs. Face-to-Face Environments. *American Journal of Distance Education* 16(4): 227–243, 2002.

48. **Grasha, A.** *Teaching with Style: A Practical Guide to Enhancing Learning by Understanding Teaching and Learning Styles*. Pittsburgh: Alliance Publishers, 1996.

49. **Weinstein, C. E., Palmer, D. R., and Schulte, A. C.** *Learning and Study Strategies Inventory*. Clearwater, FL: H and H Publishing Company, 1987.

50. **Kolb, D.** *Experiential Learning. Experience as a Source of Learning Development*. London: Prentice Hall International, 1984.

51. **Halsne, A. M. and Gatta, L. A.** Online Versus Traditionally-Delivered Instruction: A Descriptive Study of Learner Characteristics in a Community College Setting. *Online Journal of Distance Learning* 5(1): Spring, 2002. http://www.westga.edu/~distance/ojdla/spring51/halsne51.html.

52. **Nachmias, R. and Shany, N.** Learning in Virtual Courses and its Relationship to Thinking Styles. *Journal of Educational Computing Research* 27(3): 315–329, 2002.

53. **Sternberg, R. J.** Mental Self-Government: A Theory of Intellectual Styles and Their Development. *Human Development* 31: 197–224, 1988.

54. **Grady, D. B.** Mapping Online Discussions with Lexical Scores. *Journal of Interactive Learning Research* 14(2): 209–229, 2003.

55. **Blum, K. D.** Gender Differences in Asynchronous Learning in Higher Education: Learning Styles, Participation Barriers and Communication Patterns. *Journal of Asynchronous Learning Networks* 3(1): 46–67, 1999. http://www.sloan-c.org/publications/jaln/v3n1/v3n1_blum.asp.

56. **Hall, E. T.** *Beyond Culture.* Garden City, NY: Anchor Press, 1977.

VII. ABOUT THE AUTHOR

Karen Swan is Research Professor in the Research Center for Educational Technology at Kent State University and the Learning Effectiveness Editor for the Sloan Consortium. Dr. Swan's research is in the general area of media and learning. She has published and presented nationally and internationally in the specific areas of programming and problem solving, computer-assisted instruction, hypermedia design, technology and literacy, and technology professional development. Her current research focuses on student learning in technology rich environments and on online learning, in particular, on interactivity, social presence, and interface issues. Dr. Swan has authored several hypermedia programs, as well as three online courses, and co-edited a book on Social Learning from Broadcast Television. She is the Special Issues Editor for the Journal of Educational Computing Research, and a member of the national advisory board of the Ubiquitous Computing Evaluation Consortium. Contact: Karen Swan, Research Center for Educational Technology, 201 Moulton Hall, Kent State University, Kent, OH 44242. kswan@kent.edu

THE PSYCHOLOGY OF E-LEARNING: WHY, WHAT, AND HOW?

Zheng Yan
University at Albany, SUNY

- E-learning has been studied from technological, economical, administrative, and pedagogical perspectives. E-learning is also an *important* psychological phenomenon.

- The psychology of E-learning is an *emergent* field rather than an established one.

- The psychology of E-learning is an *interdisciplinary* field rather than one single psychological discipline.

- To maximize students' cognitive capacity, pictorial and verbal information should be presented concurrently rather than successively to minimize the likelihood of cognitive overload.

- Verbal information through auditory rather than visual channels should be presented with the pictorial information.

I. INTRODUCTION

The diversity and pervasiveness of E-learning deserves systematic examination from the psychological perspective. What are important characteristics of the psychology of E-learning as a field? How can psychological insights and evidence really bring significant benefits to the E-learning community? This paper addresses these important questions. It first calls for a systematic examination of E-learning from the psychological perspective to improve the current practice of E-learning. It then presents the emergent and interdisciplinary features of the psychology of E-learning as a field. It finally demonstrates how the psychology of E-learning can inform the E-learning practice with three empirical examples of psychology studies. The paper concludes with suggestions for what the E-learning community could do to further develop the psychology of E-learning.

II. WHY SHOULD E-LEARNING BE STUDIED PSYCHOLOGICALLY?

E-learning has been studied from technological, economical, administrative, and pedagogical perspectives. E-learning is also an *important* psychological phenomenon because it concerns how best to learn and teach new knowledge with information technologies. Since learning and teaching are essentially human behaviors, it is important to study people's psychological factors (e.g., perception, memory, attitude, and motivation) and psychological processes (e.g., group dynamics of online courses or visual and auditory information processing) to promote science-based E-learning practice.

E-learning is a *complex* psychological phenomenon. With traditional human learning systems, knowledge is presented, stored, and delivered mainly through the medium of speech (e.g., giving a lecture) or paper (e.g., reading a book). However, with the E-learning system, knowledge is presented, stored, and delivered through the medium of electronics (e.g., browsing a web-based course) and/or speech and paper. As a result, the process of E-learning becomes extraordinarily complicated, involving multiple types of information (verbal and pictorial), multiple modes of processing (auditory and visual), and multiple manners of learning (successively or concurrently). It takes place much differently from traditional learning in terms of speed, timing, space, accuracy, and efficiency. Thus, the psychological complexity of E-learning challenges existing learning theories and current learning practice. It may not be adequate to rely on the existing learning theories or current learning practice to meet the challenge.

Since the E-learning process is mainly based on the medium of electronics, for instance, students' expectation of the feedback turnaround time in online courses might be substantially higher than in regular courses. They might not be satisfied if a teacher provides feedback on their homework assignments even within one week. Since students in the online course will read the learning materials on the screen for long periods of time, visual fatigue or so-called Computer Visual Syndrome might become a large concern. Since students in the online course will have to process multimedia information, some might become more frustrated with the cognitive overload and others might experience more enjoyment with more learning flexibility. However, current knowledge of the complex psychological process of E-learning is still limited, and consequently the current practice of E-learning is still not well grounded. Thus, it is timely to study the psychology of E-learning, synthesize the current understanding of E-learning from the psychological perspective, facilitate exchanges and collaboration among psychological researchers and E-learning practitioners, and develop strong and innovative psychological research to inform millions of e-learners in their everyday E-learning experiences.

III. WHAT ARE IMPORTANT CHARECTERISTICS OF THE PSYCHOLOGY OF E-LEARNING?

Emergent and *interdisciplinary* are terms that describe the psychology of E-learning.

The psychology of E-learning is an *emergent* field rather than established one. In a recent paper, Mayer [1] explicitly proposed the concept of the *science of E-learning* for the first time and presented his theory of E-learning based on his 15 years of research on this area, an important theorizing achievement in the psychology of E-learning.

A recently completed special issue of Journal of Educational Computing Research, *The Psychology of E-learning: A Field of Study*, is one of the first efforts in gathering systematic psychological studies of E-learning, and it provides an authentic window on the current status of psychological understanding of E-learning. The special issue assembles a collection of 9 articles explicitly concerned with the psychological factors and processes of E-learning, with 4 theoretical reviews and 5 empirical studies. Most of the papers in this special issue examine cognitive psychology issues (e.g., effects of multimedia learning, visuospatial cognition, judgment of learning, and navigation strategies). Only three of the papers touch upon non-cognitive issues (e.g., social success, gender differences, and collaborative study). To some extent, the special issue reflects the overall status of the psychology of E-learning as a field that is currently taking shape rather than in full bloom.

The psychology of E-learning is an *interdisciplinary* field rather than one single psychological discipline. E-learning is a complex learning phenomenon that needs to be studied in its multiple aspects from multiple angles. Thus, as shown in Figure 1, the factors and processes of E-learning can studied across multiple psychological disciplines, such as cognitive psychology, developmental psychology, social psychology, educational psychology, and neurological psychology.

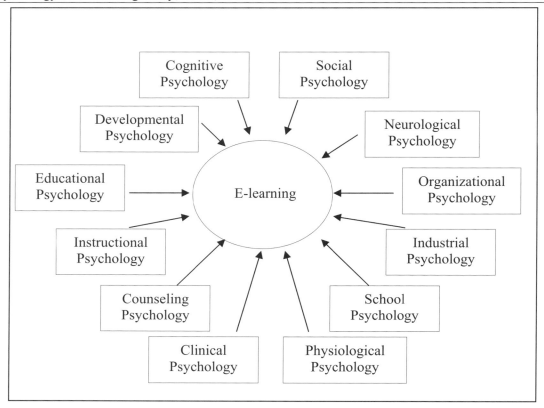

Figure 1. The psychology of E-learning as an interdisciplinary field

IV. HOW CAN THE PSYCHOLOGY OF E-LEARNING INFORM THE E-LEARNING PRACTICE?

The text that follows presents three examples to demonstrate how empirical studies in cognitive psychology, social psychology, and developmental psychology can help improve the E-learning practice in important ways.

A. Cognitive Psychological Studies of E-learning

One of the most productive areas of the psychology of E-learning is the cognitive aspect of E-learning. Two classic theories, the cognitive load theory [2, 3, 4] and the dual-coding theory [5, 6] were advanced a decade ago. The empirical research conducted by Richard Mayer and his collaborators at University of California at Santa Barbara since the 1980s can be considered as one of the earliest, largest, and strongest research programs in this area [7]. Many research groups conducted a wide variety of representative research on the cognitive psychology of E-learning, such as John Black's at Teacher's College, John Branford's at Vanderbilt, Christopher Dede's at Harvard, Roy Pea's at Stanford, and Roger Schank's at Northwest, just to name a very few. This is an area of study where many "superstars" exist and more rise above the horizon. It might continue to be "the crown jewel" of the psychology of E-learning in the future. E-learning practitioners can substantially benefit from this line of research.

Mayer and Moreno [8], for example, conducted two psychological experiments to investigate how college students learned about the formation of lightning or the operation of a car's braking system by viewing short computer-generated animation programs. In the study, about 150 college students were randomly assigned to two groups. One group of students viewed the animation with *concurrent narration*, and another group viewed the animation with *concurrent on-screen text* using the same words and timing. Students' learning outcomes were assessed with three tasks, the retention task (recalling what had been learned), recognition task (identifying what had been learned), and transfer task (solving new problems). They found that students receiving the narration outperformed students reading the on-screen text, a finding highly consistent across the three different tasks in the two experiments.

Why did students receive the narration consistently perform significantly better than students reading the on-screen text given the exactly same words and timing? According to Mayer and Moreno, this robust experimental evidence demonstrates a well-known split-attention effect [3, 4]. Students who viewed the animation with the on-screen test have to split their limited cognitive resources (e.g., attention and working memory) to process both the animation images and the corresponding text in *visual* working memory at the same time. Thus, their visual working memory became overloaded and their performance levels were decreased. In contrast, students who viewed the animation with the narration processed the animation images in *visual* working memory and processed the corresponding narration in *auditory* working memory. Consequently, they built more referential connections between the visual information and the auditory one, and their cognitive resources were not split up but rather fully used to process information coming from two different modalities simultaneously.

The experimental finding of the split-attention effect can has specific and important implications for the E-learning practice. In designing the E-learning courseware and websites in higher education settings, we often present multimedia information to students. To have a good effect on students' learning, we need to consider carefully not only which content should be included, but also when (concurrently or successively) and how (using words or pictures) to present the content. Based on the current cognitive psychological theories [5, 7, 9], to maximize the use of students' cognitive capacity, pictorial and verbal information should be presented concurrently rather than successively; to minimize the likelihood of cognitive overload, verbal information through auditory rather visual channels should be presented with the pictorial information.

Note that split-attention effect or modality effect is just one of nine major psychological effects (modality effect, contiguity effect, multimedia effect, personalization effect, coherence effect, redundancy effect, pre-training effect, signaling effect, and pacing effect) of multimedia learning that Mayer and his collaborators have been investigating for almost two decades [7, 8]. Furthermore, the Mayer research group is only one of the many research centers around the world conducting cognitive psychological studies that are directly relevant to E-learning. There is rich psychological knowledge of how to best teach and learn knowledge through information technologies. Thus, it is important to study cognitive process of E-learning to undertake activities on the basis of solid scientific evidence rather than popular folk theories.

B. Social Psychological Studies of E-learning

Another particularly active area in the psychology of E-learning is studying the social process of E-learning. Among leading researchers in this area are Linda Jackson and her collaborators at Michigan State University, Everett Katz and Ronald Rice at Rutgers, Robert Kraunt, Sara Kiesler, and their associates at Carnegie Mellon, Sheryl Turkle at MIT, Joseph Turow at University of Pennsylvania, and Patricia Wallace at John Hopkins. Based on both the growing amount of the research literature and the growing number of research groups in the area, the social psychology of E-learning is likely to become one of the most influential areas of studies.

The research work by Jackson and her collaborators provides good examples of how social psychological studies of E-learning can inform the E-learning practice [10, 11, 12, 13, 14]. In one of recently published studies [14], Jackson and her team examined the relationship between home Internet use and Internet attitude with a sample of 117 adults from in low-income families. Specifically, they automatically recorded participants' daily Internet use in terms of number of minutes spent on the Internet, number of sessions logged on to the Internet, number of Web domains visited, and number of e-mails sent. They also surveyed participants' attitudes toward the Intenet in terms of their positive Internet attitudes (e.g., believing that using the Internet helps children to do better in school or Internet skills will be necessary to getting good jobs) and negative Internet attitudes (e.g., believing that children can come to harm if they use the Internet or there is no privacy on the Internet). One the major surprising findings of this study is that the more participants believed that there is no privacy on the Internet, the *more* they used the Internet, even after controlling for demographic characteristics (race and age), previous experience using the Internet, and actual Internet use during the study. Roughly speaking, one level of increase in believing that there is no privacy on the Internet was significantly associated with about 30 minutes more spent online per day, about 2 more sessions logged on to the Internet per day, and about 4 more domains visited on the Web per day.

How do we explain this seemingly peculiar finding that the more skeptical attitude about online privacy leads to greater Internet use? Jackson and her collaborators believed that after nine months of experience using the Internet the participants in the study developed more realistic and sophisticated understanding of the Internet, particularly about online privacy. Thus, these participants' *skeptical* attitude about online privacy actually could be interpreted as *informed* attitudes about the Internet. The informed attitude motivated these participants to use the Internet more actively rather than being frightened away from the Internet. This finding about attitude and Internet use seems somehow counter-intuitive, but in fact is consistent with the literature on the *novelty effect*. The novelty effect refers to a psychological phenomenon observed when individuals initially have positive emotional responses to the new technology but gradually lose their initial excitement [15, 16, 17]. This phenomenon has been repeatedly found within cultures when computer users develop negative attitudes after gaining more computer experience [18, 19, 20, 21] and across cultures when computer learners from less technologically advanced cultures generally have a naïve but positive attitude to a new technology [15, 22, 23, 24].

Although the population involved in the study was not college students and the target of the study was not about online learning at universities, there are several potentially important implications of this social psychological study to the E-learning practice in higher education. Firstly, the Jackson study suggests that students' online participation is substantially influenced by students' Internet *attitudes* more than by their increased experience of using the Internet. Thus, it is important to motivate students by improving their attitudes toward E-learning. Secondly, with the increased online experience, students' attitudes might *change* dramatically, moving from a naïve positive attitude to a realistic informed attitude, which is a healthy indication rather than an alarming signal. Thirdly, the better way to motivate students to participate actively in online learning is to provide a realistic picture of the Internet rather than to paint a rosy image. When students are well informed about the positive and negative sides of the Internet, they will likely sustain their active participation for longer period of time.

C. Developmental Psychological Studies of E-learning

E-learning can also be studied from the perspective of developmental psychology. The leading research groups at least include Sandra Calvert's at Georgetown, Rodney Cocking's at NSF, Michael Scaife's at Sussex University, Patricia Greenfield's at UCLA, Michael Resnick's at MIT Media Laboratory, Aletha Huston and John Wright at the University of Texas at Austin, and Dorothy Singer and Jerome Singer at Yale. The existing developmental psychological studies of E-learning have demonstrated how cognitive development, social development, and physical development play a role in the process of E-learning for both children and adults. Researchers have studied, for example, how *cognitive* development of children and adults is associated with their ability to navigate on the Internet [25–29]. There are developmental studies investigating how online activities are related to *social* identity and personality of children and adults [30–32]. Research literature has also documented various concerns of *physical* development for E-learners, especially for the young adult population at universities, including concerns about repetitive strain injury (RSI) [33], computer vision syndrome (CVS) [34], and the readability of computer screen [35–37].

The Internet loneliness literature [38–44] has substantially increased in recent years, suggesting that greater use of the Internet among teenagers is associated with increases in loneliness and depression. Almost all of these studies, however, exclusively focused on the relationship between Internet use and Internet loneliness at one time, but have not examined whether and how this relationship would change over time. In contrast, the longitudinal project called HomeNet [45–47] examined change of effects of using the Internet on people's psychological well-being over years and found a complex but informative pattern.

In this longitudinal study, Kraut and his associates examined 93 families in the Pittsburgh area to see family use of the Internet in 1995 and 1998. More than 100 children and adolescents ranging in age from 10–19 years participated in the study. The first year of the study indicated that the more hours the children and adolescents used the Internet, the more their psychological well-being declined, consistent with many non-developmental studies. The second year of the study suggested, however, that further use of the Internet was associated with smaller declines or even noticeable improvements in psychological well-being. Over the period of two years, there existed a dramatic shift in the relationship between social loneliness and Internet use among these children and adolescents in Pittsburgh.

Four explanations for this shift in the Internet loneliness are given [47]. First, this group of children and adolescents may have adjusted themselves and learned to use the Internet more wisely over time rather than excessively as they did initially. Second, the Internet technology per se has changed dramatically since 1995, especially in terms of easy access and effective usage for a wide variety of individuals. Third, the online population has grown rapidly over the past few years, and these children can now easily talk to many of their good friends and close relatives through Instant Messaging or Buddy Lists. Fourth, early exposure to a novel phenomenon such as the Internet might have larger impact on behaviors than later exposure. Here, multiple internal factors (e.g., children learned to use the Internet wisely over time) and external factors (e.g., the Internet technology developed over time) changed over time and consequently contribute to the shift in the Internet loneliness. While more longitudinal data in this study will be available to show further change in the Internet loneliness, one can clearly see how important and revealing it is to study changes of the Internet loneliness over time from the developmental perspective, even just with two years of investigation. Developmental psychologists do very often examine developmental differences across different age groups. But most importantly, the real power of developmental research is to reveal macro- and micro-developmental changes over different time points [48, 49]. Developmental psychological insights and methods will really help develop online courses that are developmentally appropriate rather than merely user-friendly.

The above discussion focuses only on the studies of cognitive psychology, social psychology, and developmental psychology. It by no means exhausts all the important studies relevant to E-learning across over 50 psychological disciplines. Other promising areas of research, for example, are (a) neurological psychology of E-learning [54–57]; (b) industrial psychology of E-learning [58, 59]; and (c) physiological psychology of E-learning [34, 40, 60]. It is clear that there is rich literature about E-learning in a wide variety of psychological disciplines. More interdisciplinary psychological studies of E-learning will help improve E-learning practice.

V. CONCLUSIONS

To further build the psychology of E-learning as a field of study, we should move forward in two directions: bringing in sound psychological research and reaching out to collaborate with psychologists to improve the E-learning practice.

To bring psychological studies into the practice of E-learning, we first need to identify sound *theories* in the psychological science that are relevant to E-learning. The E-learning community should be well equipped with these psychological theories to guide E-learning practice and research. Second, we need to pay close attention to empirical psychological *research* to study explicitly various psychological factors, processes, and mechanisms that underlie the E-learning process. We should know better how and why some E-learning programs are successful and others are not. Third, we need to examine effective research *methods* that are used in the psychological studies [61] to advance the research methodology of E-learning. We should develop the E-research methodology that really takes full advantage of information technologies to collect and analyze quality data on E-learning effectively.

Intellectual exchanges and dialogues between the E-learning community and the psychology community should be reciprocal rather than one-sided. Thus, the E-learning community should reach out and work with the psychology community. First, we as the E-learning community need to reach out by challenging psychologists with intriguing and complex research *questions* that are encountered in the real-world experience of E-learning. These questions, however small (e.g., designing an icon for a courseware) or large (e.g., finding changing patterns of societal attitudes toward new technologies in the history), might influence the current research agendas of different psychological disciplines. Second, we need to reach out by *testifying* existing psychological theories or studies with the daily E-learning practice and informing psychologists whether these psychological findings really work or not for hundreds of E-learning practitioners. Third, we need to reach out by asking specific practical *implications* and direct *applications* of the psychological research.

In conclusion, it is important to both bring in theories, methods, and studies from a wide variety of psychology disciplines and reach out to ask psychological scientists for their collaborations in addressing challenging research questions and conducting practice-oriented applied research. We should develop interdisciplinary research agendas, conduct interdisciplinary research programs, and build interdisciplinary research community to develop the psychology of E-learning, a fascinating field that will have distinctive intellectual identity and broad social impacts and that will inform current E-learning practices.

VI. REFERENCES

1. **Mayer, R. E.** Elements of a Science of E-Learning. *Journal of Educational Computing Research* 29: 297–313, 2003.
2. **Chandler, P., and Sweller, J.** Cognitive Load Theory and Format of Instruction. *Cognition and Instruction* 8: 293–332, 1991.
3. **Chandler, P., and Sweller, J.** The Split-Attention Affect as a Factor in the Design of Instruction. *British Journal of Educational Psychology* 62: 233–246, 1992.
4. **Sweller, J., and Chandler, P.** Why is Some Material Difficult to Learn? *Cognition and Instruction* 12: 185–233, 1994.
5. **Paivio, A.** *Mental Representations: A Dual Coding Approach.* Oxford, UK: Oxford University Press, 1986.
6. **Claik, J. M., and Paivio, A.** Dual Coding Theory and Education. *Educational Psychology Review* 3: 149–210, 1991.

7. **Mayer, R. E.** *Multimedia Learning.* New York: Cambridge University Press, 2001.

8. **Mayer, R. and Moreno, R.** A Split-Attention Effect in Multimedia Learning: Evidence for Dual Processing Systems in Working Memory. *Journal of Education Psychology* 90: 312–320, 1998.

9. **Sweller, J.** Cognitive Load During Problem Solving: Effects on Learning. *Cognitive Science* 12: 257–285, 1988.

10. **Jackson, L. A.** Social Psychology and the Digital Divide. Paper presented at the symposium titled "The Internet: A place for social psychology." The 1999 Conference of the Society of Experimental Social Psychology. St Louis, MO, October 14–16, 1999a.

11. **Jackson, L. A.** Who's on the Internet: Making Sense of Internet Demographic Surveys. Paper presented at the symposium titled "Conducting Research on the Internet." American Psychological Association Convention. Boston, MA, August, 1999b.

12. **Jackson, L. A., Ervin, K. S., Gardner, P. D. and Schmitt, N.** The Racial Digital Divide: Motivational, Affective, and Cognitive Correlates of Internet Use. *Journal of Applied Social Psychology* 31: 2019–2046, 2001.

13. **Jackson, L. A., von Eye, A., Biocca, F. A., Barbatsis, G., Fitzgerald, H. E. and Zhao, Y.** Personality, Cognitive Style and Internet Use. *Swiss Journal of Psychology* 62(2): 79–90, 2003.

14. **Jackson, L. A., von Eye, A., Biocca, F., Barbatsis, G., Zhao, Y.; and Fitzgerald, H. E.** Internet Attitudes and Internet Use: Some Surprising Findings from the HomeNetToo Project. *International Journal of Human Computer Studies* 59(3): 355–382, 2003.

15. **Knezek, G. A., Miyashita, K. T. and Sakamoto, T.** Information Technology from the Child's Perspective. In Collis, B. A., Knezek, G. A., Lai, K., Miyashita, K. T., Pelgrum, W., Plomp, T., and Sakamoto, T., *Children and Computers in School,* 69–104. Mahwah, NJ: Lawrence Erlbaum, 1996.

16. **Krendl, K. A. and Broihier, M.** Student Responses to Computers: A Longitudinal Study. *Journal of Educational Computing Research* 8(2): 215–227, 1992.

17. **Salomon, G.** Computers in Education: Setting a Research Agenda. *Educational Technology* 24: 7–11, 1984.

18. **Rosen, L. D., Sears, D. C. and Weil, M. M.** Computerphobia. Behavior Research Methods, *Instruments and Computers* 19: 167–179, 1987.

19. **Rosen, L., and Maguire, P.** Myths and Realities of Computerphobia: A Meta-Analysis. *Anxiety Research* 3: 175–191, 1990.

20. **Rosen, L. and Weil, M.** Computer Anxiety: A Cross-Cultural Comparison of University Students in Ten Countries. *Computers in Human Behavior* 11: 45–64, 1990.

21. **Weil, M. and Rosen, L.** The Psychological Impact of Technology from a Global Perspective: A Study of Technological Sophistication and Technophobia in University Students from 23 Countries. *Computers in Human Behavior* 11: 95–133, 1995.

22. **Durndell, A., Cameron, C., Knox, A., Stocks, R. and Haag, Z.** Gender and Computing: West and East Europe. *Computers in Human Behavior* 13(2): 269–280, 1997.

23. **Martin, D., Heller, R. and Mahmoud, E.** American and Soviet Children's Attitudes Towards Computers. *Journal of Educational Computing Research* 8(2): 155–185, 1992.

24. **Li, N., Kirkup, G. and Hodgson, B.** Cross-Cultural Comparison of Women Students' Attitudes toward the Internet and Usage: China and the United Kingdom. *Cyber Psychology & Behavior* 4(3): 415–426, 2001.

25. **Chiu, C. H. and Wang, F. M.** The Influence of Navigation Map Scope on Disorientation of Elementary Students in Learning a Web-Based Hypermedia Course. *Journal of Educational Computing Research* 22(2): 135–144, 2000.

26. **Head, M., Archer, N. and Yuan, Y.** Word Wide Web Navigation Aid. *International Journal of Human-Computer Studies* 53(2): 301–330, 2000.

27. **McDonald, S. and Stevenson, R. J.** Navigation in Hyperspace: An Evaluation of the Effects of Navigational Tools and Subject Matter Expertise on Browsing and Information Retrieval in Hypertext. *Interacting with Computers* 10(2): 129–142, 1998.

28. **Park, J. and Kim, J.** Contextual Navigation Aids for Two World Wide Web Systems. *International Journal of Human-Computer Interaction* 12(2): 193–217, 2000.

29. **Xu, W., Dainoff, M. J. and Mark, L. S.** Facilitate Complex Search Tasks in Hypertext by Externalizing Functional Properties of a Work Domain. *International Journal of Human-Computer Studies* 11: 201–229, 1999.

30. **Turkle, S.** *Life on the Screen: Identity in the Age of the Internet.* New York: Simon & Schuster, 1995.

31. **Turkle, S.** *The Second Self: Computers and the Human Spirit.* New York: Simon and Schuster, 1984.

32. **Ike, C. A.** Development through Educational Technology: Implications for Teacher Personality and Peer Collaboration. *Journal of Instructional Psychology* 24(1): 42–49, 1997.

33. **Harwin, R. and Haynes, C.** Healthy Computing: Risks and Remedies Every Computer User Needs to Know. NY: American Management Association, 1992.

34. **American Optometric Association (AOA).** *Guide to the Clinical Aspects of Computer Vision Syndrome.* St. Louis: American Optometric Association, 1995.

35. **Dyson, M. C. and Haselgrove, M.** The Influence of Reading Speed and Line Length on the Effectiveness of Reading from Screen. *International Journal of Human Computer Studies* 54(4): 585–612, 2001.

36. **Feldmann, S. C. and Fish, M. C.** Reading Comprehension of Elementary, Junior High and High School Students on Print vs. Microcomputer-Generated Text. *Journal of Educational Computing Research* 4(2): 159–166, 1988.

37. **Grabinger, R. S.** Computer Screen Designs: Viewer Judgments. *Educational Technology Research and Development* 41(2): 35–73, 1993.

38. **Amichai, H. Y., & Ben, A. E.** Loneliness and Internet Use. *Computers in Human Behavior* 19: 71–80, 2003.

39. **Caplan, S. E.** Problematic Internet Use and Psychosocial Well-Being: Development of a Theory-Based Cognitive-Behavioral Measurement Instrument. *Computers in Human Behavior* 18: 53–575, 2002.

40. **Cui, L. and Liu, L.** The Influence of the Internet on the Sociality Development of Undergraduates. *Psychological Science China* 26: 64–66, 2003.

41. **Anshel, J.** *Visual Ergonomics in the Workplace.* Philadelphia, PA: Taylor & Francis, 1997.

42. **Gross, E. F., Juvonen, J. and Gable, S. L.** Internet Use and Well-Being in Adolescence. *Journal of Social Issues* 58(1): 75–90, 2002.

43. **Waestlund, E., Norlander, T. and Archer, T.** Internet Blues Revisited: Replication and Extension of an Internet Paradox Study. *Cyber Psychology and Behavior* 4: 385–391, 2001.

44. **Weiser, E. B.** The Functions of Internet Use and Their Social and Psychological Consequences. *Cyber Psychology and Behavior* 4: 723–743, 2001.

45. **Moody, E. J.** Internet Use and its Relationship to Loneliness. *Cyber Psychology and Behavior* 4: 393–401, 2001.

46. **Kiesler, S., Lundmark, V., Zdaniuk, B. and Kraut, R.** Troubles with the Internet: The Dynamics of Help at Home. *Human Computer Interaction* 15: 223–352, 2000.

47. **Kraut, R., Patterson, M., Lundmark, V., Kiesler, S., Mukophadhyay, T. and Scherlis, W.** Internet Paradox: A Social Technology that Reduces Social Involvement and Psychological Well Being? *American Psychologist* 53: 1017–1032, 1998.

48. **Subrahmanyam, K., Greenfield, P., Kraut, R. and Gross, E.** The Impact of Computer Use on Children's and Adolescents' Development. *Journal of Applied Developmental Psychology* 22: 7–30, 2001.

49. **Yan, Z. and Fischer, K. W.** How Children and Adults Learn to Use Computers: A Developmental Approach. In D. Sharma (Ed.), *New Directions for Child and Adolescent Development.* San Francisco, CA: Jossey-Bass, in press.

50. **Yan, Z. Fischer, K. W.** Always Under Construction: Dynamic Variations in Adult Cognitive Development. *Human Development* 45: 141–160, 2002.

51. **Kosslyn, S. M., Pascual-Leone, A., Felician, O., Camposano, S., Keenan, J. P., Thompson, W. L., Ganis, G., Sukel, K. E. and Alpert, N. M.** The Role of Area 17 in Visual Imagery: Convergent Evidence from PET and rTMS. *Science* 284: 167–170, 1999.
52. **Gazzaniga, M. S.** (Ed.) *The New Cognitive Neurosciences* (2nd ed.). MIT Press, 2000.
53. **Von Melchner, L., Pallas, S. L. and Sur, M.** Visual Behavior Mediated by Retinal Projections Directed to the Auditory Pathway. *Nature* 404: 871–876, 2000.
54. **Rose, D. H. and Meyer, A.** *Teaching Every Student in the Digital Age: Universal Design for Learning.* Alexandria, VA: Association for Supervisors of Curriculum Development, 2002.
55. **Gerlič, I. and Jaušovec, N.** Differences in EEG Power and Coherence Measures Related to the Type of Presentation: Text Versus Multimedia. *Journal of Educational Computing Research* 25: 177–195, 2001.
56. **Gerlič, I. and Jaušovec, N.** Multimedia: Differences in Cognitive Processes Observed with EEG. *Educational Technology Research & Development* 47: 5–14, 1999.
57. **McCluskey, J. J.** An Exploratory Study of the Possible Impact of Cerebral Hemisphericity on the Performance of Selected Linear, Non-Linear, and Spatial Computer Tasks. *Journal of Educational Computing Research* 16: 269–279, 1997.
58. **Mikropoulos, T. A.** Brain Activity on Navigation in Virtual Environments, *Journal of Educational Computing Research* 24: 1–12, 2001.
59. **Norman, D.** *The Psychology of Everyday Things.* NY: Basic Books, 1988.
60. **Shneiderman, B.** *Designing the User Interface: Strategies for Effective Human-Computer Interaction* (3rd ed.). Reading, MA: Addison-Wesley, 1998.
61. **Quilter, D.** *The Repetitive Strain Injury Recovery Book.* NY: Walker, 1998.
62. **Birnbaum, M. H.** (Ed.). *Psychological Experiments on the Internet.* New York: Academic Press, 2000.

VII. ACKNOWLEDGMENTS

I would like to thank Dr. Kurt Fischer, Dr. Paul Hallis, Dr. Karen Swan, Dr. Caral Miskill, Dr. Robert Bangert-Drowns, Dr. David Dai, Heping Hao, Larry Jon Hobbs, and Ning Wen for their advice, scaffolding, and assistance.

VIII. ABOUT THE AUTHOR

Zheng Yan, Assistant Professor, Department of Educational and Counseling Psychology, University at Albany. Contact: Zheng Yan, Department of Educational and Counseling Psychology, University at Albany, Albany, 12222. E-mail: zyan@uamail.albany.edu.

USING ADAPTIVE HYPERMEDIA TO MATCH WEB PRESENTATION TO LEARNING STYLES

Michael M. Danchak
Computer Science, Rensselaer Polytechnic Institute

- The fundamental attraction of adapting web content to individual learning styles is to improve learning.

- Since a teacher cannot realistically have multiple designs for the same topic, researchers advocate adopting a cyclic design whereby each lesson has elements of interest to all styles. Tailoring can be done for various individual traits, such as prior knowledge and preferences for certain kinds of media. We can now have designs for individuals and their learning styles.

- The Kolb Learning Cycle includes activities from all four quadrants. Starting with Concrete Experience, the cycle moves through Reflective Observation, Abstract Conceptualization, and ends with Active Experimentation.

- Each learner finds something attractive to his or her style, but is also exposed to the way other people learn.

- Style changes according to personality, educational specialization, career choice, current job role, and current task or problem to solve.

I. INTRODUCTION

Teaching and learning has remained surprisingly static, with the dominant model being that of the master-apprentice. While this model allowed for individual attention, it was also very teacher-centered. When a small number of masons or physicians were needed, the master-apprentice model worked. However, scaling up to accommodate a large number of students was impossible. The need to scale introduced the classroom and the lecture method of teaching. Information transmission was emphasized over individual attention, placing even more emphasis on the teacher and teacher-centered activities.

Early in the twentieth century, educators began to investigate the potential of process-based models of learning. Dewey, Piaget, Lewin, and others recognized the value of experiential learning and the shift to a learner-centered approach that emphasized individualized, concrete, and self-directed study. Not everyone learns the same way or at the same pace. Furthermore, learners have diverse backgrounds as well as prior and contextual experiences.

There are many different definitions of learning style and almost as many dimensions used to describe them. However, there is consensus that learning styles and educational performance are tightly linked [1] and that attention must be paid to the match between teaching styles and learning styles. When one relies on the instructor's instinctive style, the lesson will resonate only with those students having that same style. Even within narrow disciplines such as engineering and science, there is still a diversity of styles.

Instructional methods changed to accommodate different learning styles. Today the "reflective teacher" [2] observes his/her students, reflects on their needs, and then makes adjustments in his/her teaching style to accommodate those needs. Since a teacher cannot realistically have multiple designs for the same topic, researchers [3, 4, 5] advocate adopting a cyclic design whereby each lesson has elements of interest to all styles. Further justification for the cycle [3, 5] makes the argument that exposing students to styles other than their own will give those students different ways of solving problems. This means that learning styles dominate rather than teaching styles. Instructors should ensure that *their* teaching styles address all of their students' learning styles.

Today, we have more information, by orders of magnitude, available at our fingertips than at any time in history. If you want to know something, just "Google" it and follow the links! You can get an explanation, a lesson, a course, and even an entire degree online. Even face-to-face classes have web-augmented components that complement the classroom activities. However, when repurposing content for web-based delivery, course developers often overlook what was learned about student differences in the classroom and neglect to apply sound instructional design principles to the online environment [6]. Although online instructional materials may include animations or graphics, they often remain fixed, unvaried and static; adaptive to learner needs only in minor ways [7]. Even the concept of a cycle that addresses all styles gets lost in translation.

This "one size fits nobody" approach of the WWW is especially troubling in science, technology, engineering and mathematics (STEM) education. We know that students shy away from STEM courses in college and one of the major reasons for this avoidance is "style" [8]. Changing the medium from face-to-face classroom to WWW should not cause us to regress to methods that were proven marginal years ago. Techniques for adaptive presentation, content selection and sequencing (collectively called adaptive hypermedia [9]) are just becoming feasible.

For instance, when you log onto Amazon.com and allow cookies in your browser, the information presented is tailored to your previous purchases and responses. It is personalized. Can these same techniques be used for learning? If this adaptability can be done for each learner, we can realize the dream of individualized learning. Tailoring can be done for various individual traits, such as prior knowledge and preferences for certain kinds of media. We can now have designs for individuals and their learning styles.

II. LEARNING AND LEARNING STYLES

Learning styles were implicitly understood, but ill defined, for many years. More recently, researchers explicitly codified learning style concepts and developed instruments to measure or categorize the learners. This section first introduces examples of learning styles developed for face-to-face environments and then explores learning style validity in online applications. Adaptive hypermedia is then introduced, and the potential and problems with that technology are explored.

A. Face-to-Face Experience

Unfortunately, there is no single universally accepted definition of learning style. Authors do agree that people learn in different ways, but the factors that influence the differences vary. We use the definition of Curry [10] and Riding and Cheema [11], which says that a learning style is the act of "adopting a habitual and distinct mode of acquiring knowledge."

The whole personality approach, exemplified by the Myers-Briggs Type Indicator (MBTI) [12], is based on Jung's theory of psychological types. It uses four scales with two extremes each, resulting in 16 possible categories. The first scale is Extroversion-Introversion, which indicates how a person is energized. Sensing-Intuition is the second scale and reflects what a person pays attention to. The Thinking-Feeling scale indicates how a person makes decisions, while the Judgment-Perception scale points to a person's life style. An instrument that can only be administered by a licensed practitioner determines type. The Sensing-Intuition scale predominantly influences learning style, since it emphasizes to what people attend. David Keirsey [13] takes a similar approach in his Keirsey Temperament Sorter.

Another personality-based model is that of Long [14], popularized by Chuck Dziuban [15]. Long evolved his theory while working with normal adolescents for over twenty-five years. There are two reactive behavior dimensions with extremes labeled aggressive/passive and dependent/independent. Aggressive students have high amounts of energy while passive students are much calmer. Dependent students need instructor approval while independent students are more self-motivating. The two dimensions result in four possible reactive behavior patterns: Aggressive-Independent, Aggressive-Dependent, Passive-Independent, and Passive-Dependent.

Both the Gregorc [16] and the Dunn and Dunn [17] models draw on the senses and environmental factors as their scales. The Dunn and Dunn Learning Style Model uses five different categories: environmental, emotional, sociological, physiological, and psychological. The model has widespread use with adult learners and is just being applied to science, technology, engineering and mathematics [4].

Attitudes and affective dimensions serve as the basis for the third category of learning styles, as represented by Canfield [18] and Grasha-Riechmann [19]. Grasha emphasized styles of classroom participation and their attitudes toward learning, both negative and positive. The negative-positive pairs in the Grasha-Reichmann Learning Style Scales (GRSLSS) are competitive-collaborative, avoidant-participant, and dependent-independent. Ninety items are contained in the survey instrument for this method.

The information processing category is probably the largest, best known, and most frequently used, since it focuses strictly on acquiring knowledge. For the sake of brevity, we will mention only the methods that are mostly associated with web-based learning. These include the Kolb Learning Style Inventory [3] and the Felder-Silverman Index of Learning Styles [20]. A number of other information processing classifications are derived from Kolb, so we will discuss his approach in more detail.

The Kolb Learning Style Inventory is perhaps the best known of this type and is based on Kurt Lewin's Experiential Learning Theory. There are a number of experience factors that shape a learning style, namely: personality type, educational specialization, professional career choice, current job role, and current task/problem. These factors will be especially important later in our discussion.

Kolb states that people prefer to *grasp* information either through apprehension or comprehension, Figure 1. In effect, Kolb says that the grasping activity is either concrete or theoretical, or someplace in between. Once the information is grasped, people *transform* it into knowledge either through intention or extension. In other words, they need to think about it or they need to try it out. A simple example occurs when you get a new piece of software. Do you immediately rip off the shrink-wrap and try it out or do you read the manual first?

As shown in Figure 1, these two dimensions, with their extremes, identify four quadrants that Kolb labels as diverging, assimilating, converging, and accommodating. A diverging learner grasps information from concrete experience and transforms it into knowledge through reflection. A converging learner is more comfortable with grasping theoretical constructs and then transforms those constructs into knowledge through experimentation.

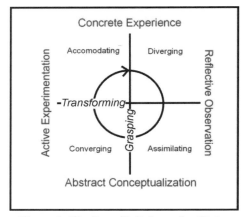

Figure 1. The Four Kolb Learning Styles

Hence, diverging learners asks the "Why" questions; they like to reason from concrete specific information and to explore what a system has to offer. They prefer to have information presented to them in a detailed, systematic, and reasoned manner and combine feeling and watching by viewing a problem from various perspectives. On the other hand, converging learners ask "How." They gain knowledge by understanding the details about the system's operation and combine experiential thinking and doing learning modes. While lecture works well for divergers, convergers prefer a more hands-on approach.

Kolb says that a learning experience designed for a specific learning style is optimal for the short run. However, he is also concerned about long term effects on problem solving and advocates that people learn to work in different ways to expand these skills. The Kolb Learning Cycle includes activities from all four quadrants. Starting with Concrete Experience, the cycle moves through Reflective Observation, Abstract Conceptualization, and ends with Active Experimentation. The idea here is that each learner finds something attractive to his or her style, but is also exposed to the way other people learn. This exposure may result in gaining additional tools or styles for learning. McCarthy [5] extends Kolb's cycle with her 4MAT system. She divides each of Kolb's quadrants in two, introducing consideration for left and right brain processing techniques. The resulting octants will be described in more detail later.

The Felder-Silverman model [20] developed within the realm of engineering education and is based both on Jung's theory and that of Kolb. Felder also has a two-step process involving reception of information and information processing. The original model had five dimensions: perception (sensory/intuitive), input (visual/auditory), organization (inductive/deductive), processing (active/reflective), and understanding (sequential/global). A recent update [21] deletes the organization dimension to yield 16 categories and re-labels visual/auditory as visual/verbal. The model achieved great success in the engineering education community and continues that success today. Felder also connected faculty teaching styles with student learning styles, pointing out mismatches and potential problems.

B. Web-based Experience

The potential of the World Wide Web for learning was immediately recognized and many educators rushed to post courses in that medium. Unfortunately, most course developers were either unaware of or ignored the findings on learning style when they designed the web sites [6, 7]. Perhaps another reason might be that they were overwhelmed with trying to establish good multimedia design principles before considering learning styles. Clark and Mayer [22] maintain that individual differences are secondary to prior knowledge. Students who are new to the content learn more than students who have prior experience. However, Ford and Chen [23] state that among the variables important to learning success, such as gender, age group, prior experience and discipline of study, learning styles are particularly important.

Empirical studies of the web and learning styles concentrated mostly on the retention question, i.e., which learning styles are most amenable to web based delivery. Dziuban and colleagues [24] used the Long-Dziuban Reactive Behavior Protocol and determined that, contrary to expectation, students in online courses tend not to be independent learners. Federico [25] found that students in the Kolb assimilating and accommodating quadrants had more positive attitudes toward online learning than those with converging and diverging learning styles.

Riding and Grimley [26] used Cognitive Styles Analysis to determine that there are distinct gender differences with different types of media (picture-sound, picture-text, and picture-text-sound) and cognitive style, but all groups did better with picture, text, and sound. Ford and Chen [27] matched and mismatched instructional materials with cognitive styles. Students whose cognitive style matched the material scored significantly higher in conceptual knowledge than those whose style was mismatched. In a practical test, performance was more a function of gender than cognitive style.

Despite the lack of extensive empirical testing of learning styles and content design, there is little reason to expect that online learning will differ from the face-to-face results. Students working with an online course designed to match their learning style should perform better than a mismatched design. Style may influence their motivation to participate as well. The question is how to accommodate styles online. If the Kolb styles were adopted, four different designs would be needed, along with a mechanism for deciding which style to use. It is here that a new technology, called adaptive hypermedia, may provide a solution.

C. The Potential of Adaptive Hypermedia

Adaptive hypermedia, as defined by Brusilovsky [28], "builds a model of goals, preferences and knowledge of each individual user, and uses this model throughout the interaction with the user, in order to adapt to the needs of that user." The pre-web versions focused on user knowledge and goals to adapt presentation and navigation support, whereas the web versions added content selection and adaptive recommendation [29]. The review here concentrates on web versions that use learning style as an individual trait, in addition to the other personal characteristics already mentioned. In other words, learning styles are the next individual trait to be considered. However, the previous traits remain part of the user model.

The common design elements for these systems require some mechanism to gather data about the user and then incorporate that data into a user model. The model then directs the adaptation of content for that particular person. What user data one looks at and how it is used to modify the presentation can vary with author. In most cases mentioned below, the user is pre-screened using a questionnaire to determine learning style. The implication here is that an instrument, a questionnaire, must be available in order to categorize the user as having a certain learning style.

Carver and colleagues [30] used the Felder-Silverman [21] model to determine learning style and then matched appropriate media to those styles. Anecdotal evidence indicated that the best students benefited the most from hypermedia courseware, whereas the worst students benefited least. This study also found that the shift of responsibility for learning to the student was a bit unsettling for the students. Any new approach requires training of both faculty and students. Danielson [31] also concentrated on media but used the Dunn model [17] to determine learning style. This work in progress posed interesting concepts, but the group was not able to produce a prototype.

Gilbert and Han [32] took a more flexible approach to learning styles. They assumed that different instructors would inherently have different styles and use different media. Three instructors each created a module for a given concept, and a number of concepts comprised the course. Rather than pre-screening for learning styles, Gilbert and Han's course system, *Arthur,* randomly assigned a student to one of the instructor's modules. Since the *Arthur* course is based on mastery learning, a quiz was given at the completion of the module. If the student scored 80 or higher, he/she was presented the next concept module by same instructor. If the student scored less than 80, she/he repeated the concept module with a different instructor's style. An additional failure at mastery resulted in a third instructor's module for that concept. No formal assessment of this technique was available in the literature.

Del Corso, and colleagues [33] based their 3DE system on the Honey and Mumford [35] model, a variant of Kolb, which categorizes learners as Activists, Reflectors, Theorists, or Pragmatists. 3DE pre-screens learners with the Learning Style Questionnaire (LSQ), but modeled the user's style as a tuple (A, B, C, D) rather than one predominant style. This provided finer resolution in determining what content was presented. Content is stored in a library of micro modules that are specifically designed for each learning style. A course is created for an individual using the Custom Course Compiler, under the supervision of a qualified teacher.

Paredes and Rodríguez [34] developed a system that pre-screened learners using the Felder-Silverman questionnaire. The learning style data was used to adapt the exposition-example sequencing in the case of moderate and extreme sensing-intuitive learners. For sensing types, example was followed by exposition. The sequence was reversed for intuitive learners. Moderate and extreme sequential-global learners received a fixed or flexible structure of content respectively. No formal assessment of this work was reported.

Another system, described by Peña [36], also used the Felder-Silverman model. Pre-screening determined the initial classification of the student. Case-Based Reasoning techniques [37] then fine-tuned the student's profile to automatically recommend subsequent teaching units, and navigation tools and techniques. This is also a work in progress.

INSPIRE [38] is the last system to be described. This took a rather unique approach in that it allowed for adaptivity as well adaptability. With adaptivity, the system adapts its output using data about the user in a *system controlled* way. Adaptability supported end-user modifiability, which qualifies as *student control*. Adaptivity uses goals, learning style and knowledge level to change curriculum sequencing, navigation support, and presentation. Pre-screening for Honey and Mumford Learning Style determined the presentation according to a fixed set of rules for each style. The also collected both satisfaction scores and performance data to guide future work.

D. Are Learning Styles Fixed?

The fundamental attraction of adapting web content to individual learning styles is to improve learning. As discussed earlier, the reflective teacher should be sensitive to the needs of her students and modify her teaching methods to match those needs. In an ideal world of one-on-one teaching, the teacher could continually modify the lesson to match those needs. However, that is just not possible with larger groups. Can adaptive hypermedia make this possible? Pre-screening for learning styles makes selecting sequence and content possible. But that raises two other questions. Does learning style remain fixed so the one pre-screening is valid forever? Does focusing on a particular learning style deprive the student of acquiring additional problem solving strategies?

One of the most common ways to determine a person's learning style is to analyze his or her responses to a questionnaire, according to some rubric. Students are rarely aware of the concept of learning styles, and most certainly do not know their own particular style within a given model. Asking them to provide this piece of information is problematic, to say the least. A better alternative is to survey them before the learning experience and use the analysis to determine style. This works well if learning styles are static—not changing over time.

But Kolb's model is experiential; style changes according to personality, educational specialization, career choice, current job role, and current task/problem, as previously mentioned. Obviously, the first three factors do not change radically over time, but job function and task certainly do. Will a person adopt the same style when studying tax law as he/she does when studying basket weaving? If we accept the possibility that learning styles may change over time, how do we ensure that we are working with the current and correct style? Surveying each time would definitely be irksome and unacceptable to students.

The second question is equally perplexing. Predefined sequences for each style could easily be stored for presentation. However, concentrating or emphasizing one dominant style may diminish the learners' ability to function in other styles. The seemingly good idea of optimizing may, in fact, be suboptimal for the long run. The recommendation for executing a cycle [3, 5, 34] that includes all styles is strong and justifiable.

So if adaptive behavior is desirable, how do we do it? As pointed out by Brusilovsky [28], "it still is not clear which aspects of learning style are worth modeling and what can be done differently for those users."

The next section hopes to answer these questions.

III. MATCHING STYLE TO PRESENTATION: EXPLANAGENT

The ExplanAgent approach uses the Kolb Style as the learning model because of its extensive use and grounding in information processing. We use the 4MAT variant developed by McCarthy [5] because it has a strong emphasis on traversing all octants—offering something for everyone, at least initially. This decision is for research purposes only and does not preclude using other learning styles or individual traits once we have proof-of-concept. The 4MAT approach takes the Kolb Cycle in Figure 1 and divides each quadrant in two to educate the "whole brain," both left side and right. This division identifies eight instructional events that should occur in sequence:

Connect: Create a concrete experience.

Attend: Reflect on the experience and analyze what happened.

Imaging: Picture the concepts, as students understand them.

Inform: Define theories and concepts.

Practice: Apply the defined concepts and givens, as is.

Extend: Experiment with the concepts and add to them.

Refine: Evaluate the extensions and modify as necessary.

Perform: Apply the learning to the learners' world and share with others.

Not every student relates to all the events in this cycle, nor needs to. We record various student interactions during each octant, such as time spent in the octant and performance, and use this data to infer student preferences and modify subsequent presentations based on those inferences. More theory and less reflection may be appropriate for some students and less theory, more reflection better for others. The ExplanAgent continually monitors student progress and adapts as the student interacts with the lessons and courses. Particular learning style at the time does not matter, successful performance does. Figure 2 illustrates how a course might adapt over three lessons. This pattern might represent a converging learner who prefers more theory and less reflection. Pattern 1 is the initial 4MAT layout; pattern2 shows a preference for less reflection; whereas pattern 3 returns to some reflection. We believe that this design addresses the questions raised in the previous section.

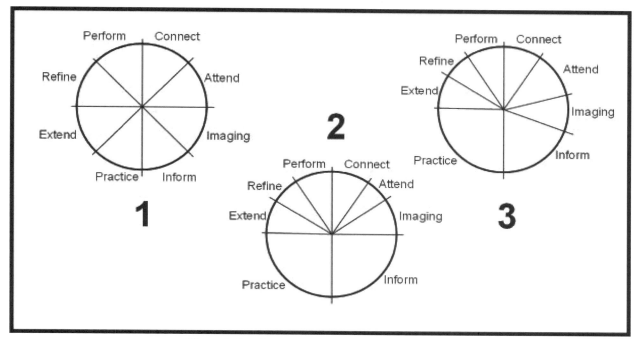

Figure 2. Possible patterns for a converging learner.

This approach has an ancillary benefit that results from "Gain/Loss" theory [39], which says that adjustment is the ultimate form of flattery. A human appreciates when another human accommodates to their personality or style. Moon and Nass [40] applied this concept to computer personalities. They gave the computer either a dominant or submissive personality by selecting appropriate verbs in message strings. They also categorized human participants according to these personality extremes. Not surprisingly, they found that "likes attract"—dominant people like computers with a dominant personality and vice versa. But in a related test, they had the computer start in the opposite personality, (i.e. dominant), and change to match the human (submissive). The human liked this accommodation better than starting out with the same computer personality. Therefore, we postulate that students will sense the computer modifying the presentation to match their learning styles and the system will achieve a "gain" in satisfaction.

We are conducting a pilot study to test the basic hypotheses about matching versus mismatching learning styles and presentation before starting implementation. Full implementation will be followed by extensive assessment in web-based explanations and, eventually, full lessons and courses.

A. Architecture

The architecture of our system follows one that is standard in the literature [29] and is shown in Figure 3. Developing an adaptive ExplanAgent requires the ability to take the information from a digital repository (the domain model) and provide the content in various ways that adapt to different users. Many models were developed to encapsulate the elements of a class and a classroom environment. These "pedagogical models" [41] describe the learning environment and define the roles of each person, such as the instructor, coach, learner, and so on. Research groups, such as EDUCAUSE's Information Management Systems [42], were working to create specifications for learning design models that incorporate packaging and sequencing systems using common Web markup languages. This effort spawned the IMS Global Learning Consortium a few years ago. We make an explicit attempt to adhere to existing and evolving standards, especially in the case of learning objects. Learning objects are any entities, digital or non-digital, that can be used, re-used, or referenced during technology-supported learning [41]. The following paragraphs discuss each model of Figure 2 in detail.

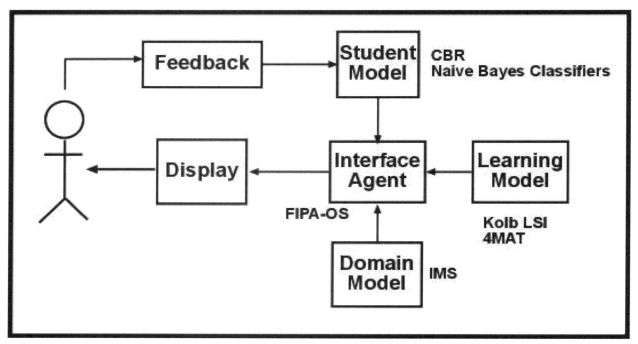

Figure 3. ExplanAgent Architecture

B. Content Organization

The first challenge in establishing such a system is to decide on how the data will be organized and stored, be it content or user characteristics. An Educational Modeling Language (EML) contains learning metadata, learning objects or "units" of study in courses along with the methods to store such information in databases and other repositories [41]. EML was defined as "a semantic information model and binding, describing the content and process within a 'unit of learning' from a pedagogical perspective in order to support reuse and interoperability" [12]. We analyzed several EMLs and projects to investigate the potential advantages and disadvantages and decided on OUNL-EML as the best choice for this project.

OUNL-EML was a project created by a team of approximately thirty specialists from the Open University of the Netherlands and was in development for the past four years. Its first official release was in December 2000. The model takes into account the people in the learning process, requirements and rules of the learners, the domain, and the context in which learning objects are used in the learning environment. Using XML and domain-specific vocabularies, instructional scenarios or complete description of all activities can be carried out by all the roles in a logical relationship. The activities and events, educational content, and tasks that occur in a traditional learning environment can be modeled using OUNL-EML, with the relationships of these occurrences in a network of inter-dependent activities that determine the sequence. Since development, over 50 courses have been using OUNL-EML as the method of providing educational information to users. IMS selected OUNL-EML as the base for the IMS Learning Design specification [42].

Since our project consists of an agent that encompasses all roles in the learning environment (learners, instructors, etc), we allow for semantic richness in which the content sequencer can correctly pick which media to present and which remains hidden from the learner. These media elements form low granularity learning objects, such as text bundles, graphics, animations, etc. For this, the IMS Learner Information Package is a good choice. Following the IMS Learning Design specification, our project will be compatible with the Content Packaging, Simple Sequencing, and Meta-Data Design Specification which already has international support, adding opportunities for further extensibility in the future.

C. User Modeling and Adaptivity

According to Beck and Stern [43], the student model stores specific information about each learner, such as their current knowledge state and learning preferences. Abou-Jaoude and Frasson [44] define three different layers of a student model: Knowledge Level, Learning Profile, and Emotion and Believability. The Knowledge Level stores the student's understanding about the domain. The traditional approaches used for representing the Knowledge Level are Bayesian Networks (BN) [45, 46, 47], the Overlay Model (OM) [48, 49], and Stereotyping [50, 44, 47]. The OM is a good representation of the Knowledge Level, comparing the student's knowledge to the domain knowledge

The Learning Profile layer contains the student's learning preferences. Two potential techniques can be used for adaptation: Naïve Bayes Classifiers (NBC) and Case-Based Reasoning (CBR). NBC is very fast for both learning and predicting [51]. The learning time is linear with the number of examples, and the prediction time is independent of the number of examples. This allows NBC to be used in real time and is particularly valuable for situations where additional knowledge about the user is added to the model incrementally. It also works well even if only a small amount of data is available [52]. This is very important, since we want to be able to predict the correct learning style after a few interactions. Student Modeling using CBR is based on the notion that student's problem solving capabilities can be evaluated by looking at how the student accesses past solved problems (cases) which are similar to their current situation [53]. Gilbert and Han [32] and Weber and Sprecht [54] apply CBR to model the Knowledge Level. In Peña [36], CBR techniques fine-tune the student's profile to gradually reflect more faithfully his/her learning style.

We adopt these approaches for the Learning Profile Level, observing which parts of the cycle are attended to most. We do not intend to address the aspects of emotions and believability (the third layer) in our initial prototype. Implementation of the ExplanAgent is currently underway and will be followed by extensive assessment. In the future, we hope to investigate the impact of affective computing [55] and animated pedagogical agents on explanations and web-based learning.

D. Pilot Study

In order to verify our assumptions about learning styles and web presentation, we are conducting a "paper and pencil" pilot study that looks at these issues. This study asks the following research questions:

- Do learning styles make a difference in the effectiveness of presentation of content in online learning?
- Are there effective guidelines for the selection and sequencing of learning objects to account for differences in learning style?

We hypothesize that learning with a presentation that matches the participant's style will score highest; the 4MAT design will be second best; followed by the opposite style design. We will also measure "gain" and "loss" achieved while moving between the presentations. This pilot study will give us solid data upon which to base the building of the adaptive system.

The first activity was to search for adequate guidelines to design the presentations. While we found excellent empirically based recommendations for multimedia design from Mayer [56], selecting and sequencing recommendations were definitely lacking. Kolb talks about grasping and transforming and McCarthy advocates the eight steps listed earlier. However, detailed application of these guidelines is still a challenge. Polhemus [57] created a series of principles that meet these criteria and these will be published soon.

Another necessary decision was the form and content of the testing examples. To which domain do we apply these principles and how do we know the tests are valid? An entire course would take too long. We chose to follow the work of Mayer who focused on explanations: messages about cause and effect systems. With permission, we used three of his examples: lightning formation [56, 58], the human respiratory system [56], and pump functioning [56, 59]. These are multimedia animations that explain how each concept works. As such, they satisfy Kolb's *Abstract Conceptualization* and McCarthy's *Inform* events. We wrapped the other events advocated by Kolb and McCarthy around each explanation. We then proceeded with the formal testing.

1. Test Design

The actual testing of these concepts is currently in progress in late 2003. Participants are screened for two opposite Kolb [3] learning styles (convergers and divergers.) and given pretests to determine prior knowledge of how lightning, the human lungs, and a bicycle pump works. The sequence is shown in Table 1.

Lightning Explanation	Respiratory Explanation		Bicycle Pump Explanation	
4MAT	Same Style	Converger	Opposite Style	Diverger
		Diverger		Converger
	Opposite Style	Converger	Same Style	Diverger
		Diverger		Converger

Table 1. Treatment Conditions for the Prototype

Participants are later given a "lesson" on each of these topics. The lightning explanation uses the 4MAT design, accounting for all styles. Then half the group receives an explanation of how the lungs work using a web presentation hard coded for their particular style, while the other half receives the explanation using a style opposite to theirs. The situation is reversed for the explanation of bicycle pumps. For instance, one Diverger gets the Lightning Explanation in the 4MAT style, the Respiratory Explanation in Diverger style and the Bicycle Pump Explanation in the Converger style. Another Diverger has the same Lightning Explanation but is presented the Respiratory Explanation in a Converger style followed by the Bicycle Pump Explanation in the Diverger style. After each explanation, participants are tested for retention and transfer. A final debriefing asks about overall satisfaction and the "fit" of presentation to the participant's comfort level

2. Results

Thirty-two participants are used in this study, 16 each in the Diverger and Converger styles. The preliminary results of this pilot study indicate that there is no difference in retention testing and preference, but there is a significant difference ($p < 05$) in transfer testing when matched presentation is used. This may indicate that matching presentation to learning style promotes deeper understanding. The complete results will be published shortly [57].

Given positive results of the pilot, we will implement the ExplanAgent based on the IMS specifications, Naïve Bayes Classifiers and Case-Based Reasoning, and the continually modified 4MAT cycle. More experimentation will be done on which events to attend to in establishing the user model. As this work progresses, we see obvious extensions to the work and to the development of related, but much more sophisticated, systems.

IV. FUTURE EXTENSIONS: QNAGENT

The ExplanAgent focuses on the output of information. While learning styles are one characteristic, our approach lends itself to tailoring on many different dimensions. For instance, providing alternatives to graphics for the visually impaired could extend accessibility. Cultural issues, such as those raised by Morse [60], could also be addressed using the same adaptability. An important issue not addressed is the ease with which courses could be created to allow for adaptability. If the concept proves viable, an authoring system will have to be devised to take advantage of the concept—no mean task itself. We would also like to test animated pedagogical agents [55] as a way of bringing the affective dimension to web-based learning.

Beyond the ExplanAgent is the QnAgent. An adaptive QnAgent is an intelligent agent that allows a student to ask questions related to web-based course content in a variety of ways and view the answers in a manner that best matches their learning style or purpose. The corpus of knowledge for that course is accumulated over time from both the instructor and the students, establishing a collaboration that results in a richer and more diverse knowledge base than otherwise possible.

V. CONCLUSIONS

Learning styles definitely need to be attended to in any learning experience. We hope the pilot study confirms our hypothesis that a matched design was best, with a cyclic design following closely. By using a cyclic design at the outset, we can modify content and sequence based on performance. The practitioner would be well served by adopting the learning cycle approach now, looking forward to greater adaptability in the future. Once out of the research stage, an authoring system will aid instructors in developing adaptive courses. The continually monitored approach allows for evolving learning styles driven by changing job roles and task/problems. We anticipate that extensive assessment will confirm this approach.

VI. REFERENCES

1. **Rutz, E.** Learning Styles and Educational Performance — Implications for Professional Development Programs. *CIEC Conference*, Tucson, AZ, 2003.
2. **Zeichner K. M. and Liston, D. P**. *Reflective Teaching: An Introduction*. Mahwah, NJ: Lawrence Erlbaum Associates, 1996.
3. **Kolb, D. A.** *Experiential Learning: Experience as the source of learning and development*. Englewood Cliffs: Prentice Hall, 1984.
4. **Hein, T. L. and Budny, D. D.** Teaching to Students' Learning Styles: Approaches That Work, *29th ASEE/IEEE Frontiers in Education Conference*. San Juan, Puerto Rico, 1999.
5. **McCarthy, B.** The 4MAT System: Teaching to learning styles with right/left mode techniques. Barrington, IL: Excel, Inc., 1981, 1987.

6. **Gunawardena, C. and Boverie, P. L.** Impact of Learning Styles on Instructional Design for Distance Education. Paper presented at *World Conference of the International Council of Distance Education*, 1993.

7. **McGloughlin, C.** The Implications of the Research Literature on Learning Styles for the Design of Instructional Material. *Australian Journal of Educational Technology* 15(3): 222–241, 1999.

8. **Tobias, S**. They're Not Dumb, They're Different: Stalking the Second Tier. Tucson, AZ: Research Corporation, 1990.

9. **Brusilovsky, P.** Adaptive Hypermedia. *User Modeling and User-Adapted Interaction* 11: 87–110, 2001.

10. **Curry, L.** Patterns of Learning Style Across Selected Medical Specialties. *Educational Psychology* 11: 247–278, 1991.

11. **Riding, R. and Cheema, I.** Cognitive Styles: An Overview and Integration. *Educational Psychology* 11: 193–215, 1991.

12. **Briggs, K. C. and Myers, I. B.** *Myers-Briggs Type Indicator.* Palo Alto, CA: Consulting Psychologist Press, Inc., 1977.

13. **Keirsey, D. and Bates, M.** *Please Understand Me.* Prometheus Nemesis Book Company, 1984.

14. **Long, W. A.** Personality and Learning. 1988 John Wilson Memorial Address. *Focus on Learning Problems in Mathematics* 11(4): 1–16, 1989.

15. **Dziuban, J. I. and Dziuban, C. D.** Reactive Behavior Patterns in the Classroom, *Journal of Staff, Program, and Organizational Development* 15(2): 85–91, 1997.

16. **Gregorc, A.** *Gregorc Style Delineator.* Columbia, CT; Gregorc Associates, Inc., 1982.

17. **Dunn, R. and Griggs, S. A..** *Synthesis of the Dunn and Dunn Learning-Style Model Research: Who, What, When, Where and so What?* New York, NY: St. John's University's Center for the Study of Learning and Teaching Styles, 2003.

18. **Canfield, A.** *Learning Styles Inventory Manual.* Ann Arbor, MI: Humanics Media, 1980.

19. **Grasha, A.** Learning Styles: The Journey from Greenwich Observatory to the College Classroom. *Improving College and University Teaching* 22: 46–53, 1984.

20. **Felder, R. M. and Silverman, L. K.** Learning and Teaching Styles in Engineering Education. *Engineering Education* 78(7): 674, 1988.

21. **Felder, R. M. and Silverman, L. K.** Learning and Teaching Styles in Engineering Education. *Engineering Education* 78(7): 674, 1988. http://www.ncsu.edu/felder-public/Papers/LS-1988.pdf.

22. **Clark, R. C. and Mayer, R. E.** *e-Learning and the Science of Instruction.* San Francisco, CA: Jossey-Bass/Pfeiffer, 2003.

23. **Ford, N. and Chen, S. Y.** Individual Differences, Hypermedia Navigation and Learning: An Empirical Study. *Journal of Educational Multimedia and Hypermedia* 9(4): 281–312, 2000.

24. **Dziuban, C. D., Moskal, P. D. and Dziuban, E. K.** Reactive Behavior Patterns Go Online. *Journal of Staff, Program, and Organizational Development* 17(3): 171–182, 2000.

25. **Federico, P. A.** Learning Styles and Student Attitudes Toward Various Aspects of Network-Based Instruction. *Computers in Human Behavior* 16: 359–379, 2000.

26. **Riding, R. and Grimley, M**. Cognitive Style, Gender and Learning from Multi-Media Materials in 11-Year-Old Children. *British Journal of Educational Technology* 30(1): 43–56, 1999.

27. **Ford, N. and Chen, S. Y.** Matching/Mismatching Revisited: An Empirical Study of Learning and Teaching Styles. *British Journal of Educational Technology* 32(1): 5–22, 2001.

28. **Brusilovsky, P.** Adaptive Hypermedia. *User Modeling and User-Adapted Interactions* 11: 87–110, 2001.

29. **Brusilovsky, P. and Maybury, M. T.** From Adaptive Hypermedia to the Adaptive Web. *Communications of the ACM* 45(5): 31–33, 2002.

30. **Carver, C. A., Howard, R. A. and Lane, W. D.** Enhancing Student Learning Through Hypermedia Courseware and Incorporation of Student Learning Styles. *IEEE Transactions on Education* 42(1): 33–38, 1996.

31. **Danielson, R. L.** Work in Progress: Learning Styles, Media Preferences and Adaptive Education. Proceedings of the workshop "Adaptive Systems and User Modeling on the World Wide Web." *Sixth International Conference on User Modeling.* Chia Laguna, Sardinia, 2–5 June, 1997.

32. **Gilbert, J. and Han, C.** Arthur: Adaptive Instruction to Accommodate Learning Styles. *Proceedings of the WebNet Conference of the WWW and Internet.* Honolulu, Hawaii, 1999.

33. **Del Corso, D., Ovcin, E., Morrone, G., Gianesini, D., Salojarvi, S. and Kvist, T.** 3DE: An Environment for the Development of Learner-Centered Custom Educational Packets. *31st ASEE/IEEE Frontiers in Education Conference.* Reno, NV: Session F2C, 21–26, October 10–13, 2001.

34. **Honey, P. and Mumford, A.** *The Manual of Learning Styles.* Maidenhead, Berkshire: Peter Honey, 1992.

35. **Paredes, P. and Rodriguez, P.** Considering Learning Styles in Adaptive Web-based Education. *Proceedings of the 6th World Multiconference on Systemics, Cybernetics and Informatics.* Orlando, Florida, 481–485, July 2002.

36. **Peña, C., Narzo, J. and de la Rosa, J.** Intelligent Agents in a Teaching and Learning Environment on the Web. *International Conference on Advanced Learning Technologies (ICALT2002).* Kazan, Russia, September 9–12, 2002.

37. **Kolodner, J.** *Case-Based Reasoning.* Morgan Kaufmann, 1993.

38. **Papanikolaou, K. A., Grogoriadou, M., Kornilakis, H. and Maloukas, G. D.** Personalizing the Interaction in a Web-based Educational Hypermedia System: The Case of INSPIRE. *User Modeling and User-Adapted Interaction* 13: 213–267, 2003.

39. **Aronson, E. and Linder, D.** Gain and Loss Esteem as Determinants of Interpersonal Attractiveness. *Journal of Experimental Psychology* 1: 156–171.

40. **Moon, Y. and Nass, C.** How 'Real' Are Computer Personalities? *Communication Research* 23(3): 651–674.

41. **Rawlings, A., van Rosmalen, P., Koper, R., Rodriguez-Artacho, M. and Lefrere, P.** *Survey of Educational Modeling Languages.* http://www.cenorm.be/isss/Workshop/LT/eml-version1.pdf, 2001.

42. *IMS Learning Design Information Model.* Version 1.0 Public Draft Specification, http://www.imsglobal.org/learningdesign/, 2002.

43. **Beck, J., Stern, M. and Haugsjaa, E.** Applications of AI in Education. *ACM Crossroads Student Magazine,* 1996.

44. **Abou-Jaoude, S. C. and Frasson, C.** Integrating a Believable Layer into Traditional ITS. *AIED '99 - 9th International Conference on Artificial Intelligence in Education.* Le Mans, France, 1999.

45. **Conati, C., Gertner, A. and VanLehn, K.** Using Bayesian Networks to Manage Uncertainty in Student Modeling. *User Modeling and User-Adapted Interaction* 12: 371–417, 2002.

46. **Henze, N. and Nejdl, W.** Adaptivity in the KBS Hyperbook System. *ASUM99—Second Workshop on Adaptive Systems and User Modeling on the World Wide Web, UM99—7th International Conference on User Modeling.* Banff, Canada, 1999.

47. **Millán, E. and Pérez-de-la-Cruz, J. L.** A Bayesian Diagnostic Algorithm for Student Modeling and its Evaluation. *User Modeling and User-Adapted Interaction* 12: 281–330, 2002.

48. **Virvou, M. and Moundridou, M.** Student and Instructor Models: Two Kinds of User Model and Their Interaction in an {ITS} Authoring Tool. *Lecture Notes in Computer Science 2109.* Springer Verlag, 2001.

49. **Weber, G. and Specht, M.** User Modeling and Adaptive Navigation Support in WWW-Based Tutoring Systems. *UM97 — 6th International Conference on User Modeling.* Chia Laguna, Sardinia, Italy: Springer Wien New York, 1997.

50. **Brailsford, T., Ashman, H., Stewart, C., Zakaria, M. R., and Moore, A.** User Control of Adaptation in an Automated Web-Based Learning Environment. *ICITA 2002 — 1st International Conference on Information Technology & Applications.* Bathurst, Australia: IEEE, 2002.

51. **Billsus, D. and Pazzani, M. J.** Learning Probabilistic User Models. *Workshop on Machine Learning for User Modeling. UM97 - 6th International Conference on User Modeling,* Chia Laguna, Sardinia, Italy: Springer Wien New York, 1997.

52. **Langley, P., Iba, W. and Thompson, K.** An Analysis of Bayesian Classifiers. *The 10th Conference on Artificial Intelligence*. San Jose, CA: AAAI Press, 1992.

53. **Shiri, M. E., Aïmeur, E. and Frasson, C.** Case-Based Student Modelling: An accessible Solution Model. *NTICF '98 - Conference Internationale sur les nouvelles technologies de la communication ET de la formation*. Rouen, France, 1998.

54. **Weber, G., Kuhl, H. C. and Weibelzahl, S.** Developing Adaptive Internet Based Courses with the Authoring System NetCoach. *3rd Workshop on Adaptive Hypertext and Hypermedia, UM2001—8th International Conference on User Modeling*. Sonthofen, Germany: Springer, 2001.

55. **Picard, R.** *Affective Computing*. Cambridge, MA: The MIT Press, 1997.

56. **Mayer, R. E.** *Multimedia Learning*. New York: Cambridge University Press, 2001.

57. **Polhemus, L., Danchak, M. M. and Swan, K.** *Adaptive Presentations for Learning Styles: Reflective Online Teaching*. Submitted to American Educational Research Association (AERA). San Diego, CA, 2004.

58. **Mayer, R. E. and Moreno, R.** A Split-Attention Effect in Multimedia Learning: Evidence for Dual Processing Systems in Working Memory. *Journal of Educational Psychology* 90(2): 312–320, 1996.

59. **Mayer, R. E. and Anderson, R. B.** The Instructive Animation: Helping Students Build Connections between Words and Pictures in Multimedia Learning. *Journal of Educational Psychology* 84(4): 444–452, 1992.

60. **Morse, K**. Does One Size Fit All? Exploring Asynchronous Learning in a Multicultural Environment. *Journal of Asynchronous Learning Networks* 7(1): 37–55, February 2003.

VII. ACKNOWLDGEMENTS

I would like to acknowledge the excellent work of my graduate students: Alessandro Assis, Derek Carey, Linda Polhemus, Andrew Sheh, and Michael Vanne. Without their help, none of this would be possible.

VIII ABOUT THE AUTHOR

Dr. Michael Danchak is Professor of Computer Science at Rensselaer Polytechnic Institute. He is both a researcher in and practitioner of distributed education. Recently he turned his attention to increasing the efficacy of the web for learning through appropriate application of computing technology. His course, GUI Building, was selected as a WebCT Exemplary Course in 2003. Contact: Michael M. Danchak, Ph.D., Computer Science, Rensselaer Polytechnic Institute, Troy, New York, 12180. Telephone: 518-276-6583; FAX: 518-276-4033. Email: danchm@rpi.edu

ALN RESEARCH: WHAT WE KNOW AND WHAT WE NEED TO KNOW ABOUT CONTEXTUAL INFLUENCES

Starr Roxanne Hiltz
Information Systems Department, NJIT

J. Ben Arbaugh
University of Wisconsin at Oshkosh

Raquel Benbunan-Fich
CUNY

Peter Shea
SUNY

- Generalizations can only be made if previous results can be replicated in subsequent multi-course, multi-discipline studies.

- Research aimed at increasing generalizability should be a high priority in the next decade.

- Comparisons across institutions with similar ALN environments may highlight specific institutional factors that contribute to the success of ALNs.

- Four course characteristics have been identified as relevant for successful implementation of ALNs: demographics (class size, level, course length, participant dispersion, etc.), mode of delivery, and discipline.

- Additional studies on how best to design, develop, and scale online learning at the institutional level are needed.

I. INTRODUCTION

What is the best way to set a research agenda for ALN effectiveness to move the field forward?

With support from the Alfred P. Sloan Foundation, many of the leading researchers on ALN, judged by their production of refereed published articles thus far, were invited to a workshop at NJIT in the Spring of 2002 to share ideas and reach consensus on the top research concerns for the next five to ten years, and then to develop a collaboratively written book which describes what we know based on past research, what we need to know, and the methodological techniques (both quantitative and qualitative) that are needed to improve our knowledge about ALN effectiveness. *Learning Online Together: Research on Asynchronous Learning Networks* is scheduled to be published in the fall of 2004 by Lawrence Erlbaum Associates, Inc. This paper summarizes some of the main findings in two of the key chapters of the book about the influence of context and moderating factors on the effectiveness of ALN: characteristics of the technology, the institution and the course in which it is used, the instructor's pedagogy and the students enrolled in the course.

II. THEORETICAL FRAMEWORK: ONLINE INTERACTION LEARNING THEORY

The authors of the book use an integrated theoretical model to organize what research shows and where research is going. We call this model "Online Interaction Learning Theory." An extension of preliminary frameworks that have been included in past Sloan-C research papers (for example, [1]), it models the variables and processes that are important in determining the relative effectiveness of communities of online learners. These communities of learners are working to reach a deep level of understanding by interacting with each other and with the materials under investigation. The framework, and its relationship to chapters in the book, is shown in Figure 1. This paper covers the "input" or contextual factors shown at the top of the diagram.

Any use of ALN technology is located within a particular social context. The characteristics of the user and of the hardware-software system shape the dynamics of human-computer interaction during a session in which a teacher or student uses a system.

In the model, the "inputs" or moderators include the characteristics of:
- the technology (in particular, the media mix);
- the group (course or class), and the organizational setting (college or university), which define the context in which the technology is used;
- the instructor; and
- the individual student.

These four sets of factors are expected to act as "moderator" variables [2] that influence how the technology is adapted for a particular course [3]. The model is based on contingency theory. These "input" or moderator variables must be present at least at a minimal level, so that online interaction and communication can occur and lead to the outcomes. For example, if the technology used is unreliable, or difficult to learn and use, or requires hardware or software that many of the students do not have, then the barriers to a successful online course are almost insurmountable. A second example is the experience and effort of the instructor. If the instructor has no experience and no training on how to design and teach online, then he or she is not likely to be able to use ALN effectively. Likewise, if the instructor in essence "misses class" by failing to evidence a daily and active guiding online presence, then most students will stop participating, too, just as they will leave an empty classroom if the instructor does not show up within a certain time of the scheduled start of class. Finally, unless the student has at least a minimal level of motivation and ability to do the required activities in a course, he or she will fail to reach a satisfactory level of learning. As an extreme example, if the student is unable to read or write at even an eighth grade level in the English language, he or she will not do well in an ALN course, which is based almost totally on reading and writing in English.

Each of the contextual factors listed can be logically assumed to be related to the probability that the interaction within an ALN will be lively and productive of desirable learning outcomes. However, the relative importance of the variables, individually and as they may interact, is a question for research. The contextual or "input" factors lead to the communication and social and learning processes within the online classroom: the amount and type of communication, the nature of the activities conducted there (individual and/or collaborative learning), and perceptions of the environment by the participants (e.g., perceived social presence and media richness/sufficiency; perceived sense of community). Favorable outcomes of the ALN educational process are contingent upon the nature of the actual process that occurs within a specific "virtual classroom." How many people are actively participating, how often, and with what kinds of activities and communications patterns? To what extent does a learning community actually emerge from the collection of people, resources, and media assembled for the course?

The intervening variables, in turn, are conceptualized as leading to the attainment of the desired outcomes, particularly learning and satisfaction. These are referred to by the ALN research community as the "five pillars of quality" [4]: learning effectiveness, cost effectiveness, access, student satisfaction and faculty satisfaction. They are described and discussed at: http://www.sloan-c.org/effective/index.asp.

III. TECHNOLOGY

Many attributes define the characteristics of the technology. From the technical point of view, functionality, usability, and reliability and media bandwidth determine the capabilities of the system. From a communications perspective, the system can be classified in terms of its ability to be used from different times and places.

From their beginnings as extensions of proprietary Computer-Mediated Communication Systems or combinations of electronic tools such as e-mail, web pages, and newsgroups [5], delivery platforms for ALNs have evolved into fairly sophisticated, increasingly interactive software packages. Research on these commercial platforms (e.g., WebCT, Blackboard, Lotus Learning Space) is growing but still sparse.

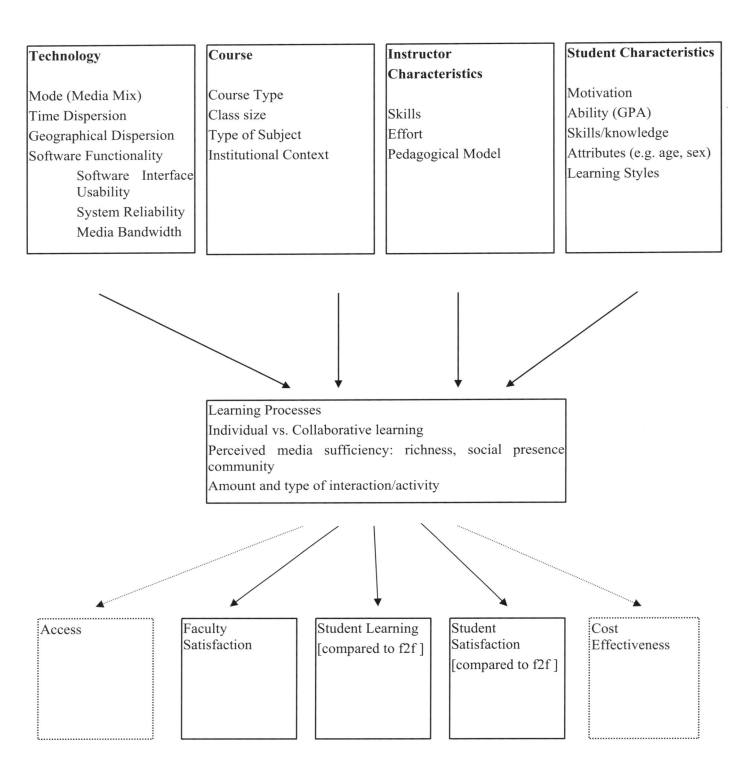

Figure 1: Correspondence between the Online Interaction Learning Model and Book Topics

For instance, studies of WebCT to date have generally been favorable, particularly in situations where it is used to supplement classroom courses [6, 7, 8] or synchronous online course offerings [9], while results of research on ALN courses using LearningSpace have been mixed. While it has compared favorably in comparisons of student performance in ALNs and classroom courses [10, 11, 12], it also has been associated with increased interaction difficulty [10, 13], scored significantly lower in user friendliness compared to other software packages [14, 15], and has required the installation of Lotus Notes on student machines to ensure that they did not lose their work [16]. Generally, while individual software platforms have received varying degrees of research attention, comparative research on the effectiveness of these software packages is rather limited [17].

The quality and reliability of any ALN environment is critical especially when it is used as the only instructional delivery medium. Technology-mediated distance courses in which the technology is reliable and of high quality tend to be more successful [18]. However, the effects of system quality and/or reliability typically have not been measured in the design of most ALN research. This is likely because intentionally varying system quality and reliability would be inappropriate in actual educational environments. However, if researchers considered and designed their studies for the possibility that systems may not work as planned, they could produce useful research on the management of technological crises in the delivery of education via ALN.

In terms of media mix, very few studies have included systematic comparisons among the three modes of course delivery: traditional, "mixed" mode and pure ALN. Most of them present two-way comparisons (traditional vs. mixed or distance vs. mixed). The empirical evidence suggests that due to its hybrid nature mixed mode courses may combine the "best of both worlds." Due in part to these encouraging initial findings, some researchers have called for the mixed mode model to play an increasingly prominent role in the development of future courses and degree programs [19]. Another area related to media mix that has been notable for the absence of research is the question of the effects of different types and amounts of use of digital multi-media (e.g., student presentations via PowerPoint plus digital audio files) in addition to text-based discussions. This is because until most students have broadband connections (which are becoming increasingly prevalent), digital multimedia are not practical. At the present time there isn't enough research to help us determine whether additional media produce enough student learning and course satisfaction benefits to merit the additional time and expense required to develop and incorporate them into courses.

IV. COURSE CHARACTERISTICS

Four course characteristics have been identified as relevant for successful implementation of ALNs: demographics (class size, level, course length, participant dispersion, etc.), mode of delivery, and discipline.

The number of students enrolled in a course produces different group dynamics. If it is too few, then "critical mass" will not be reached; the online learning space may seem empty. If too many, then the amount of postings online may lead to information overload and confusion, particularly if no technological features or pedagogical interventions are made to structure and organize the interactions of a large number of students. Using a sample of courses with enrollments of up to 50 students, Arbaugh and Duray [15, 20] have found that class section size was negatively associated with student learning. Other studies with class sizes of thirty or less have found that class size was not a significant predictor of student learning or satisfaction [14, 21, 22].

These findings prompt at least two possible explanations or solutions to the class size issue. One possibility is that the class size-outcome relationship is curvilinear in nature [12]. That is, increasing class size improves student learning to a point, but adding students beyond that point reduces the quality of the course experience. A possible solution for this issue may be through adding additional instructional support personnel as class sizes increase. Andriole [23] proposed maximum instructor/course quality ratios: 1 instructor for every 30 students, 1 instructor + 1 ALN assistant for every 50 students, 1 instructor + 2 ALN assistants for every 75 students, and so on. Additional research is needed to identify optimal student-instructor ratios in ALN settings.

The level of the students enrolled in a course (undergraduate or graduate) also may dictate different approaches to the use of ALNs. Unfortunately, our present ability to make inferences about this factor is inhibited by the fact that most ALN studies have examined either undergraduate or graduate samples without combining the student populations. In one of the few comprehensive studies using both student groups in their sample, Benbunan-Fich & Hiltz [25] studied 1974 undergraduate and graduate students in several traditional, pure ALN and mixed mode courses. They found that graduate students in hybrid courses had the highest levels of perceived learning, while undergraduates in hybrid courses had the lowest scores in perceived learning. However, other studies using both groups suggest that undergraduates may be more excited about the use of technology for learning [8] and more playful in their use of the Internet and therefore possibly better able to use it as a learning tool [26]. Clearly, this limited pool of research suggests that the relationship between student educational level and course outcomes is an area where additional study is needed.

In terms of subject matter or academic discipline, it appears that to date ALN research has been conducted to a widely varying extent within disciplines. While some disciplines such as information systems have been the subject of extensive ALN research, others such as the humanities have received little research attention. Therefore, while ALNs appear to be effective in a number of educational settings, making generalizations as to the applicability of ALNs across disciplines (and across different types of institutions) may be premature. These generalizations can only be made if previous results can be replicated in subsequent multi-course, multi-discipline studies. Certainly research aimed at increasing the generalizability of these findings should be a high priority in the next decade.

V. INSTITUTIONAL SUPPORT

The broader contextual factor influencing ALN effectiveness is the institution. Unfortunately, most of the literature on asynchronous learning networks (ALNs) deals with the pedagogical and technological advantages of this environment while ignoring the institutional obstacles that may prevent the widespread implementation of ALNs [27, 28]. The existing research regarding institutional characteristics is mostly prescriptive. Different authors advise institutions on how to embrace the promises of the technology and improve teaching and learning productivity without sacrificing the quality of instruction. However, some authors argue that in order to reap the benefits of the new technology a total institutional restructuring must occur [29, 30].

Typical institutional challenges can be classified in three critical areas: technological support, administrative support and policy issues. For example, a recent multi-institutional study of technology-mediated learning suggests that colleges and universities tend to underestimate the cost of providing the additional technical support for implementing ALN initiatives [25]. Increased demand to access the ALN system and other campus computing facilities may cause slowdowns or service outages that inconvenience students and faculty [31]. Likewise, attacks on central servers that host ALN platforms may slow or completely halt their operation; the speed of recovery depends on the size and competence of the technical support staff. If the technological infrastructure is not adequate, it may be necessary to invest in new servers, more or better technical support staff, security measures, support and help desks, and high speed and high capacity networks [32]. Hardware, software and telecommunication upgrades must be constantly evaluated, not only because of increasing demand but also due to the rate of technical change.

Another key element for the success of an ALN environment is administrative support. Institutions must examine if the current infrastructure is adequate to deal with the new demands of ALN courses and degrees. For example, will special marketing efforts be needed to enroll students in ALN courses? How to project the demand for this new type of course? Hiltz [31] suggests the development of new marketing strategies for this new mode of delivery. Another administrative issue deals with the proper training and supervision of adjuncts or teaching aides assigned to online sections.

Faculty new to online teaching need training and support as they develop and deliver online courses. This should include short courses in use of the technologies, e.g., the ALN platform, how to create and update course web pages and multimedia online lectures or simulations via the variety of software packages licensed by the institution. In addition, both new and more experienced faculty need to learn about, develop, and share experiences with appropriate pedagogical principles, such as how to develop, facilitate and grade collaborative assignments, and how to facilitate high-quality online discussions [27, 33].

As a new teaching/learning environment, ALNs challenge some of the existing practices and policies on campuses [31]. In particular, issues such as faculty workload and compensation, intellectual property and degree policies must be re-examined and adapted to the new context. How efforts related to teaching online are related to merit ratings, promotion and tenure decisions must be clarified.

Another complex policy issue deals with the intellectual property rights associated with the development of online learning materials. Who is the owner of the content of ALN courses, the institution, the faculty member, or both? What type of ownership is the most appropriate to deal with ALN materials, copyright or patent? Many faculty will be unwilling to teach via ALN if they do not feel that the institution's intellectual property rights are fair.

VI. INSTRUCTOR CHARACTERISTICS AND PEDAGOGY

The mode of adaptation of technology in different courses by different instructors, in particular their actions in terms of pedagogical design (instructivist or constructionist/collaborative), the degree and nature of "structuring" or "scaffolding" of the course, and the instructor's "style," will be key factors in determining the nature of the educational processes and outcomes. For example, what is the balance between individual and collaborative assignments and activities, and how does the instructor grade or reward students for class discussion participation, and for group projects? Another example is the clarity of the course requirements. Can the student see a syllabus or calendar from the beginning of the course, to know what is expected and when? In terms of an online persona or teaching style, does the instructor act so as to establish "swift trust" during the first week of the course [34], by establishing a lively and responsive environment and working to establish an online learning community from the start?

Besides course design, other attributes of the instructor's behavior also crucially affect the process and outcome for students. How much skill and experience does the instructor have with online learning? Does he or she even know how to use the technologies without fumbling? Does he or she have any training, if not experience, in the role changes that must be made in moving towards becoming a "virtual professor?" And very importantly, how "present" is the instructor in the virtual classroom? If the instructor is not

115

"there," then very shortly, the students will not participate either, just as students leave a physical classroom if the instructor does not show up within 10–20 minutes of the scheduled start of the class.

Pedagogy emphasizing the one-way transmission of concepts (instructivist approach) calls for the use of a system that improves the efficiency of this transfer in the lecturing process. In contrast, constructivist models call for learner-centered applications where students can construct their own knowledge by formulating ideas into words, and building upon these ideas through discussions, reactions and responses of their peers. For constructivist methods based on collaborative group assignments, the technological platform should above all support communications among students [35].

A significant question meriting future research attention is whether either of these approaches or a combination of them best predicts student learning and/or satisfaction in the ALN environment. Evidence to date is somewhat mixed. Some studies report that collaborative learning approaches should be the foundation to design and deliver online courses because they result in better student performance and perceptions [36, 37, 38, 39]. Others have shown collaborative learning techniques to be negatively associated with student learning in web-based courses [41]. The inconclusive nature of this research to date suggests that determining which pedagogical approaches are most appropriate or the contextual factors that make one more appropriate than another is a topic meriting extensive research.

While the most appropriate pedagogy model for ALNs remains in question, one variable that has been well established is the extent to which quality interaction takes place amongst course participants [17, 41, 42, 43]. Some studies suggest that it is the instructor's role in course interaction that is most critical [33, 41, 44, 45], while others suggest that the students' role in interaction most significantly predicts student learning and/or satisfaction [9, 43, 46, 47], and still others suggest that they are equally important [17, 34, 48, 49]. However, it is not certain whether this interaction should be primarily between the instructor and the students, or among the students themselves. Although the prominence of the instructor's role in course interaction remains unclear, the nature of instructor interaction is becoming well established. The extent to which an instructor engages in immediacy behaviors appears to be strongly associated with student outcomes. Originally conceptualized by Mehrabian [50], immediacy refers to communication behaviors that reduce social and psychological distance between people [51]. In the ALN context, immediacy describes behaviors such as including personal examples, using humor, providing and inviting feedback, and addressing students by name [52]. There is increasing evidence that these behaviors are positively associated with student learning and satisfaction with the course format [21, 22].

One of the most glaring gaps in the ALN literature is the lack of studies conducted at the institutional level. Comparisons across institutions with similar ALN environments may highlight specific institutional factors that contribute to the success of ALNs. An example of how institutions might be studied in an ALN context is the extent to which their structures, behaviors, and decision making processes encourage ALN research. For instance, some longitudinal studies have attempted to measure student characteristics and preferences for ALNs only to find that the institution's decision to delegate the decision to offer online courses to the individual departments resulted in too few online courses being offered to generate statistically significant results for the study [53, 54].

VII. STUDENT CHARACTERISTICS AND ALN EFFECTIVENESS

At the core of the concept of an Asynchronous Learning Network is the student as an active—and socially interactive—learner. Individual characteristics of the students such as learning style, cultural values, cognitive ability and motivation will also influence the processes and will determine outcomes.

A. What We Know About Student Characteristics

On the individual level, students who are motivated, self-directed and confident about having the computer skills necessary to use the technology are those who are most likely to thrive in the ALN environment. Often these are students who are older than traditional on-campus undergraduates. Females seem on the average to be somewhat more comfortable in ALN courses than males, perhaps because of their generally higher verbal skills and their greater tendency to like collaborative learning styles.

Students tend to prefer to process information in different ways; this is referred to as "learning style" or "cognitive style." The learning style construct assumes that a student's preferred mode for obtaining knowledge affects how well he or she interacts and learns via different media. There are many different classification schemes for learning style and cognitive style, and a lack of agreement on measures. There is also a great deal of controversy about whether aspects of cognitive style significantly predict learner success. A notable study from Diaz [55] used a simple one-dimensional classification of the degree to which learners prefer "independent" learning vs. "dependent" learning (tied to desire to receive guidance from their teacher). He found that successful online students (defined as those who received a grade of C or better) were more strongly independent learners than those who were not successful. Another learning style classification is verbal vs. non-verbal learners: the former feel more comfortable with text-based information while the latter prefer non-verbal materials, such as images [56]. The text-based communication that is predominant in ALN currently may place non-verbal learners at a disadvantage. A study by Leuthold [57] used the Gregorc model that includes a classification of how learners tend to organize information, sequentially or randomly. She found that sequential learners prefer computer-based instruction while random learners tend to prefer traditional instructional techniques. Random learners seem to have more problems navigating and using the web-site and are bothered more by access problems than are the sequential learners. Sequential learners reported feeling strongly that interaction, particularly with the instructor, is improved with computer-based learning. Sequential learners also experienced increased motivation to learn and their familiarity and knowledge of computers increased with computer-based instruction.

Many student characteristics appear to have some influence on ALN outcomes, when examined individually, but they are often so weak that they disappear when other factors are taken into account. Lim [58] reports a multivariate analysis of correlates of outcomes for undergraduate and graduate students at five universities. Personal variables were age, gender, computer self-efficacy, academic self-concept, and academic status. Experiential variables were years of computer use, frequency of computer use, computer training, Internet experience in a class, and participation in a workshop to prepare for a Web-based course. The criterion variables were satisfaction levels with the Web-based distance education courses and intent to participate in future Web-based courses. There was a significant relationship between computer self-efficacy and satisfaction. Years of computer use, Internet experience in a class, and academic self-concept had positive relationships with satisfaction. Computer self-efficacy was significantly related to years of computer use ($r=.452, p<.001$), frequency of computer use ($r=.305, p<.001$), academic self-concept ($r=.224, p<.001$), age ($r=-.187, p=.002$), and academic status ($r=-.139, p=.017$). The combination of all these predictor variables produced a predictive model for satisfaction of adult learners in their Web-based distance education course. The results of the multiple regression analysis revealed that 15% of the variability in the dependent variable (satisfaction) was explained by these predictor variables. Entering all predictor variables, the percentage of observed variability in intent to take future Web-based courses is 12%. So, while individual student characteristics are important, they do not explain the majority of the variance in outcomes.

B. What We Need To Know

In looking at gender, most studies examine either interaction modes or course outcomes. We need more studies that look at the relationship among characteristics that may be associated with gender (e.g., verbal skills, learning styles, independence, and family responsibilities), interaction patterns online, and course outcomes.

We could use more longitudinal and multivariate studies, across a variety of disciplines and institutions and cultural/national backgrounds of students, which look at how characteristics of the students interact with pedagogy and interaction patterns online to produce course outcomes. Most studies are of a small number of students at one institution (and often in one class), are based only on a cross sectional questionnaire, and look at only a few variables.

While examinations of student characteristics may allow us to understand a little about who is likely to succeed in online learning environments, the larger and more important issues may be about how we can help most or all students seeking online education to succeed [59]. Motivated, self-directed, self-disciplined students are likely to succeed in any learning environment, but we need to know more about how to support weaker students—online environments pose additional challenges and opportunities in this regard. We need additional inquiry in at least three areas: student support, faculty support and institutional alignment for online learning.

Additional studies of approaches to online learning environments need to focus on student outcomes relative to the existence of support services. Student support services such as the technology helpdesk, academic advisement, orientation, tutoring, and library services are all considered essential in F2F learning environments. Additional study of how best to provide these to online learners may prove fruitful in reducing failure for students with less than ideal levels of motivation, self-direction and self discipline.

We also need additional studies on the impact of faculty support. Focusing solely on student traits, without also examining faculty behaviors is unlikely to provide a complete analysis of how best to facilitate success. Clearly, systematic approaches to faculty development and support have positive consequence on effective online course design and management [60, 61, 63], which, in turn, are likely to result in higher rates of student success.

VIII. CONCLUSIONS AND FUTURE RESEARCH DIRECTIONS

ALN research would be greatly strengthened if researchers would simultaneously consider some of the topics we have mentioned here to help increase our understanding of how contextual factors may moderate relationships between particular variables and ALN effectiveness. Research of this nature will likely require the increased use of multi-course and multi-institutional research samples, as well as case studies that include qualitative research methods.

For example, we have stated that the studies thus far suggest a curvilinear relationship between online class size and effectiveness, with classes in the 25–30 range being most successful. However, this "average," in turn, depends on the other contextual factors, such as:

> What is the subject matter? Perhaps science classes with a great deal of "objective" knowledge to impart, can use "objectivist" delivery techniques such as tutorials, simulations, and self-testing via quizzes, and be very successful as large online courses. An account of an introductory physics

class for 500 students [64] gives an example.

What level of skills and motivation and experience with online learning do the students bring to the course? And what kind of training and support does the institution offer? If students are skilled in online interaction and/or have extensive technical or content tutoring available from sources other than the instructor, class sizes can be larger.

What is the pedagogical model used by the instructor, and how experienced is the instructor with teaching online? For example, "fully" collaborative learning in which students explicitly share responsibility for facilitating discussion and activities in the course can help the faculty to accommodate more.

What functions are available in the software to help the instructor with her job? For example, is there a built in gradebook and/or quiz function? Can she easily obtain a weekly summary of participation by student rather than having to search and count by hand?

What training and support are provided by the institution? For instance, are there teaching assistants who can help with leading break-out discussion groups and with grading? This would make it much easier to handle classes of 50 or more online.

Finally, additional studies on how best to design, develop, and scale online learning at the institutional level are also needed. This will require a "case study" approach that includes extensive personal interviews, as well as the use of more quantitative data. Identifying, understanding, and confronting common institutional barriers that inhibit the overall growth of online learning environments will result in higher quality and more sustainable models for online learning—ultimately a key beneficiary will be the online student.

To illustrate, "optimal class size" is an example of how current findings also point to challenges for both research and practice. For many institutions, there are insufficient resources to permit an average class size of 25–30 students per full time faculty member. We need research on how to scale up the size of ALN courses and still teach them effectively. We need more case studies of effective "large" ALN classes. (See Turoff and Hiltz [65] for one example.)

A second major area in which current findings showing a "weakness" in the effectiveness of ALN and point to a priority area for future research is related to student characteristics. How can ALN be made more effective for students who lack the motivation, self-discipline, computer self-efficacy and verbal skills that characterize the most successful online students? Some of the possible areas for exploration include other contextual factors:

Would changing the media mix, e.g., including some remedial tutorials in the form of animations, help certain types of students?

Would institutional provision of online and telephone student peer tutoring help, particularly for certain types of subject matter such as mathematics?

Would a "pre-course" in basic skills for online learning help? (Many institutions now provide such an introduction).

Thus, the gaps and negative findings of the ALN research thus far points the way to important research issues for the future.

IX. ACKNOWLEDGEMENTS

The material in this chapter is adapted from Starr Roxanne Hiltz and Ricki Goldman, Eds., *Learning Online Together: Research on Asynchronous Learning Networks*, scheduled to be published by Lawrence Erlbaum Associates, Inc. in fall 2004, and used with permission by the publisher. This work was partially supported by grants from the Alfred P. Sloan Foundation, and the New Jersey Center for Pervasive Information Systems. Eunhee Kim and Yi Zhang assisted in the compilation of studies of learning styles and of gender differences in ALN. Linda Harasim collaborated on the theoretical framework chapter of the book. Ricki Goldman and David Spencer have made editorial contributions to the entire volume, including the chapters from which this paper is drawn. Zheng Li assisted with the editing of this paper.

X. REFERENCES

1. **Turoff, M. and Hiltz, S. R.** Effectively Managing Large Enrollment Courses: A Case Study. In J. Bourne and J.C. Moore, Eds, *Online Education, Vol 2: Learning Effectiveness, Faculty Satisfaction, and Cost Effectiveness. Proceedings of the 2000 Summer Workshop on Asynchronous Learning Networks*. Needham, MA: Sloan-C, 2001.
2. **Baron, R. M. and Kenny, D. A.** The Moderator-Mediator Variables Distinction in Social Psychology Research: Conceptual, Strategic and Statistical Considerations. *Journal of Personality and Social Psychology* 51(6): 1173–1182, 1986.
3. **Dennis, A. R., Wixom, B. H. and Vandenberg, R. J.** Understanding Fit and Appropriation Effects in Group Support Systems Via Meta Analysis. *MIS Quarterly* 25(2): 167–193, 2001.
4. **Mayadas, F., Bourne, J. and Moore, J. C.** Introduction. In J. Bourne & J. C. Moore (Eds.), *Elements of Quality of Online Education*, 7–11. Needham, MA: Sloan-C, 2002.
5. **Dumont, R. A.** Teaching and Learning in Cyberspace. *IEEE Transactions on Professional Communication* 39(4): 192–204, 1996.
6. **Hartman, J., Dziuban, C. and Moskal, P.** Faculty Satisfaction in ALNs: A Dependent or Independent Variable. *Journal of Asynchronous Learning Networks* 4(3): 2000.
7. **Sandercock, G. R. H. and Shaw, G.** Learners' Performance and Evaluation of Attitudes Towards Web Course Tools in the Delivery of an Applied Sports Medicine Module. *ALN Magazine* 3: 1999.
8. **Wernet, S. P., Olliges, R. H., & Delicath, T. A.** Postcourse Evaluations of WebCT Classes by Social Work Students. *Research on Social Work Practice* 10: 487–514, 2000.
9. **Borthick, A. F., & Jones, D. R.** The Motivation for Collaborative Discovery Learning Online and its Application in an Information Systems Assurance Course. *Issues in Accounting Education* 15(2): 181–210, 2000.
10. **Arbaugh, J. B.** Virtual Classroom Characteristics and Student Satisfaction in Internet-Based MBA Courses. *Journal of Management Education* 24(1): 32–54, 2000a.
11. **Alavi, M., Yoo, Y. and Vogel, D. R.** Using Information Technology to Add Value to Management Education. *Academy of Management Journal* 40(6): 1310–1333, 1997.
12. **Piccoli, G., Ahmad, R. and Ives, B.** Web-Based Virtual Learning Environments: A Research Framework and a Preliminary Assessment of Effectiveness in Basic IT Skills Training. *MIS Quarterly* 25: 401–426, 2001.

13. **Yoo, Y., Kanawattanachai, P. and Citurs, A.** Forging into the Wired Wilderness: A Case Study of a Technology-Mediated Distributed Discussion-Based Class. *Journal of Management Education* 26: 139–163, 2002.

14. **Arbaugh, J. B.** A Longitudinal Study of Technological and Pedagogical Characteristics of Web-Based MBA Courses. In D. Nagao (Ed.), *Academy of Management Best Papers Proceedings* Vol. MED: A1–A6, 2002a.

15. **Arbaugh, J. B. and Duray, R.** Class Section Size, Perceived Classroom Characteristics, Instructor Experience, and Student Learning and Satisfaction with Web-Based Courses: A Study and Comparison of Two Online MBA Programs. In D. Nagao (Ed.), *Academy of Management Best Papers Proceeding* Vol. MED: A1–A6, 2001.

16. **Smith, L. J.** Content and Delivery: A Comparison and Contrast of Electronic and Traditional MBA Marketing Planning Courses. *Journal of Marketing Education* 23(1): 35–44, 2001.

17. **Palloff, R. and Pratt, K.** *Building Learning Communities in Cyberspace.* San Francisco: Jossey-Bass, 1999.

18. **Webster, J. and Hackley, P.** Teaching Effectiveness in Technology-Mediated Distance Learning. *Academy of Management Journal* 40(6): 1282–1309, 1997.

19. **Alavi, M., & Leidner, D. E.** Research Commentary: Technology-Mediated Learning—A Call for Greater Depth and Breadth of Research. *Information Systems Research* 12(1): 1–10, 2001.

20. **Arbaugh, J. B. and Duray, R.** Technological and Structural Characteristics, Student Learning and Satisfaction with Web-Based Courses: An Exploratory Study of Two MBA Programs. *Management Learning* 33: 331–347, 2002.

21. **Arbaugh, J. B.** How Instructor Immediacy Behaviors Affect Student Satisfaction and Learning in Web-Based Courses. *Business Communication Quarterly* 64(4): 42–54, 2001.

22. **Arbaugh, J. B.** Managing the Online Classroom: A Study of Technological and Behavioral Characteristics of Web-Based MBA Courses. *Journal of High Technology Management Research* 13: 203–223, 2002b.

23. **Andriole, S. J.** Requirement-Driven ALN Course Design, Development, Delivery, & Evaluation. *Journal of Asynchronous Learning Networks* 1(2): 1997.

24. **Benbunan-Fich, R. and Hiltz, S. R.** Correlates of Effectiveness of Learning Networks: The Effects of Course Level, Course Type and Gender on Outcomes. In *Proceedings of the 35th Hawaii International Conference on System Sciences HICSS-35.* Hawaii, 2002.

25. **Alavi, M. and Gallupe, R. B.** Using Information Technology in Learning: Case Studies in Business and Management Education Programs. *Academy of Management Learning and Education* 2(2): 139–153, 2003.

26. **Atkinson, M. and Kydd, C.** Individual Characteristics Associated with World Wide Web Use: An Empirical Study of Playfulness and Motivation. *The DATA BASE for Advances in Information Systems* 28(2): 53–62, 1997.

27. **Alavi, M. and Gallupe, R. B.** Using Information Technology in Learning: Case Studies in Business and Management Education Programs. *Academy of Management Learning and Education* 2(2): 139–153, 2003.

28. **Jaffee, D.** Institutionalized Resistance to Asynchronous Learning Networks. *Journal of Asynchronous Learning Networks* 2(2): 1998.

29. **Graves, W. H.** "Free Trade" in Higher Education: The Meta University. *Journal of Asynchronous Learning Networks* 1(1): 1997.

30. **Moore, M. G.** Institutional Restructuring: Is Distance Education Like Retailing? *American Journal of Distance Education* 13(1): 1999.

31. **Hiltz, S. R.** *The Virtual Classroom: Learning Without Limits Via Computer Networks.* Norwood, New Jersey: Ablex Publishing Corporation, 1994.

32. **Hawkins, B.** Distributed Learning and Institutional Restructuring. *Educom Review* 34(4): 1999.

33. **Brower, H. H.** On Emulating Classroom Discussion in a Distance-Delivered OBHR Course: Creating an Online Community. *Academy of Management Learning and Education* 2(1): 22–36, 2003.

34. **Coppola, N. W., Hiltz, S. R. and Rotter, N.** Becoming a Virtual Professor: Pedagogical Roles and Asynchronous Learning Networks. *JMIS* 18(4): 169–190, 2002.

35. **Benbunan-Fich, R.** Improving Education and Training with IT. *Communications of the ACM* 45(6): 94–99, 2002.

36. **Alavi, M., Wheeler, B. and Valacich, J.** Using IT to Reengineer Business Education: An Exploratory Investigation to Collaborative Telelearning. *MIS Quarterly* 19(3): 294–312, September 1995.

37. **Card, K. A.** Providing Access to Graduate Education Using Computer-Mediated Communication. *International Journal of Instructional Media* 27: 235–245, 2000.

38. **Hiltz, S. R., Coppola, N., Rotter, N., Turoff, M. and Benbunan-Fich, R.** Measuring the Importance of Collaborative Learning for the Effectiveness of ALN: A Multi-Measure, Multi-Method Approach. *Journal of Asynchronous Learning Networks* 4(2): 2000.

39. **Arbaugh, J. B. & Benbunan-Fich, R.** Testing the Applicability of Learning Theories to Web-Based MBA Courses. *Proceedings of the 2003 Academy of Management Meeting.* Seattle, WA, August 2003.

40. **Swan, K.** Building Learning Communities in Online Courses: The Importance of Interaction. *Education Communication and Information* 2(1): 23–49, 2002.

41. **Fredericksen, E., Pickett, A., Shea, P. and Pelz, W.** Student Satisfaction and Perceived Learning with Online Courses: Principles and Examples from the SUNY Learning Network. *Journal of Asynchronous Learning Networks* 4(2): 2000.

42. **Hiltz, S. R., & Turoff, M.** What Makes Learning Networks Effective? *Communications of the ACM* 45(4): 56–59, 2002.

43. **Nulden, U.** Thematic Modules in an Asynchronous Learning Network: A Scandinavian Perspective on the Design of Introductory Courses. *Journal of Group Decision and Negotiation* 8(5): 391–408, September 1999.

44. **Arbaugh, J. B.** Virtual Classroom Characteristics and Student Satisfaction in Internet-Based MBA Courses. *Journal of Management Education* 24(1): 32–54, 2000a.

45. **Arbaugh, J. B.** How Classroom Environment and Student Engagement Affect Learning in Internet-Based MBA Courses. *Business Communication Quarterly* 63(4): 9–26, 2000c.

46. **Arbaugh, J. B.** Virtual Classrooms Versus Physical Classrooms: An Exploratory Study of Class Discussion Patterns and Student Learning in an Asynchronous Internet-Based MBA Course. *Journal of Management Education* 24(2): 207–227, 2000b.

47. **Smith, G. G., Ferguson, D. L. and Caris, M.** Teaching College Courses: Online vs. Face-to-Face. *T.H.E. Journal* 28(9):18–24, 2001.

48. **Hiltz, S. R.** Correlates of Learning in a Virtual Classroom. *International Journal of Man-Machine Studies* 39(1): 71–98, 1993.

49. **Jiang, M. and Ting, E.** A Study of Factors Influencing Students` Perceived Learning in a Web-Based Course Environment. *International Journal of Educational Telecommunications* 6(4): 317–338, 2000.

50. **Mehrabian, A.** *Silent Messages.* Belmont, CA: Wadsworth Publishing Co., 1971.

51. **Myers, S. A., Zhong, M. and Guan, S.** Instructor Immediacy in the Chinese College Classroom. *Communication Studies* 49: 240–253, 1998.

52. **Gorham, J.** The Relationship between Verbal Teacher Immediacy Behaviors and Student Learning. *Communication Education* 37(1): 40–53, 1988.

53. **Fornaciari, C. J.** *Student Personality Types and Enrollments in Distance Education: A Longitudinal Study.* Paper presented at the Academy of Management, Denver, CO, 2002.

54. **Fornaciari, C. J. and Matthews, C. S.** Student Personality Types and Predispositions toward Distance Education. In S. J. Havlovic (Ed.), *Academy of Management Best Papers Proceedings*, 2000.

55. **Diaz, D. P.** *Comparison of Student Characteristics, and Evaluation of Student Success, in an Online Health Education Course.* Unpublished doctoral dissertation, Nova Southeastern University, Fort Lauderdale, FL, 2000.

56. **Monaghan, P. and Stenning, K.** *Effects of Representation Modality and Thinking Style on Learning to Solve Reasoning Problems.* Paper presented at the 20th Annual Meeting of the Cognitive Science Society, Madison, Wisconsin, 1998, August 1–4.

57. **Leuthold, J. H.** Is Computer-Based Learning Right for Everyone? In *Proceedings of, 32nd Hawaii International Conference on Systems Sciences* (Vol. CD Rom, pp. 8). Washington, DC: IEEE Computer Society Press, 1999.

58. **Lim, C. K.** Computer Self-Efficacy, Academic Self-Concept, and Other Predictors of Satisfaction and Future Participation of Adult Distance Learners. *The American Journal of Distance Education* 15(2): 41–51, 2001.

59. **Wahlstrom C., Williams B. and Shea, P.** *The Successful Distance Learning Student.* Belmont CA: Wadsworth/Thomson Learning, 2003.

60. **Frederickson, E., Pickett, A., Shea, P., Pelz, W. and Swan, K.** Factors Influencing Faculty Satisfaction with Asynchronous Teaching and Learning in the SUNY Learning Network. In J. Bourne & J. C. Moore (Eds.), *Online Education, Volume 1 in the Sloan-C Series*, 239–267. Needham, MA: Sloan-C, 1999.

61. **Hartman, J., Dziuban, C. and Moskal, P.** Faculty Satisfaction in ALNs: A Dependent of Independent Variable. In J. Bourne & J. C. Moore (Eds.), *Online Education, Volume 1 in the Sloan-C Series,* 151–172. Needham, MA: Sloan-C, 1999.

62. **Frederickson, E., Pickett, A., Shea, P., Pelz, W. and Swan, K.** Student Satisfaction and Perceived Learning with Online Courses: Principles and Examples from the SUNY Learning Network. *JALN* 4(2): 2000.

63. **Shea, P., Swan, K., Fredericksen, E. and Pickett, A.** Student Satisfaction and Reported Learning in the SUNY Learning Network. In J. Bourne & J. C. Moore (Eds.), *Elements of Quality Online Education, Vol 3 in the Sloan-C Series*, 145–155. Needham, MA: Sloan-C, 2002.

64. **Thoennessen, M., Kashy, E., Tsai, Y. and Davis, N. E.** Impacts of Asynchronous Learning Networks in Large Lecture Classes. *Group Decision and Negotiation* 8(5): 371–384, September 1999.

65. **Hiltz, S. R., Coppola, N., Rotter, N., Turoff, M. and Benbunan-Fich, R.** Measuring the Importance of Collaborative Learning for the Effectiveness of ALN: A Multi-Measure, Multi-Method Approach. *Journal of Asynchronous Learning Networks* 4(2): 2000.

XI. ABOUT THE AUTHORS

Dr. Starr Roxanne Hiltz is Distinguished Professor of Computer and Information Science, New Jersey Institute of Technology, where she also directs the Ph.D. in Information Systems. She received her A.B. from Vassar and her M.A. and Ph.D. from Columbia. She has spent most of the last 20 years engaged in research on applications and social impacts of computer technology. Her research interests include educational applications of computer-mediated communications, human-computer interaction, and computer support for group decision making. In particular, with major funding from the Corporation for Public Broadcasting and the Alfred P. Sloan Foundation, in the 1980s and early 1990s she created and experimented with a Virtual Classroom® for delivery of college-level courses. This is a teaching and learning environment which is constructed, not of bricks and boards, but of software structures within a computer-mediated communication system. Her publications include six books and over 150 articles and professional papers.

Dr. J. B. (Ben) Arbaugh (B.B.A., Marshall University, M.B.A., Wright State University, M.S., Ph.D., The Ohio State University) is an Associate Professor of Strategy and Project Management in the College of Business Administration at the University of Wisconsin Oshkosh. His current research interests include the delivery of education via the internet, international entrepreneurship, project management, and the intersection of spirituality and strategic management research. His recent publications include articles in the Journal of Management Education, the Journal of High Technology Management Research, Management Learning, Frontiers of Entrepreneurship Research, the Blackwell Handbook of Entrepreneurship, Business Communication Quarterly, the Academy of Management's Best Papers Proceedings, and the Academy of Management Learning and Education Journal. Ben's recent research on characteristics of effective ALNs have allowed him to win the Academy of Management's Best Paper in Management Education in 2001 and 2002, along with the 2001 Fritz Roethlisberger Award for the best article in the Journal of Management Education.

Dr. Raquel Benbunan-Fich is an Assistant Professor of Information Systems at the Zicklin School of Business, Baruch College, City University of New York (CUNY). She received her Ph.D. in Management Information Systems from Rutgers University – Graduate School of Management, in 1997. She got her MBA (1989) from IESA, the leading Venezuelan business school, and her B.S. in Computer Engineering (1986) from Universidad Simon Bolivar in Caracas, Venezuela. Her research interests include Asynchronous Learning Networks, Computer-Mediated Communication Systems, evaluation of Web-based systems and e-commerce. She has published articles on related topics in Communications of the ACM, Group Decision and Negotiation, Information & Management, Journal of Applied Management and Entrepreneurship, Journal of Computer Information Systems and Journal of Computer-Mediated Communication and has forthcoming articles in the Case Research Journal and Decision Support Systems.

Dr. Peter Shea is the Director of the SUNY Teaching, Learning, and Technology Program for the 64 campuses of the State University of New York. He is also Director for SUNY's participation in the Multimedia Educational Resource for Learning and Online Teaching (MERLOT), an international collaboration for peer review of discipline specific online learning resources. Formerly Lead Instructional Designer for the SUNY Learning Network (SLN) he has assisted in the design of more than 100 online courses and provided training in online pedagogy to instructional designers for SLN. His research interests include student satisfaction and learning in internet-based distributed education and he has published a number of studies on this topic. He has also published and presented the results of research on computer assisted learning both nationally and internationally. Dr. Shea is also a Visiting Assistant Professor at the University at Albany, State University of New York.

Blended Environments

THREE ALN MODALITIES:
AN INSTITUTIONAL PERSPECTIVE*

*Charles Dziuban, Joel Hartman, Patsy Moskal, Steven Sorg, and Barbara Truman**
University of Central Florida
*authors appear alphabetically

- "Traditional" roles change as instructors becomes more facilitative while students assume greater responsibility for learning.

- Students focus on flexible thinking, problem solving, and new social and behavioral skills.

- Instructors acknowledge that their current personal and professional theories of teaching may be challenged and altered.

- Courses are designed more as communication and collaboration environments than as repositories for content.

- By dropping the "E" designation, face-to-face and E courses are becoming indistinguishable—a problem for evaluation but a clear sign of institutional transformation.

I. INTRODUCTION

The use of online or Web-enhanced courses is increasing at a dramatic rate and predictions are that this trend will continue in the foreseeable future [1]. The term asynchronous learning networks (ALN) has become synonymous with Web-based learning in which self study combines with computer-mediated interactivity.

Making the online learning environment successful requires change and commitment. Both faculty and students must realize that their "traditional" roles change as instructors becomes more facilitative and students assume greater responsibility for his or her learning. While the online learning environment provides the advantage of more convenient course access, challenges are apparent as well. Students must relearn how to learn and instructors must reexamine their face-to-face courses, and even their personal theories of teaching—evaluating each component for instructional design and ALN compatibility.

In this new environment, students focus on flexible thinking, problem solving, and new social and behavioral skills. Instructors acknowledge that their current personal and professional theories of teaching may be challenged and altered. The nature of ALN requires amended course design and the addition of student and faculty support mechanisms not customarily found in the face-to-face environment. Universities must commit substantial financial and technical support if students and faculty are to succeed online. However, as the data are beginning to show, the opportunities for transformation of teaching and learning are significant.

In 1996 UCF began offering online courses to address the needs of nontraditional students while alleviating a shortage of classroom space and increasing course offerings. Since that time, the number of online courses has grown rapidly. The university administration quickly realized the need for assessment and began a distributed learning impact evaluation as the online learning initiative began. In offering Web-based alternatives to students, UCF has developed three online instructional models, each of which is designed to serve specific institutional, faculty, and student needs. All three models are formally recognized and supported throughout the institution; and they afford a continuum of online activity bridging the fully face-to-face classroom with the fully online experience.

A. Web-Enhanced Courses

Web-enhanced courses ("E" courses) are fully face-to-face course offerings that include a substantive, required online component, for example: online course materials; links to other course-related Websites; use of computer-mediated conferencing, e-mail or chat facilities; and online testing. E courses are the largest and most rapidly growing online learning format at UCF, and they are indicative of a general trend toward pedagogically-related use of the Web and Internet resources in instruction throughout the university. Faculty or departments can implement an E course at will, and course accounts in the university's course management system are provided upon request. The university strongly recommends—but does not require—that all E courses be supported in a Course Management System (CMS) environment to ensure that a full range of functional capabilities and support resources are available, and to maintain consistency between E courses and the other online modalities discussed below.

There is an unusual relationship between the rapid growth of E courses and the September 11, 2001 terrorist attack on the World Trade Center. Following September 11, tourism in Florida declined, leading to state budget reductions, and restricted university operating budgets. Because of the ease with which E courses could be established, many departments shifted from printing and distributing course materials to placing them online through the creation of E courses. In fall 2001, more than 300 new E course requests were received. By fall 2002, the state budget picture had improved somewhat, and we expected the number of E course requests to diminish. Instead, they again increased, with more than 145 new E course sections implemented for the fall 2002 semester. In retrospect, it appears that the budget-induced E course ramp-up in 2001 led to greater faculty awareness of this format, and E course activity continues to expand. The E modality is not transformative, but rather enriching, providing any regular face-to-face class with tools to support online collaboration, learning communities, and access to online resources.

The increased level of E course activity at UCF has been a mixed blessing. On the positive side, it signifies greater faculty and student acceptance of online learning, and ultimately provides students with increased flexibility, and an opportunity to learn new technical and information processing skills. The extraordinarily high volume of E course activity has expanded to a level that is beginning to overwhelm support resources, requiring the development of more efficient faculty orientation and course development processes.

B. Mixed-Mode Courses

Mixed-mode courses ("M" courses) combine face-to-face instruction and online activity with reduced requirements for classroom attendance: reduced "seat time." A typical M course meets once a week, with the remaining course activity occurring online. Thus, a course that holds live class meetings two or three times a week in traditional face-to-face mode would meet only once when redesigned as an M course. This allows scheduling one or two additional M course sections in the original one-course classroom slot, yielding a 50% to 67% increase in scheduling efficiency.

The M modality is very flexible, and can also be used to scale up or down course enrollment with the potential to positively impact student learning. For example, a course that has three sections of 100 enrollments each can be aggregated into a single M section of 300. Three 100-student face-to-face sections are held each week (typically, MWF), and all 300 students share a common online experience. When increasing the number of students in the online segment of an M course, it is highly desirable to provide additional support resources such as graduate or undergraduate teaching assistants. Instructional benefits of this M format include smaller face-to-face live course sections and reduced instructional costs (cost reductions of 30% to 50% are possible). In a reverse example, a very large enrollment course could be delivered in M format with smaller face-to-face sections, with an associated improvement in the live classroom experience and increased opportunities for student interaction.

The university began aggressively developing M courses in 1997 after discovering that more than 75 percent of students taking the initial fully online courses were also enrolled on campus-based face-to-face classes. Results from the initial student assessments revealed that these campus-based students had sought the online courses primarily because of their accessibility and convenience, and secondarily because of their novelty. The M format was the university's response to the needs of on-campus or near-campus students for increased flexibility and convenience. In addition, the M format addressed the university's classroom space shortage. Because of rapid enrollment growth, UCF has experienced periodic shortages of classroom space. As noted above, the M model affords the opportunity to double or triple the number of courses that can occupy a traditional classroom scheduling block, or to achieve other efficiencies through aggregating or disaggregating course sections.

The institutional strategies supporting M courses are to increase access and convenience for students, and to improve student retention and enhancement of student learning in high-enrollment courses through increased interactivity and active student learning [2, 3]. Many faculty and students regard the M format as the "best of both worlds," optimizing the use of both classroom and virtual environments. In the words of one M course instructor, the M format is best conceptualized as a "classroom-enhanced Web course," rather than a "Web-enhanced classroom course." However it is conceptualized, the university's M courses have consistently demonstrated the ability to produce higher student learning outcomes than any other mode of instruction, combined with very low withdrawal rates.

A question commonly asked by faculty when they begin transforming their face-to-face courses into the M modality is how to divide course activities and learning objectives between the live and online segments of the course. Although requirements vary, instructors are typically advised to use face-to-face classroom time for answering questions, reviewing content, fostering student learning communities, and assessment activities.

C. Web-Based Courses

Web-based courses ("W" courses) are fully online courses that require no face-to-face or classroom-based attendance. Like the M format, W courses emphasize student learning communities, computer-mediated communication, and active student learning. With few exceptions, W courses are offered only as part of a fully online degree or certificate program. The university's current online degree and certificate offerings and those in development include:

1. Undergraduate Programs

B.S. in Health Services Administration;

B.S. and B.A. in Liberal Studies;

RN to BSN Program in Nursing;

B.S. in Vocational Education and Industry Training;

2. Graduate Programs

M.Ed. in Educational Media;

M.S. in Forensic Science;

M.A. and M.Ed. in Vocational Education and Industry Training;

M.A. in Instructional/Educational Technology;

M.S. in Criminal Justice;

M.S. in Nursing;

M.A. in Education, Curriculum and Instruction;

M.S. in Special Education

3. Graduate Certificate Programs

Graduate Certificate in Professional Writing;

Graduate Certificate in Community College Education;

Graduate Certificate in Nonprofit Management; and

Graduate Certificate in Instructional/Educational Technology.

Graduate Certificate in Computer Forensics;

Graduate Certificate in Criminal Justice;

Graduate Certificate in Domestic Violence;

Graduate Certificate in Engineering Management; and

Graduate Certificate in Special Education

Current online program information can be found on the UCF Center for Distributed Learning's Web site at http://online.ucf.edu.

II. A CONTINUUM OF ONLINE ALTERNATIVES

The E, M, and W modalities provide a hierarchy of online options, each increasingly displacing classroom meeting time, as illustrated in Figure 1.

Figure 1. A F2F-online continuum.

The M and W formats are regarded as transformed teaching and learning environments, not only because they replace face-to-face classroom time with online learning activities, but also because they are highly interactive, student-centered learning environments. The E modality although not transformative, provides students in any regular face-to-face course with tools to support online collaboration, learning communities, and access to online resources. Because the M and W formats are regarded as transformative, faculty must participate in an intensive faculty development program (IDL6543, which will be discussed in Section V) in order to teach a course in one of these modalities. Faculty development for the E format is provided through *Essentials*, a self-paced online course that prepares faculty to use WebCT and includes the basics of online pedagogy. *Essentials* is supplemented with additional skill development classes including WebCT Academy and Web101, which focus on the mechanical aspects of WebCT and Web site development. Priorities for course development in M and W modalities are established by the respective college deans and chairpersons through consultations that occur once each academic term. Faculty responsible for the courses selected for online development are identified by the academic units and scheduled for participation in an upcoming IDL6543 faculty development session.

III. COURSE DESIGN ELEMENTS

To maintain consistency and quality, all M and W courses are designed with a set of standard structural elements. Each course has a public main Web page that is placed outside the course management system containing an identification of the instructor and his or her photograph; office and e-mail addresses; required text(s); a course overview that articulates the basic scope, intent, and learning goals of the course; a protocols section that spells out instructor expectations for individual and group class participation, attendance (if required), grading policy, expectations for instructor interaction, and attitudinal expectations; a course syllabus and schedule; and links to student support pages, such as the library, eCommunity, and the Learning Online Website (discussed below). These pages are deliberately placed outside the password-protected body of the course to allow students an opportunity to review course content and expectations before enrolling, and to serve as an advance organizer for the students that can be readily accessed without the delay of logging into the course. The body of the course is secured within the course management system to prevent individuals not registered in the course from interacting with the class. Guest "presenters" can be easily granted course access to allow them to participate.

IV. COMMUNICATION AND COLLABORATION-CENTRIC DESIGN

UCF online courses are designed more as communication and collaboration environments than as repositories for content. Thus, extensive use of e-mail, discussion groups, and live chat features of the course management system are standard design elements. Multiple discussion groups are established to accommodate general course discussion; problem reporting and response; a "coffee shop" or "lounge" area for social, non-course related discourse; and individual discussion areas for student teams or projects. Multiple live chat rooms can also be established; however, this capability is used only when deemed pedagogically necessary to keep course communication as fully in the asynchronous domain as possible.

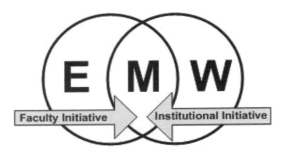

Figure 2. Source of initiative for online learning modalities.

Within the institution, drivers and incentives for faculty participation in each of the three modalities vary, as illustrated in Figure 2. With few exceptions, W courses exist as program elements undertaken as initiatives of the colleges, with extensive institutional support. E courses, on the other hand, are created solely upon the request of individual faculty. From an institutional perspective, M courses facilitate more efficient classroom utilization and have been demonstrated to result in improved or comparable student learning outcomes. From a faculty perspective, M courses are a natural extension of the E format, and also allow greater flexibility and convenience for both instructors and students. The growth in M courses is thus a result of both institutional and faculty initiative.

V. FACULTY DEVELOPMENT

The University of Central Florida's faculty support for online program development features systematic design, delivery, and evaluation. The payoff for this investment in faculty is systemic transformation of the teaching culture and practice. The faculty development process and instructional model have remained stable as online learning has been expanded and extended over the past seven years. At UCF, Course Development and Web Services (CDWS) is the unit responsible for leading the design and development of ALN learning, including faculty (http://teach.ucf.edu) and learner support systems (http://learn.ucf.edu), course development, and production processes (see http://cdws.ucf.edu).

A. Initial Assumptions and Evolutionary Change of Faculty Support

The cornerstone of faculty support has been, and continues to be, facilitated instructional design. CDWS staff do not advocate teaching software in a vacuum devoid of appropriate instructional context. Other units on campus teach basic PowerPoint, and word processing. CDWS staff focuses on teaching the basics of UCF's course management system and Web editing software in the context of deliberate application of best practice as advocated by the unit's instructional designers.

Developing an instructional design team has focused on finding instructional designers with the following characteristics: team-oriented, enjoy working with faculty, advocate relationship management (vs. customer service), are restrained in designing instruction (vs. appropriately empowering the faculty), and are gentle agents of change. We prefer to think of our instructional designers as the "wizards" that magically orchestrate all the talents of faculty and production staff. The team's ability to build strategic support systems and diffuse innovation enables increased service to greater numbers of faculty. This strategy is not necessarily transportable to other university cultures, which is the reason why we have generally declined requests to license our faculty development courses.

Early experiences in supporting faculty producing online courses were painful. From the start, a cohort approach was adopted, enabling faculty from diverse disciplines to learn together in developing online learning environments based on computer-mediated communication. UCF is a large metropolitan university with about 18% of students living in university housing. Thus, an instructional model that enables social constructivism empowers students to enrich courses with their experiences. The same learning community philosophy was applied to faculty development although the approach was initially very difficult. Our expectations for faculty to learn from attending workshops resulted in enormous support requirements resulting from dealing with faculty one at a time. Faculty also needed more time to conceptualize their instruction and examples to which they could react.

In January 1998, CDWS launched its flagship faculty development offering—a six week M course called IDL6543 (http://reach.ucf.edu/~idl6543), which incorporated online modules and face-to-face seminars. Later, as more instructional designers were hired, each faculty member participating in IDL6543 was assigned an instructional designer to improve faculty support, facilitate change, and build trust. The IDL6543 course provided experiential learning for faculty and enabled them to act as an advisory group for campus services such as online learner support. Another critical support factor was that of course development. We felt that if faculty were required to build their own courses and master the requisite technology skills, then they could not focus on interaction with their students nor their instructional activities. CDWS had to develop course support that was cost-effective and systematic. A team of especially talented students (the Techrangers™) build the online courses designed by instructional designers and faculty. Over time, as faculty have become comfortable teaching online, they have been encouraged to attend further training to enable them to assume responsibility for ongoing maintenance of their courses. UCF's approach to course development has resulted in more students successfully taking online courses and has allowed departments to reuse more online materials among faculty members. Creating, maintaining, and upholding Web standards for course production continues to be a challenge. As CDWS evolved into a production unit, it became necessary to operate as an appointment-only operation. This requirement has often put us at odds with faculty expectations for walk-in, boutique service. One-on-one support is best bundled with participation in the IDL6543 faculty development process; however, the scale to which the course design and development process has grown precludes fully individualized approaches.

In 1997, UCF launched its initial hybrid course development experiment. We focused on faculty teaching

133

these M courses, engaging them in a new faculty development program. What resulted was an inevitable combination of faculty teaching fully online and some teaching in the hybrid M model. Fortunately, design is design. Our faculty development course IDL6543 served appropriately for both modalities, and was itself structured as a model M course. The examples emphasized for M courses were different than for W sections and are too numerous to describe in this article. Resistance to our faculty development program was expected and came in the form of challenges ranging from the day and time of IDL6543 classes, to the staff's authority to conduct faculty development, to the selection of course management system, and even in the unit's responsibility in handling faculty support. In the end, IDL6543 and its methods have become fully accepted and institutionalized.

As increasing numbers of faculty arrived at UCF from other institutions where they had taught online, a need developed for creating the means to assess and support these experienced faculty. Many UCF faculty are motivated to develop one online course and then go on to develop other courses with appropriate online activities. Often, these faculty agree to hand off the delivery of one of their online courses to adjuncts, graduate teaching assistants, or other instructors. To meet this need, CDWS developed a fully online faculty development course called ADL5000 (http://reach.ucf.edu/~adl5000), which prepares faculty to deliver a previously-developed UCF online course. The IDL6543 and ADL5000 course experiences focus on common objectives:

1. Develop a personal professional theory about distributed learning's contribution to higher education;

2. Develop an understanding of UCF's course development process for online courses;

3. Develop a reflective practice about current teaching strategies and their suitability for online teaching and learning; and

4. Collaborate with colleagues and facilitate using distributed learning technologies to design an online course consistent with best practice by:

   • Formulating student centered learning objectives,

   • Composing appropriate web-based content,

   • Creating activities and assignments that correspond to one's learning objectives,

   • Developing valid assessment strategies,

   • Designing effective grading strategies,

   • Selecting instructional graphics and media that demonstrate visual literacy,

   • Developing effective student interaction protocols,

   • Developing a tactical plan for course-based learning communication, and

   • Developing a learner support system.

Increasingly, faculty on campus wish to enhance their face-to-face courses with a Web presence and the course management system. To deal with the rapid increase in E course demand, CDWS created a program called Essentials (http://teach.ucf.edu) to provide the basics necessary to teach an enhanced course. The Essentials program launched in fall 2003 with the following objectives:

   • To impart the essential skills needed by faculty members to set-up and deliver web-enhanced courses using WebCT,

   • Provide a supportive environment for faculty members to develop their skills, and

   • Allow faculty members to demonstrate mastery.

B. Scope and Scale of UCF's Online Initiative

As of July 2003, more than 900 UCF faculty members have become involved in online learning, producing a total of over 2,000 online courses. This number reflects the total online activity by faculty requesting service and online accounts by departments scheduling courses. Figure 3 illustrates total courses by college.

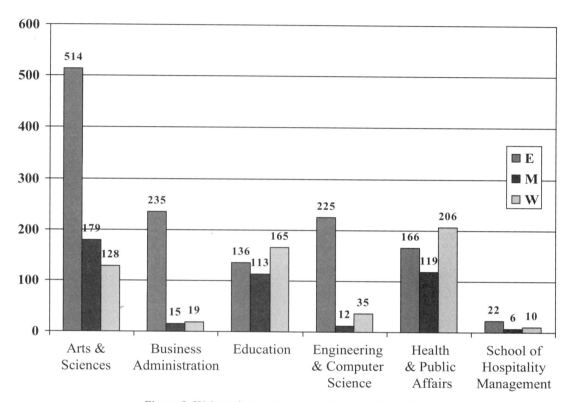

Figure 3. Web environment courses developed by college

VI. PROGRAM GROWTH

UCF's significant growth coupled with the formalized online faculty development has contributed to extensive growth of the university's three online delivery models from the first offering in 1996 to the present (shown in Figures 4 and 5).

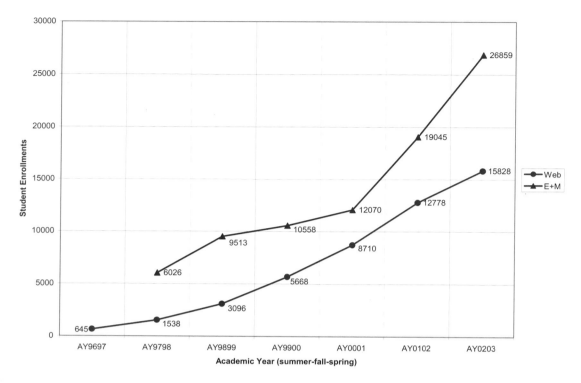

Figure 4. Growth of UCF online learning enrollments—1996–2003.

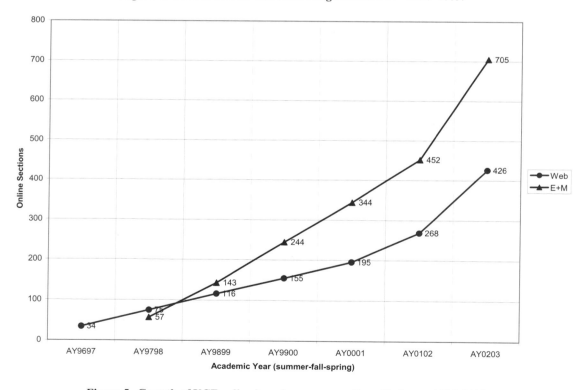

Figure 5. Growth of UCF online learning course section offerings—1996–2003.

VII. DEMOGRAPHICS OF ONLINE LEARNING

Since 1996, UCF faculty have developed more than 2,000 fully online (W) and mixed mode/reduced seat time (M) online courses. During the 2002–2003 academic year:

- UCF offered 1,930 course sections via Distributed Learning, a 29% increase over 2001–2002.

- Distributed Learning course sections accounted for over 46,000 enrollments, a 32% increase over 2001–2002.

- Distributed Learning course sections accounted for 13.8% of the university total student credit hours production, up from 10.6% in 2001–2002.

- Web-based course modalities were the largest and fastest growing segment of Distributed Learning, accounting for nearly 58% of the Distributed Learning course sections and almost 93% of the enrollments.

- 38% (17,734) of UCF students enrolled in at least one totally web-based (W) or mixed-mode (M) web course section, reflecting 27,794 total enrollments, up from 13,197 students in 2001–2002.

- 20% (9,442) of UCF students enrolled in a fully Web-based (W) course section, up from 19% (8,304) in 2001–2002.

- Enrollments in Web-based (M and W only) courses accounted for 7.55% of the total university student credit hours production, up from 6.2% in 2001–2002.

- All Web-based and Web-enhanced course enrollments account for 12.7% of the total university student credit hours production up from 9.64% in 2001–2002.

VIII. CHANGE IS CONSTANT

As online enrollment data were reviewed, it became clear that the number of E course sections appearing in the schedule and the enrollments did not match data from WebCT server logs. Other aspects of E courses were scrutinized as we tried to develop strategies for dealing with the under reporting of E courses in the schedule. We found that:

- E course sections were consistent only in regard to their use of WebCT.

- Student support problems did not increase even though most E courses had not been identified as such in the schedule. We understand this to mean that the concept of a course utilizing the Internet has become commonplace to students.

Beginning in the summer of 2004, we plan to eliminate the E course designation from the schedule. At that time, WebCT server data will be used to identify sections and enrollments for all E courses, which will yield more accurate representation of the number of Web-enhanced courses, the number of faculty and students who need support, and the infrastructure required to support Web-based and Web-enhanced instruction.

IX. EVALUATING THE W, M, AND E EXPERIENCES

The UCF Distributed Learning Impact Evaluation began in 1996 at the inception of the university's online learning initiative. Interestingly, the program evaluation aligns itself with at least four of the five Sloan quality pillars [4]: learning effectiveness, student satisfaction, access, and faculty satisfaction. The changing nature of the evaluation components, however, makes assessment transformative in nature [5] in that it supports, and in some cases initiates, transformation. This notion seems consistent with what one would expect in a setting such as in Forrester's [6] theory of intervention in complex systems (systems dynamics) and Senge's [7] development of systemic change.

Research on online learning is forcing change in the evaluation model because other, more historically used, approaches show little promise for informing policy. A prime example of this might be found in the early use of quasi-experimental designs to evaluate the effectiveness of distance education. Many of these studies used course mode as a treatment effect (which it wasn't) and tested point hypotheses without considering effect sizes that would add value. In addition, most of these studies used intact groups with small sample sizes that produced low power. These were the artifacts that lead to the "no significant difference," phenomenon [8]. The trouble with these findings was that those who were philosophically opposed to the ALN movement used them to dismiss the initiative as ineffective and costly. Alternatively, proponents of distributed learning largely ignored the findings and went about their business. In a real sense, this is a classic example of how research informed nothing.

We have come to realize that research focusing on varying course modalities is a complex problem in which control of extraneous variables is nearly impossible. Further, those making decisions about funding and implementing ALN programs are not interested in findings from artificially contrived situations. For example, faculty satisfaction is both a dependent and independent variable, impacting and being impacted by the educational environment [3]. Probably the best one can do is model what is happening in a very complex system with the hope of identifying interactions and relationships that cannot be observed with traditional hypothesis tests.

Evaluating Web teaching uncovers unanticipated outcomes along with side effects that may be more informative than the original evaluation objectives. Therefore, we have reformulated our Distributed Learning Impact Evaluation approach to the following principles—derived from continually changing evaluation demands [5] by suggesting that UCF's evaluation is:

A. Always Formative [9]

The university system in which we operate is so complex that considering components independently underinforms policy decisions. Every outcome is deeply nested in the university so that any meaningful result must be reported as a complex series of interactions. These complex patterns are neither "bottom line" nor straightforward. They are, however, an authentic portrayal of how the W, M, and E experiences play out at UCF.

B. Opportunistic [10]

The evaluation process must be flexible enough to take advantage of opportunities that present themselves. Very often, an intervention produces an unexpected, non-intuitive result. Usually, these side effects are the precursors to systemic transformation.

C. Facilitative [11]

Instead of evaluating "effectiveness," the assessment procedures must facilitate change by: sharing an inspiring vision; focusing on results, process and relationships; seeking maximum possible involvement; designing pathways to action; bringing out the best in others; celebrating accomplishment; and modeling behaviors that facilitate collaboration. These principles form the basis of facilitative leadership and, in our experience, serve to enhance evaluation effectiveness.

D. Multifaceted (Multicultural) [12]

Effective assessment models feature many templates, some of which are complimentary, some competitive, and some cobbled together. This multiplicity is a characteristic of ALN in the university setting.

E. Autocatalytic [13]

Effective assessment creates its own synergy that transfers energy and enthusiasm to the constituents in a cyclic fashion that expands on each cycle. Without this energy and interaction the evaluation becomes an add-on component with little added value—serving to deplete resources that might be better directed elsewhere.

Additionally, the UCF evaluation model is characterized by:

F. Uncertain Mediation [14]

Evaluators must make decisions in the face of incomplete information and lack of closure. Those seeking summative (is it or is it not effective?) decisions will be disappointed because the morphing nature of ALN programs defies traditional summative evaluation statements.

G. Continual Feedback [15]

Effective evaluation must engage in a continual exchange of information through recursive cycles. These cycles produce incremental results that are neither comprehensive nor sweeping. Worthwhile information is iterative, occurring when a preliminary result is derived, presented to a constituency that poses several additional questions generated from the results. The multifaceted nature of the evaluation comes into play here, and the meaningfulness of information depends on the context in which it is received.

X. SOME MEDIATED RESULTS

After reading Section VIII of this paper one should not be surprised that considering the E course designation as a distinct nominal category for evaluation purposes is a tenuous proposition at best. Categorization is necessary for any effective evaluation plan but wrestling with the "correct" classifications becomes a daunting task. One metric for course modality is the degree to which seat time is replaced by Web-based instruction; but this is where boundaries blur. Are they distinct categories? Are they subsets of a more comprehensive classification scheme? Are there more valid ways to make classifications?

Lakoff [16] addresses the problem of classification in his book *Women, Fire, and Dangerous Things*. He defines the classic approach to classification as assuming that correct categories exist naturally, with the task of the investigator being proper identification. This long-accepted approach assumes that misclassification fails to recognize some preexisting underlying structure. One other interesting property of classical theory is that no member of a particular group has any special status because all members share the properties in the category. Rosch [17] and Lakoff [16], however, challenge this assumption with their prototype theory. They assert that, on a perceptual basis, certain individuals or objects better represent their category. They demonstrate prototyping by asking individuals to rate how good an example of a category is. For instance, evaluating robin, ostrich, and penguin as examples of the category "bird" will consistently give the highest rating to robin. The connection here is that when considering the W, M, and E experiences, the W mode is the prototype ALN course and the E designation is the least representative example.

This leads us to the conclusion that the E classification is no longer viable for evaluation purposes. The fact that there are so many fewer declared E sections (E courses scheduled as such) than there are WebCT accounts (actual E courses) suggests that our attempts to draw distinctions between E course sections and face-to-face sections are no longer useful. The two designations are merging so that maintaining the separation will misrepresent the impact of either mode. Therefore, UCF plans to discontinue use of the E designation for evaluation purposes, realizing that face-to-face courses are rapidly blending with E courses in practice.

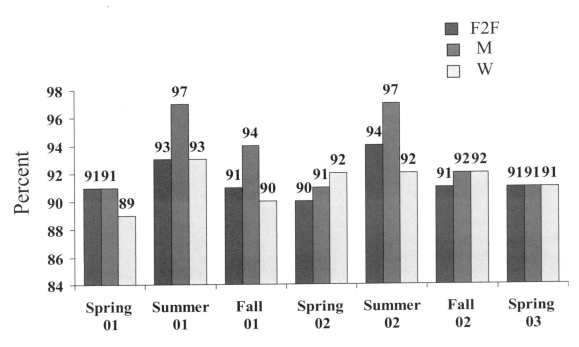

Figure 6. Success rates by modality and semester: Spring 2001–Spring 2003

A. Learning outcomes

Figure 6 presents the success rates for W, M, and loosely coupled face-to-face (F2F) courses (where student success is defined as an A, B, or C grade). The most prominent features are that, in general, the success rates are high with an average level of success across all semesters and modes of 92.1%. The second noteworthy feature is that there is a leveling effect for the fall 2002 and spring 2003 semesters across the modalities. Figure 7 presents another perspective on success that takes into account college, gender, and modality. These success data were analyzed using decision trees based on the CHAID model (Chi Square Automatic Interaction Detection) [18]. This approach develops a predictive model that accounts for all possible interactions thereby giving some indication of the complexity embedded in the findings. The process examines each predictor for its relationship to the dependent measure (in this case, "success"), choosing the one with the strongest predictive capacity. Secondly, the algorithm examines the predictor to determine which categories might be combined. The process continues under each node until no additional predictability is found in the model. Overall, the analysis determined that college was the best predictor for success with the following predicted success rates: Hospitality Management and Arts and Sciences (Combined)=90.6%, Business=87.1%, Education=88.0%, Engineering and Computer Science=88.0%, Health and Public Affairs=93.0%. A portion of the decision tree is presented in Figure 7 to show the interaction patterns. Within the College of Health & Public Affairs, gender was the best predictor of success (Females=94.3%, Males=90.5%). For the female node, M courses produced a success rate of 97.4%, W=93.1% and F2F=94.5%. The male node showed a success rate of 95.7% for M courses and 89.8% for W and face-to-face courses combined. Within this college the decision tree analysis presents a more accurate portrayal of the interactions between modality and gender. (Appendix A contains these decision rules across all colleges).

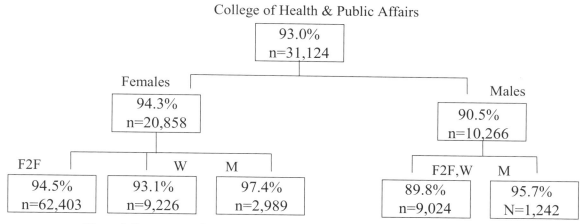

Figure 7. Success rates by college, gender, and modality: Spring 2000–Spring 2003

B. Student Satisfaction

Student satisfaction is an important component of teaching and learning success and should be indexed on a regular basis. UCF is conducting an ongoing study of student satisfaction on a database of over one million student responses to the university instrument used to evaluate teaching effectiveness. The study involves analyzing the item that measures overall course satisfaction using college, course level (lower undergraduate, upper undergraduate, and graduate), semester, and the remaining 15 items on the instrument as predictors. The decision tree showed that only the other fifteen items were predictors. The analysis led to a series of if-then decision rules. The strongest of these rules was that if an instructor received an excellent rating on the items "The instructor facilitated my learning" and "The instructor was able to communicate ideas and information effectively" then the probability of receiving an overall rating of "Excellent" was .96, irrespective of course level, college, semester, and the instructor's rating on any of the other items. Table 1 presents the percentage of overall "Excellent" ratings of instructors in W, M, and face-to-face courses. Interestingly, M and W courses experienced an approximate advantage of 4 to 5 percent. The ratings adjusted for the decision tree rule show the "Excellent" ratings increased dramatically to the 95–96% range and that differences disappeared. These data suggest that student ratings of satisfaction with their instruction are independent of course modality.

Modality	(N)	Unadjusted for rule	(N)	Adjusted for rule
W	6,847	46.9%	5,055	95.9%
M	10,830	47.2%	7,128	96.1%
F2F	207,266	42.8%	137,407	95.5%

Table 1. 2000–2002 faculty overall "Excellent" ratings by course modality unadjusted and adjusted for the decision tree rule.

C. Mediated Student Access In Terms Of Success

We completed one additional decision tree analysis, examining student success, gender, ethnicity, and course modality for the entire university. The analysis showed that gender was the best predictor for success with females succeeding at a rate of 92.8% and males showing a success rate of 88.3%. After gender, ethnicity entered the model. An example of the rule for the female node is presented in Figure 8. The success rates for female student by ethnicity were: Caucasian (W) and American Indian or Alaskan Native (I)=93.6%, Non-Resident Alien (O) or those who did not specify ethnicity (X)= 94.6%, Hispanic (H)=91.2%, Black (B)=88.5%, and Asian (A)=92.4%. Interestingly, there were only two nodes for which course modality predicted success. For Caucasian and Native American students, M courses showed a success rate of 95.7% while combined face-to-face and W students had a success rate of 93.4%. Asian students showed a success rate of 94.3% in W and M courses combined and 91.3% in face-to-face sections. These data suggest that course modality does not adversely impact student success across varying ethnicities. In fact, the minimal impact that did result favors online ALN courses. (Appendix B contains all rules for this solution.)

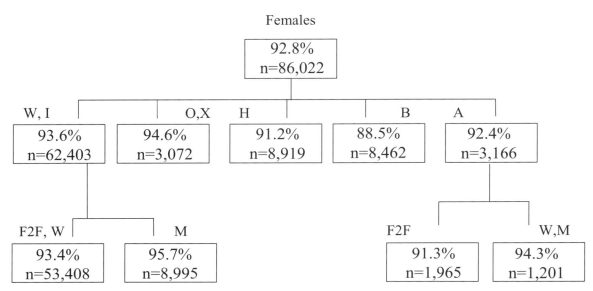

Figure 8. Success Rates by Ethnicity and Modality for Females (W=Caucasian, B=Black, H=Hispanic, A=Asian or Pacific Islander, I=American Indian or Alaskan Native, X=Ethnicity not reported, O=Non-Resident Alien)

D. Unmediated Faculty Satisfaction

Over the past seven years we have completed several faculty satisfaction surveys with essentially the same result: faculty are very satisfied with their Web experiences. To make this point we present two tables from our latest spring 2002 survey. Table 2 shows 87% of faculty were satisfied with their W courses and 88% with M courses. Table 3 shows faculty willingness to teach ALN courses in the future. Of those responding instructors, 82% would teach a W format course again while 94% would teach an M format course in the future if they had a choice.

	W	M
Very satisfied	48%	43%
Satisfied	39%	45%
Neutral	6%	7%
Unsatisfied	7%	5%
Very unsatisfied	--	--

Table 2. Faculty satisfaction with web courses

	W	M
Definitely	67%	81%
Probably	15%	13%
Neutral	--	--
Probably not	10%	2%
Definitely not	6%	4%

Table 3. Faculty willingness to teach another web course

XI. SUMMARY

A. Proactive and Reactive Models

By incorporating three modes of Web-based learning, the University of Central Florida is achieving its objective of enhancing access while maintaining and improving educational quality and increasing convenience for its metropolitan student constituency. The distributed learning initiative at UCF is proactive, having been initiated and supported at the highest administrative levels. The Web-based initiative is a good fit for the UCF's strategic plan, which stresses our mission of anticipating and responding to the central Florida community's needs. This involves offering programs that will enhance opportunity while accommodating the demands of contemporary society. That is the core mission of a metropolitan University.

A reactive component of UCF's program results from demographic inertia. The University is young, having been founded in 1963. The 2003 student population is just over 42,000, with recent projections placing that population at 58,000 in 2013. This kind of growth creates infrastructure demands that respond well to the reduced classroom component of W and M courses. In addition, world events have created the need for universities to accommodate the changing geo-political climate.

To meet both proactive and reactive requirements, UCF uses several mechanisms that support ALN efforts on our campus. These take the form of the Office of the Vice Provost for Information Technologies and Resources, the Center for Distributed Learning, Course Development and Web Services, the Computer Center, the Library, the Research Initiative for Teaching Effectiveness, the Office of Instructional Resources, and the Faculty Center for Teaching and Learning. Each organization dedicates itself to the success of faculty and students in their W, M, or E experience—or any other modality.

B. Transformation

The W, M, and E modes reveal a good deal about institutional transformation. Using social systems and spiraling change theories [19, 20], genuine change occurs at the idiographic (personal) and nomothetic (institutional) levels. The transformation discloses itself when students view the institution as more responsive to their life style demands, feel more actively involved in their learning, and experience technological empowerment. Faculty involved in Web-based teaching refocus their attention on instructional design, teaching techniques, and alternative assessment models perhaps more than they typically do in the face-to-face environment.

Institutional transformation is equally dramatic. Growth curves for Web-based and enhanced courses take on a cubic form. This means that in addition to the continuing increase, the rate of growth will rise dramatically in the next few years. Demographic data foreshadow this prediction. With the number of Web sections and students in Web sections growing by a third in a single year, and Web-based courses accounting for approximately 13% of student credit hour production, the impact of W, M, and E modalities is felt throughout the university.

The key component facilitating instructional transformation is faculty development that is tailored to the three modes. This component of UCF's model features significant and sustained support for instructors. Instructional design underpins faculty transformation in an environment that bases itself on collaboration and communication—encouraging faculty across disciplines to interact around common themes of effective teaching, active student learning, and effective learning communities.

C. Side Effects

Forrester [6] and Morris [15] forecast that when an intervention introduces itself into a complex system such as a university, unanticipated side effects will result. The emergence of the E course phenomenon is just such an occurrence. Originally, E courses were instigated by professors who, through their IDL6543 training experience for W and M sections, introduced Web enhancement into their face-to-face sections. However, the phenomenon has rapidly accelerated to a point where instructors all over campus are augmenting their programs with significant online components but are not giving their courses the E designation. The result is that there are many more E courses than designated in the published course schedule, and many courses that carry the face-to-face label should be labeled as containing some web enhancement. The positive impact of this side effect is that the E course structure is the conduit through which ALN is radiating throughout the institution. The less positive effect is that determining the proper modality for these sections is only possible by querying each instructor. A further consequence is that by dropping the E designation, face-to-face and E courses are becoming indistinguishable—a problem for evaluation but a clear sign of institutional transformation.

D. Learning Outcomes

Seven years of systematic research on the impact of W, M, and E courses gives us some insight into the evolving educational climate at the University of Central Florida. We find that learning outcome differences among Web modalities and face-to-face sections is equalizing. We view this as a positive sign because as more and more faculty and students become involved, the initiative is no longer an intervention but rather a transformation in the university culture. Considering the impact of course modalities on student achievement actually underinforms the influence of asynchronous learning networks. There are differential impacts in colleges and departments corresponding to any number of discipline characteristics. Modeling these interactions has helped us better understand what is transpiring in distributed learning.

E. Student Satisfaction

The underlying tenet in our research is that student satisfaction with all three of the Web modalities started out positive and remains very high. Once again, there has been some leveling as non-early-adopting students became involved. This is an equitable trade-off however. When one considers the large number of students in our fully online degree programs—and that they report high satisfaction, the positive impact is obvious.

Aside from general satisfaction with the Web modalities, students' ratings of the teaching and learning climate in their Web-based courses meet or exceed those of face-to-face experiences. Further, students universally value instructors who communicate effectively and facilitate learning, irrespective of teaching mode. When courses of every modality are scrutinized for those two characteristics, student satisfaction differences tend to disappear, which suggests an analogy to Tolstoy's Anna Karenina phenomenon—"All good teachers are alike. Poor teachers are poor in their own unique ways" [21].

F. Access

The data on student access are very encouraging. Consistently, we find that Web modalities do not negatively impact our minority populations. Examining the interaction of gender, ethnicity, and modality show that females succeed in all course modes at an approximately 4% higher rate then do males. Across the entire university there is a difference in success rates of various ethnic groups [22], but when modality becomes predictive Web courses generally produce slightly higher success rates for some ethnicities and have no impact on others.

G. Faculty Satisfaction

The data on faculty satisfaction are clear. The vast majority of instructors who become involved with UCF's course development activities report high satisfaction with their newly designed courses. They sustain, and upgrade this instructional approach, collaborating across disciplines and sharing promising techniques. Those IDL6543 graduates coalesce into a community devoted to the scholarship of teaching and learning and produce numerous articles and presentations at professional meetings.

XII. A FINAL THOUGHT

Three modes of online teaching and learning at the University of Central Florida are transforming the institution and will continue to do into the foreseeable future. As we move toward second generation development and research problems we do so with certainty about the longevity of the distributed learning initiative on the UCF campuses. Our students, faculty, and administrators plan their learning, teaching, and leadership lives in large measure around access & connectivity. The university strategic plan, by making numerous references to Web-based learning, recognizes that our goal of becoming a premiere metropolitan research university can be greatly accelerated by courses that have online components. This realization is a cornerstone of UCF's continuing efforts to transform and improve our institution.

XIII. REFERENCES

1. **Allen, I. E. and Seaman, J.** *Sizing the Opportunity: The Quality and Extent of Online Education in the United States, 2002 and 2003.* Needham, MA: Sloan-C, 2003.
2. **Dziuban, C. D., Moskal, P. D. and Dziuban, E. K.** Reactive Behavior Patterns Go Online. *The Journal of Staff, Program, & Organizational Development* 17(3): 171–182, Fall 2000.
3. **Hartman, J., Dziuban, C., and Moskal, P.** Faculty Satisfaction in ALNs: A Dependent or Independent Variable? *Journal of Asynchronous Learning Networks* 4(3): 155–179, 2000.
4. **Moore, J. C.** *Elements of Quality: The Sloan-C Framework.* Needham, MA: Sloan-C, 2002.
5. **National Learning Infrastructure Initiative.** *NLII Focus Session: Building a Culture for Transformative Assessment*, 2003. Available online: http://www.educause.edu/nlii/meetings/nlii033/.
6. **Forrester, J. W.** *System Dynamics and the Lessons of 35 Years,* 1991. Available online: http://sysdyn.mit.edu/people/jay-forrester.html.
7. **Senge, P. M.** *The Fifth Discipline: The Art and Practice of the Learning Organization.* New York, NY: DoubleDay Currency, 1990.
8. **Russell, T. L.** *The No Significant Difference Phenomenon: As Reported in 355 Research Reports, Summaries, and Papers.* Raleigh, NC: North Carolina State University, 1999.
9. **Buchanan, T.** The Effectiveness of a World-Wide Web Mediated Formative Assessment. *Journal of Computer Assisted Learning* 16(3): 193–200, September 2000.
10. **Beveridge, W. I. B.** *The Art of Scientific Investigation.* New York, NY: Vintage Books, 1950.
11. **Straus, D. A.** *Facilitative Leadership: Theoretical Underpinnings.* Cambridge, MA: Interaction Associates, Inc., 1988.
12. **Moskal, P. D. and Dziuban, C. D.** Present and Future Directions for Assessing Cybereducation: The Changing Research Paradigm. In *Cybereducation,* Vandervert, L, and Shavinina, eds. Larchmont, NY: Mary Ann Liebert, Inc., 2001.
13. **Diamond, J. M.** *Guns, Germs, and Steel: The Fates of Human Societies.* New York, NY: W. W. Norton & Company, 1997.
14. **Setenyi, J.** Teaching Democracy in an Unpopular Democracy. A Report from the "What to Teach About Hungarian Democracy?" Conference, Kossuth Klub, May 12, 1995.
15. **Morris, D. R.** Institutionalization and the Reform Process: A System Dynamics Perspective. *Educational Policy* 10(4): 427–447, 1996.
16. **Lakoff, G.** *Women, Fire, and Dangerous Things.* Chicago, IL: The University of Chicago Press, 1987.
17. **Rosch, E.** Prototype Classification and Logical Classification: The Two Systems. In E. Scholnick, Ed., *New Trends in Cognitive Representation: Challenges to Piaget's Theory,* 73–86. Hillsdale, NJ: Lawrence Erlbaum Associates, 1983.
18. **SPSS, Inc.** *AnswerTree 3.0 User's Guide.* Chicago, IL: SPSS, Inc., 2001.
19. **Getzels, J. W., Lipham, J. M. and Campbell, R. F.** *Educational Administration as a Social Process.* New York, NY: Harper & Row, 1968.
20. **Prochaska, J. O., DiClemente, C. C. and Norcross, J. C.** In Search of How People Change: Applications to Addictive Behaviors. *American Psychologist* 47(9): 1102–1114, 1992.
21. **Tolstoy, L.** *Anna Karenina.* New York, NY: Penguin Group (USA), Inc., 1961.
22. **University of Central Florida.** *The President's Commission on the Status of Racial & Ethnic Minorities*, 2001. Available online: http://www.diversity.ucf.edu/committees/rem_report_final.pdf.

XIV. APPENDIX A

Decision Tree Rules for College, Gender, and Mode

IF COLLEGE IS	AND GENDER IS	AND MODE IS	THEN THE PROBABILITY OF SUCCESS IS
Health and Public Affairs	Female	F2F	.96
Health and Public Affairs	Female	W	.93
Health and Public Affairs	Female	M	.97
Health and Public Affairs	Male	F2F or W	.90
Health and Public Affairs	Male	M	.96
Engineering and Computer Science	Female	F2F or M	.91
Engineering and Computer Science	Female	W	.85
Engineering and Computer Science	Male	F2F	.86
Engineering and Computer Science	Male	W	.84
Engineering and Computer Science	Male	M	.92
Arts and Sciences or Hospitality Management	Female	-----	.92
Arts and Sciences or Hospitality Management	Male	-----	.88
Education	Female	F2F or M	.98
Education	Female	W	.97
Education	Male	F2F or W	.94
Education	Male	M	.99
Business	Female	F2F	.87
Business	Female	W	.96
Business	Male	-----	.86

F2F = Face-to-Face Courses

W = Web-Based Courses

M = Mixed-Mode Courses

XV. APPENDIX B

Decision Tree Rules for Gender, Ethnicity, and Mode

IF GENDER IS	AND ETHNICITY IS	AND MODALITY IS	THEN THE PROBABILITY OF SUCCESS IS
Female	Caucasian	F2F or W	.93
Female	Non-resident alien or Declined to Respond	-----	.96
Female	Hispanic	-----	.91
Female	Black	-----	.88
Female	Asian or Pacific Islander	F2F	.91
Female	Asian or Pacific Islander	W or M	.94
Male	Caucasian	F2F or W	.89
Male	Caucasian	M	.90
Male	Non-resident alien or Declined to Respond	-----	.91
Male	Hispanic	-----	.87
Male	Black	-----	.82

F2F = Face-to-Face Courses

W = Web-Based Courses

M = Mixed-Mode Courses

USING ALN IN A BLENDED ENVIRONMENT: IMPLICATIONS FOR INSTITUTIONAL PLANNING

John T. Harwood, Ph.D.
The Pennsylvania State University

Gary E. Miller, D.Ed.
The Pennsylvania State University

- Blending can enhance instruction on campus, distribute learning more efficiently among campuses in a multi-campus system, and enrich the range of students' choices about modes of learning.

- We have been able to re-purpose "learning objects" that are appropriate in more than one content domain.

- Evaluation indicates significant learning gains and significant cost reductions, so it's clear that the innovation has become a mainstream part of the department.

- What is remarkable is the speed with which the undergraduate landscape has been transformed.

- Blending contributes to an expectation that all University locations will benefit from online courses, purposefully blurring the historic lines between distance education and resident instruction.

I. INTRODUCTION

Most institutions adopted online learning initially to extend access to new students via distance education. However, as institutions have gained experience in this new arena, it has become clear that online learning can serve several purposes, in addition to creating new avenues for access. It can be used to enhance instruction on campus, to distribute learning more efficiently among campuses in a multi-campus system, and to enrich the range of students' choices about modes of learning. These applications tend to involve what has come to be called a "blended" approach to the use of technology.

The Pennsylvania State University has a commitment to integrating e-learning into its total learning environment—on campus, among campuses, and at a distance through the World Campus. It has experimented with a wide variety of blended approaches—both at the course level and at the degree or program level. Those experiments are leading to a university-wide policy and organizational infrastructure to support the use of online learning in the university's academic mainstream. This paper will describe the variety of approaches within a single, large university, in an attempt to better define the "blended online learning" concept and to explore key institutional issues associated with the use of blended approaches.

II. BLENDED LEARNING AT THE COURSE LEVEL

To state the obvious, Penn State offers a lot of sections: 18,000 sections in a typical semester distributed among 24 campuses. We have no precise way to gauge the extent of "blended learning" across all of these sections, but our annual student and faculty surveys indicate a large fraction (~50%) of faculty use technology in teaching. In our large general education program, we have a long history of targeting courses that will affect a large number of our first-year students.

We have used support from several foundations as well as internal funding to jump start this initiative. It has made most sense to work with departments that believed that they could both increase students' learning while reducing the costs of instruction. While the goals may sound similar, the pedagogical strategies and the technological solutions are quite different.

With support from the Sloan foundation, Professor Richard Cyr and his colleagues created an alternative to the traditional lecture-based course, Biology 110, which enrolls more than 900 students per semester. Students are given the choice of attending the traditional lecture course or replacing the lectures with carefully designed web-based tutorials that cover the same material but also feature quizzes, enrichment activities, and a chance to interact with the faculty (for more information on both of these courses, see http://www.science.psu.edu/journal/Spr2002/InteractiveClasses-Sp02.htm).
Assessment data demonstrated very strong learning gains. We found that while some students preferred online tutorials to lectures, a significant fraction of students wanted both the lecture and the tutorials. (No faculty member will ever complain that students were spending too much time studying!) A very important component was low-stakes quizzing, which enabled students to review and summarize key concepts and principles in each tutorial. An unexpected benefit of this project was the creation of visual materials that the PI has allowed us to use in another wholly online course, Nutrition 100. In other words, we have been able to re-purpose "learning objects" that are appropriate in more than one content domain.

With support from the Center for Academic Transformation (http://www.center.rpi.edu/PewGrant.html), Professor Bill Harkness and his colleagues significantly reduced the number of lectures in Statistics 200 by developing computer-based games, simulations, and statistical software that led students through the key concepts in statistics. A key concept was RATS (readiness assessment tests). The faculty were convinced that mastery learning was possible and that students needed frequent feedback on how well they understood concepts or had mastered skills. These assessment activities were crucial to the success of this initiative, one that enrolls nearly 1,000 each semester. Evaluation indicated significant learning gains and significant cost reductions. This innovation is now in its fifth year, so it's clear that the innovation has become a mainstream part of the department.

Penn State's Provost, Rodney Erickson, has funded a courseware initiative that is applying the lessons learned from these two projects to four additional large-enrollment courses: Accounting 211, Nutrition 100, Landscape Architecture 060, and Biological Science 004. These efforts complement other college-based initiatives (Meteorology 101) that are already serving students at multiple campuses in one "virtual" section and several other courses being developed by Liberal Arts. It is too soon to talk about the collective impact of these courses on the experience of first- and second-year students, but it is safe to say that almost all students will complete one or more courses that are either wholly online or have a very significant portion of the instruction offered only in a blended environment. What will be critical, however, is that all of the college-developed courses conform to university-wide norms for pedagogy, technical standards, and assessment. It would be premature to suggest that all departments are equally comfortable with the idea of online undergraduate courses, but we believe that our early leaders have established solid principles that others can easily adapt.

While each of these courses represents what Bill Graves calls "random acts of progress," Penn State can also point to one unit, the School of Information Sciences and Technology (http://ist.psu.edu), which has developed a blended learning environment that is a hallmark of its undergraduate programs. The School of Information Sciences and Technology (IST) received funds from the Commonwealth of Pennsylvania with the proviso that its curriculum be made available to any institution in the Commonwealth. In addition, the School wanted to ensure that undergraduate course materials could be used equitably across 19 campuses by nearly 100 faculty with nearly 2,400 undergraduates. (We will not discuss the graduate programs in this essay.) To help a highly distributed faculty achieve common course goals, IST charged its Solutions Institute with the task of creating and distributing course materials that could be used flexibly and easily in many different ways. Some IST students will complete online versions of the five core courses, but most will complete a blended version of these courses. Course materials that have been developed to support credit instruction can then be repurposed to support non-credit or certificate programs. IST has built into its culture the expectation that blended learning will be part of the experience of every student and faculty member. If IST had not taken a systems approach to courseware development, it would have been impossible to support so many faculty and students so rapidly. Its success is not a result of "random acts of progress."

What is remarkable is the speed with which the undergraduate landscape has been transformed. The Web has created new ways to personalize instruction, provide feedback to students, foster sharing of course materials and pedagogical strategies, and encourage closer integration between departmental resources and university-wide resources (e.g., electronic materials available through the libraries). Current challenges are to find better ways to assess student learning in online environments and to ensure that students for whom online learning is not appropriate have options that are suitable to them. Assessment is particularly important since it would seem paradoxical to need a traditional classroom only for two or three periods per semester—the times when Scantron tests are administered.

III. BLENDED LEARNING AT THE PROGRAM LEVEL: FROM DISTANCE EDUCATION TO DISTRIBUTED LEARNING

Penn State has more than a century of commitment to serving distant students through correspondence study, broadcast and cable television, and satellite delivery. Over that time, it has developed an array of support services that duplicate traditional campus-based services for distant students. These include registrar and bursar functions, undergraduate advising, bookstore, and so on. These were organized as the Department of Distance Education in 1993. As a result, when the Penn State World Campus was launched in 1998, the goal was to enhance service to these distant students by offering programs that could be taken entirely at a distance. ALN was seen as a way to enhance access by giving students the ability to interact with online resource and to create highly interactive learning communities at a distance. These two capabilities allowed the World Campus to offer, completely at a distance, baccalaureate degrees and professional master's degrees that otherwise would have required residencies.

By the end of its fifth year of operation, the World Campus has worked with eleven of Penn State's academic colleges to develop 30 degree and certificate programs, including several associate degrees, two complete baccalaureate degrees and three complete master's degrees. In addition, several colleges have developed post baccalaureate certificate programs for the World Campus; these allow distant students to earn credits toward a master's degree, reducing the time they spend on campus. A critical feature of all World Campus programs is that they are programs of the university's core academic units and are comprised of the same courses that are offered on campus. This sets the stage for students to be able to blend World Campus and on campus courses to meet degree requirements.

Blending at the program level has evolved around two very different needs: (1) brief residencies in cohort-based graduate programs and (2) partnerships with traditional campuses to blend online and campus-based courses to enhance options available to students who live in local campus service areas.

A. Residencies

When the World Campus was first established, the Graduate Council debated the residency requirements for graduate degrees to be delivered at a distance. The Council determined that, while academic master's degrees (the M.A. and M.S.) require a physical presence on campus, the World Campus should be permitted to offer professional master's degrees that did not require a physical residency. The rationale is that, for academic degrees, one goal is to socialize students to professional academic life in a campus environment; this is not necessarily the case for professional degrees, where the goal is to help students become socialized to leading in the professional work environment.

Currently, the World Campus offers two professional degrees (both Masters of Education) that can be taken entirely at a distance. However, the World Campus also offers two professional graduate-level programs—the intercollege MBA and a post baccalaureate certificate in Project Management—that make different uses of short residencies. Significantly, neither residency is necessarily on a campus.

The intercollege Master of Business Administration was launched in fall 2002. It requires two brief residencies as part of the curriculum structure. Two characteristics makes these residencies both feasible and potentially valuable to the program: the iMBA serves cohorts of students who take all courses together and, second, most students are supported by their employers, including covering the cost and time away from work. We admit cohorts of up to 30 students per year. These students take all courses together on a common calendar. The residencies bring this learning community together around a particular case study. For instance, in 2003, the first cohort's residency was a two-week on-site visit to

QVC, where students learned about the integration of business functions in the company. A second residency will be held at the end of the core, before students begin specialized projects.

The post baccalaureate Certificate in Project Management is a contract program that involves employees at three multinational companies that have partnered to make this program available to their employees. All three companies have broadly distributed facilities. The residencies serve to bring employees together across the companies. Typically, the residency is held at a training center of one of the companies. It provides an opportunity for interaction, company-based meetings, testing, and, as the program has matured, graduation ceremonies in which the students are recognized by both the University and their employers. In this instance, a residency serves to build cohesion within a cohort, to reinforce the employer's commitment, and to motivate and recognize student achievement.

B. Blending Programs through Campus Partnerships

Most World Campus programs deal with fairly specialized disciplines, assuming that it will be necessary to aggregate a student population from a broad geographic region to sustain delivery over time. Students can complete entire undergraduate degree programs at a distance through a mix of online courses, web-enhanced independent learning courses, and traditional correspondence courses. The World Campus is now partnering with the University's 12-campus Commonwealth College to offer two of these specialized degree programs in a blended format that assumes that students will take the bulk of their general courses at a local campus and take the specialized courses through the World Campus. The two degrees being offered in this blended format are associate degrees in Dietetics and in Hotel, Restaurant, and Institutional Management. The blended approach allows the local campus to expand the number and variety of degree programs that it offers locally.

Within the Penn State environment, this kind of blending requires a three-way partnership among (1) the College of Health and Human Development, which is the academic home of the two degrees and which controls the curriculum and instruction, (2) the Commonwealth College, which coordinates delivery and support of the program for local students and which directly offers general education courses for the degree in the local community, and (3) the World Campus, which delivers the specialized courses in the major and provides an alternative source for general courses. The programs are difficult to deliver locally not only because of scale—the relatively small number of students in a given campus area makes it difficult to support regular faculty—but because both programs result in national accreditation and require central academic control. The programs also require students to be working in the field and to have a local mentor.

The program assumes that most students entering the program at local campuses will be adult part-time students. The students will enroll on a course-by-course basis, paying the Commonwealth College tuition for courses taken at the local campus and paying the World Campus tuition for courses taken online. The World Campus funds the College of Health and Human Development's instructional costs for the online courses out of its tuition revenue. A new policy, developed as a Course Sharing Task Force charged by the Provost in the 2002–03 academic year, will provide for full-time students at participating campuses to be able to take the World Campus courses without paying additional tuition. Under the course sharing system, the participating campus will list the World Campus course in its local schedule; the student will register locally but will receive instruction from the World Campus. The local campus will pay a per-student fee to the World Campus to support instructional costs.

This approach has benefits for all internal partners.

- The Commonwealth College is able to offer two degree programs that do not attract enough students to support the cost of dedicated campus-based faculty, allowing it to better serve the local community.

- The World Campus, which was already committed to offering these courses nationally, is able to attract more enrollments to each course, helping the financial stability of the entire program.

- The College of Health and Human Development is able to offer the program statewide without the addition of faculty and in a way that guarantees consistency and equity.

Most importantly, students gain access to a broader array of programs, with greater choice of delivery methods, than would be the case without blending. The blended approach provides for equitable access while enhancing student flexibility and choice.

Blended program delivery and course sharing were initially stimulated out of a concern over internal competition—that the World Campus would attract local students away from the regional campuses. The blended approach serves to expand the curriculum and course offerings of the local campus, while giving students greater access, flexibility, and choice. As a result, Penn State is better prepared to compete for adult students with other online and traditional providers. At the same time, blending contributes to an expectation that all University locations will benefit from online courses, purposefully blurring the historic lines between distance education and resident instruction.

IV. INSTITUTIONAL IMPLICATIONS

Several organizational characteristics and strategic decisions have strengthened Penn State's ability to innovate with both stand-alone and blended online learning.

A. Organizational Characteristics

Penn State's organizational structure is a key to understanding its approach to blended programming. While Penn State has 24 traditional campuses in addition to the World Campus, it is not a "university system." Instead, it operates as a single, highly integrated university with a single curriculum. When the Faculty Senate approves a course number for a course, any campus is able to offer that course locally, provided that it has appropriate faculty. Thus, the same course can be taught at all 25 locations and contribute equally to the student's progress toward a degree. This curricular seamlessness encourages campuses to want to share materials within courses and sets the stage for course sharing at the program level.

B. Strategic Decisions

Despite having an organizational structure that encourages blending of online and face-to-face courses, the University's business practices initially did not support course sharing. Over the past few years, Penn State has taken several steps to develop an institutional infrastructure to support the full integration of online learning into its learning environment on campus, between campuses, and off campus.

An Institution-wide Learning Management System: Beginning in the late 1990s, Penn State entered a period of innovation. While the World Campus and the on-campus Teaching and Learning Through Technology represented the major institution-wide innovations, many individual academic units and individual faculty were also innovating. The result was a mélange of technologies and little opportunity for synergy or sharing. In 2001, the Provost appointed the authors of this paper to co-chair a task force charged to recommend a single, university-wide online learning environment for Penn State. The University ultimately chose ANGEL, a product developed originally by University of Indiana/Purdue University. Like several other learning management systems, ANGEL had developed initially within a university setting; unlike some, its owners were willing to share code, making it possible for Penn State to adapt ANGEL to our unique institutional culture and to continue to evolve it. This made ANGEL perfect for the University's vision of a seamless environment in which faculty could develop online elements to support blended learning on campus or develop complete courses for distance education delivery through the World Campus and share resources between these environments.

A key component of Penn State's success in blended learning is its strong central support of a single course management system, ANGEL. Three years ago, our provost sought to ensure a "common learning environment"—the goal was to ensure that a faculty member teaching in the World Campus or in resident education would be able to use the same tools and resources. The creation of our "common learning environment" was an additional step toward making the World Campus a seamless part of the experience for both students and faculty. The adoption of ANGEL has spread very rapidly throughout resident education. From our pilot semester of 100 sections, ANGEL usage has grown to nearly 3,500 sections last spring. More than 45,000 students were using ANGEL in at least one course, and these sections were spread proportionately across lower- and upper-division courses. Clearly, the vast majority of these sections had only a part of their instruction online, but the important point is that the early adopters have been rapidly joined by the early majority of our faculty and teaching assistants. Within this context of rapid adoption on instructional technology, Penn State has also embarked on highly focused initiatives dealing with general education. We have sought to incorporate principles of "active learning" in a handful of our high-enrollment, high-impact courses. We believe that this selective investment has had a major impact on our undergraduates' expectations about their learning.

e-Learning @ PSU Cooperative: Penn State's Course Sharing Policy: Penn State's vision of distributed learning precedes the blossoming of e-learning. In the 1990s, the University adopted a "Campus Course Exchange" policy to encourage academic units to share resources across campuses. Originally, this policy envisioned that courses would be distributed via interactive video. However, the policy was quickly applied to online courses, as these became available. In 2003, the Provost charged an Online Course Sharing Task Force to review the Campus Course Exchange policy and experiences. The task force recommended that the University enhance the original policy and provide a stronger organizational structure to support it. This is a new policy, and an implementation plan is still being developed. However, a key element was to avoid creating new bureaucracy and new cost while facilitating sharing of online resource within the University.

Enhancing Student Choice: The Course Sharing Task Force report also includes a recommendation that will encourage greater blending of online learning at the program level. The recommendation allows students to declare a "home campus," so that they can more easily mix on-campus and World Campus courses in a degree program.

New Business Processes: Most of the University's business practices were created to support a well-established, routine system—the offering of semester-based classroom courses to students living on or communing to a traditional campus. Distance education operates as a cost center, generating its own tuition revenue to cover its costs. Blended programming challenges the traditional business model because it involves a different value chain: different units contribute to serving a student, in some cases requiring a different internal flow of revenue to cover expense. Penn State has created new business practices to accommodate this new channel within the mainstream. These include internal licensing of courses, new revenue sharing formulas, etc. As blended online delivery takes root and grows, it may turn out that these are temporary "fixes"—a new mainstream that seamlessly integrates these new practices may evolve over time.

III. CONTINUING CHALLENGES

A. Realizing the Full Pedagogical Potential of Blended ALN

Initially, ALN was designed to improve access. In a blended environment, this meant a more equitable distribution of courseware across multiple locations of the University. However, as we have gained experience with the online environment, it has become clear that blended online learning also has remarkable pedgagogical potential. It offers new opportunities for resource-centered, inquiry-based learning in which students become actively involved in researching issues, solving problems, and working in virtual teams on projects. It can also contribute to the globalization of the curriculum by bringing into on-campus and distant courses the perspectives of international experts and students from other institutions around the globe. Equally important, it can be an element in service learning, internships, and other community-based learning.

The blended learning environment makes these pedagogical innovations possible. However, we have not yet seen the full integration of online learning into systematic pedagogical innovations at the curricular level. We have yet to leave the "early adopter" stage.

B. Managing Online Course Assets

Like most institutions, Penn State has created new intellectual property policy to protect all parties in the online learning environment. Under the University's Courseware Copyright policy, the University retains copyright of courseware that it "commissions" from faculty members and retains use rights of courseware that faculty create on their own initiative as part of their teaching role. This policy has eased many concerns that arose in the early days of the World Campus and of distributed learning generally at Penn State.

There is, however, another dimension to intellectual property that is stimulated by blending online and traditional learning. How does the University encourage and support the sharing of online modules by multiple faculty members within a department and, perhaps more important, the sharing of course materials across academic units? To some extent, this is an intellectual property issue: just as the University created the course sharing policy to ensure a stable financial environment for sharing of courses across locations, the future will require that universities create mechanisms to support sharing of modules across disciplines. This will require that the interests of individual faculty authors and their departments be protected when other departments incorporate their materials into courses offered by the second department.

It will also require that the University create a repository for these "learning objects" and mechanisms to identify, retrieve, and publish modules. Perhaps the greatest single remaining obstacle is the absence of an institutional (or national) strategy for sharing course materials. We are convinced that if we had an easy way to share not just pedagogical ideas but actual materials (e.g., graphics, video, simulations, quiz banks, assessment rubrics, and more), faculty would find it easier to incorporate elements of blended learning. For this reason Penn State proposed to the Center for Institutional Cooperation that we create a prototype of an IMS-compliant learning repository. The verdict is not yet in, however, on how rapidly disciplinary groups will find a compelling case for sharing materials.

C. Encouraging Organizational Evolution

Penn State will soon be faced with new choices about how best to organize its resources for online learning to ensure that the benefits of blended learning are fully realized. Currently, the organizational environment is marked by two central units—Teaching and Learning through Technology and the World Campus—one created to support e-learning on campus, the other created to extend education to off-campus students. Over the past few years, several individual colleges within the University have created their own online course development capabilities. The Course Sharing Task Force report encourages evolution through closer collaboration among these existing units. This path will blur current distinctions between on campus and distance education and set the stage for the gradual evolution of new structures. Our hope is that this approach will stimulate innovation and cooperation.

At a time of very rapid social and technological change, it is easy to forget that change has been a constant for Penn State. From its first independent learning courses in 1892 to the creation of the World Campus in 1997, we have sought to find the right kind of technology to meet students' needs. The passage of the TEACH Act in 2002 promises new resources to support blended learning, but the Act also challenges us to face a new set of issues surrounding principles of "fair use." A larger challenge, though, is one posed by Carol Twigg in 1993: why is it that teaching faculty find it so hard to collaborate with their peers? Why is it that departments seem so inclined to do all parts of courseware development themselves? Clearly, no department or institution is wealthy enough to do the whole job independently. And while we may applaud the idea behind MIT's "open courseware initiative," we remain skeptical that whole courses can be built out of these materials. What will be required, we believe, is a different kind of framework for sharing ideas and materials that underlie most of our general education courses. Indeed, Penn State's recent grant from the Andrew W. Mellon Foundation will enable us to develop LionShare, a tool that permits authenticated file sharing and federated searching for instructional materials from a variety of sources – individual faculty, department or college resources, and external repositories (such as Merlot). There's no question that faculty use the same textbooks at most universities, and it's reasonable to expect faculty to adopt, not write, their textbooks. We hope that through our e-Learning Cooperative, we will learn how to nurture a culture of sharing.

IV. AUTHOR CONTACT INFORMATION

John T. Harwood, Ph.D.
Senior Director, Teaching and Learning with Technology
The Pennsylvania State University

Gary E. Miller, D.Ed.
Associate Vice President for Outreach
Executive Director, World Campus
The Pennsylvania State University

MODEL-DRIVEN DESIGN: SYSTEMATICALLY BUILDING INTEGRATED BLENDED LEARNING EXPERIENCES

Stephen Laster
Babson College

- Developing and delivering curricula that are integrated and that use blended learning techniques requires a highly orchestrated design.

- While institutions have demonstrated the ability to design complex curricula on an ad-hoc basis, these projects are generally successful at a great human and capital cost.

- Model-driven design provides a sustainable approach that reduces some of the cost of complex curriculum development and improves the sustainability of curriculum innovation.

- Systems thinking is a perspective for going beyond events, to looking for patterns of behavior, and to seeking underlying systemic interrelationships which are responsible for the patterns of behavior and the events.

- Model-driven design provides the ability to share models and learning units beyond the borders of the institution.

I. INTRODUCTION

Blended teaching and learning in an integrated curriculum creates opportunities for learning that are not found in a traditional discipline-specific, pure classroom model. These opportunities include:

- the multi-dimensional analysis of complex issues and concepts
- the exploration of discipline domain problems from new vantage points
- the ability to collaborate with students and colleagues in a geographically and socially diverse community

However, developing blended, integrated experiences is complicated and can be expensive from both work-hours and financial perspectives. For example, in an integrated experience, faculty need to spend more time coordinating materials and exercises that support the desired outcomes than they would in a more traditional stand-alone, discipline-specific classroom course. When this integrated model is delivered in a blended format, the design team needs to coordinate delivery techniques in addition to integrating the material. The result is a highly orchestrated teaching plan that rivals the design and development of any complex system.

This paper explores Babson College's experience designing, developing, and implementing blended and integrated curricula for undergraduate, graduate, and executive business education. The paper examines the process from a systems thinking approach and attempts to develop an effective, repeatable, practice: model-driven design (MDD).

This paper also includes a brief history of Babson's migration from discipline-based teaching to integrated teaching. This migration serves as the foundation for Babson's recent evolution to the blended delivery model. A review of these transitions provides the necessary context for understanding the evolution to model-driven design.

A note on language: While many definitions exist for integrated teaching, blended learning, and systems thinking, for the purpose of this paper, we will use the following working definitions:

- **Integrated teaching**: Teaching complex concepts and skills from a multi-disciplinary perspective.
- **Blended learning**: Using a mix of technologies and educational activities in support of identified learning outcomes.
- **Systems thinking**: A mindset for understanding how things work. It is a perspective for going beyond events, to looking for patterns of behavior, and to seeking underlying systemic interrelationships which are responsible for the patterns of behavior and the events. [1]

II. BABSON BACKGROUND

To understand the evolution of model-driven design at Babson, it is important to know something about Babson's history of innovation and integration. For example:

- During the early 1990s, Babson transformed the core of its course-based MBA curriculum from the traditional class/instructor model to an integrated set of experiences that immerse students in the study of business life cycles.

- During the mid 1990s, Babson transformed its undergraduate curriculum into an integrated business core/integrated liberal arts experience and migrated to a competency-based model for outcome measurement.

- In the early 2000s, Babson drew on its integrated MBA curriculum to launch a blended MBA program for corporate clients. Soon after, the College launched a similar open enrollment offering.

- Currently, Babson is redesigning its undergraduate intermediate management core experience (IME) and leveraging blended learning for integrated skills mastery and student self-service refresher requirements.

Through the early transitions from discipline-based teaching to integrated teaching, Babson's faculty developed the skills and understanding required to collaborate beyond the single instructor/single classroom model. Faculty and program administrators developed processes and language that support an integrated teaching and learning experience. This early work resulted in Babson's first model for visualizing and speaking about an integrated program.

In this early integrated model, the core of the MBA program was constructed to model the entrepreneurial life cycle. Students moved through modules that are focused on key business activities. Within each module the experience was organized in streams that cover integrated topics. Implicit in this model was a new language (i.e. module, stream) and a new visualization of the experience that was no longer tied to the semester model. The program was designed around a series of module maps that highlight and coordinate the activities of the streams within the program. These module maps are the perceptual model for the program.

When Babson designed and developed its blended MBA program, the integrated model was refined. For example, the concept of the integrated core stayed largely the same as the on-campus MBA, while the method of delivering this content shifted to a blended format. With this change came changes in the language used to discuss aspects of the program. Terms such as face-to-face days, discussion forums, and online sessions made their way into the language. Logistics also changed. While the blended MBA program planning still included content progression as it does in the on-campus programs, it also expanded to include planning the delivery of the content.

While much of the design work for both the on-campus MBA and the blended MBA was highly successful, both development efforts were time- and resource-intensive. Therefore, when the College decided to redesign the undergraduate IME program, Babson's curriculum innovation and technology group leveraged the design opportunity to develop a sustainable, repeatable process for design and implementation that was more time- and resource-efficient than the MBA programs had been. The goals were to:

- Arrive at a design that achieves the learning, teaching, quality, and cost objectives of the College.

- Develop an approach to design and development that is less resource intensive than prior design experiences.

- Develop a learning environment where the students can quickly understand how to use the technology platform and can focus on learning the curriculum content.

The result of this work is the concept and practice of model-driven design.

III. MODEL-DRIVEN DESIGN (MDD)

A. Overview

Model-driven design (MDD) is the concept of developing complex learning experiences through the use of a team model (how the team is staffed and empowered), a process model (how the experience is developed), and a perceptual model (how the experience is discussed and visualized). Model-driven design applies the basic principles of systems and software design to the creation of a complex curriculum. These systems and software design principles include:

- the creation of systems that can be visualized and understood at various levels of detail
- the assembly of larger systems from smaller re-usable components
- the ability for the system to change and adapt throughout its useful life

Successfully implementing model-driven design means committing to the following:

1. Using a common language

Within a single institution, a student may move among courses and faculty and discuss the same intellectual concepts and topics using different language. For example, in one class, the student may have "homework," while in another s/he may have "assignments." The implication in both situations is that the student has work to complete outside of class. While this language discrepancy may be acceptable in a single instructor/single class model, it creates large integration problems as we begin the development of a complex learning experience.

2. Establishing and committing to clear learning objectives

The establishment of clear learning objectives is the point from which all other curriculum decisions are made. For example, as a faculty member argues to include a certain reading or exercise that he or she has "always assigned," that professor must determine whether that activity helps the students achieve the established learning objectives. If it does, it should be assigned. If it does not, it should be cut or the objectives must be modified.

3. Working in new units of instruction

The majority of US higher education institutions structure their planning around semesters, courses, and class sessions. While this structure is, arguably, an effective one for administering the learning process, it does impose time and segmenting constraints on curriculum design. As we begin to design integrated and blended curricula, it is important to free the design from these existing constraints so that the learning objectives and the delivery model can drive the segmentation.

4. Developing content in stand-alone learning units

A stand-alone learning unit provides an entry point and exit or conclusion that allows an individual to learn content in a meaningful, discrete experience. It must set context, present information, and conduct mastery exercises such that by completing the learning unit, the individual will be able to demonstrate competency in established learning objectives.

B. MDD — Team Model

Most integrated and/or blended design initiatives require a cross-discipline, cross-functional team. Even the creation of small units of instruction delivered in a blended experience requires skills that are rarely found in a single person. Frequently the team includes a faculty member (or subject matter expert), instructional designer, and instructional technologist. Often a graphic designer is also part of the design team. In addition to these core production skills, the team must possess the understanding and authority to drive the design and the resulting implementation.

For a large-scale initiative, such as the creation of an entirely new academic program, several teams are employed at different stages of the project. As the project grows in scope, team size must be carefully balanced with the proper make-up of the faculty experts for the subject matter, administrators, and specialists versus the logistics of meeting and working together.

Successful projects leverage a sponsorship approval model. A **steering committee**, usually an academic decision-making body, sets the overall goals and directions for the program and reserves the right of final approval. This group also helps to sell the completed design to the rest of the institution.

The **high-level design team** (HLDT) is the working group that builds the perceptual model. It is driven by faculty division representatives who are empowered to commit their colleagues to the new design. It drives the project timeline and refines the goals for the implementation teams. The HLDT also includes instructional designers and technologists in an advisory capacity so that implementation feasibility and new opportunities are factored into the design. Program administrators also serve an advisory role so that logistical implications and costs are discussed during the design. The goal is to arrive at an innovative, implementable design that is made final before content development.

Development teams work within the bounds of the high-level design to find or create source materials and, where required, to create technology to support teaching and learning experiences. These development teams can work in parallel, compressing the overall time required to build out the new program.

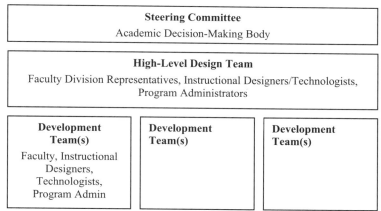

Figure 1. Large-Scale Project Team Structure

C. MDD — Process Model

In the traditional teaching model (one instructor teaching a single discipline in a classroom) many degrees of freedom exist such that just-in-time session planning or content development carries a low cost. The professor can adjust to student reaction in real time. The content can be developed "on the fly" through the use of verbal discussion and white board/PowerPoints. In this environment, the results of this technique can be positive.

Adoption of a blended model raises the costs of the just-in-time model and adds delivery risks that can be unacceptably high. A discussion forum that is not well-planned or a Web presentation that fails to communicate key information may result in student drop-out rather than student learning. Additionally, delivery requirements need to be coordinated with technology support staff to ensure the uninterrupted access to services and content. These and other risks warrant a deliberate development process that is understandable and repeatable.

While no singularly correct process model exists, it is critical that one is adopted or developed and that its constraints and requirements are respected. As a starting point, the design team can adopt a modified waterfall model, as outlined below [2]:

The waterfall approach (see below) is an established life cycle model for system development. The modified waterfall approach, when followed, provides a process for yielding a high-quality learning experience. The waterfall model follows a set of distinct prescribed steps. Each step is independent of the others. The process is document-driven, meaning that at the conclusion of a step, document(s) (physical or digital) is/are passed on. The passing of finalized documents triggers the start of the next step. Issues discovered in subsequent steps force the process back up the waterfall and the consequent modification of hand-off documents.

A modified waterfall permits the slight overlapping of steps and supports the notion of concurrent sub-projects. The concurrent running of sub-projects can reduce overall development time and can help to expose potential issues earlier in the design and development process. In the case of curriculum design the unit detailed design and development processes can generally run in parallel for each major unit of the design. This process is achievable as long as the high-level design has been completely vetted and is finalized.

While a team will want to customize its process based on the project requirements and culture, below is a skeletal process that can be used for programmatic curriculum design:

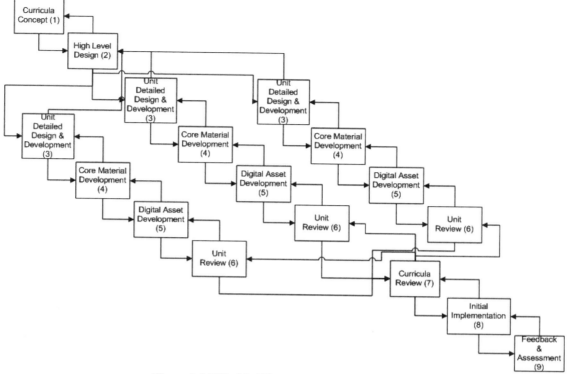

Figure 2. MDD- Modified Waterfall Process Design

1. Develop a curriculum concept. What are the major features and components for the program? What are the goals and objectives? What are the distinguishing features of this course of study? What are the assessment criteria for the project's success?

2. Develop a high-level design. Develop a language and visualization that tells the story of this program. Finalize the perceptual model.

3. Based on the perceptual model, establish a detailed design for each unit of the curriculum. This can include administrative processes.

4. Develop or identify the core or source materials for the unit.

5. Design and develop all supporting digital materials and exercises that support the learning objectives for the unit.

6. Review and refine each unit of the curriculum for completeness, effectiveness, and support of the high-level design objectives.

7. Review the entire curriculum for completeness, effectiveness, support of the high-level design objectives and overall quality.

8. Implement (teach) the new program.

9. Based on the initial and ongoing teaching experiences, assess the program's effectiveness for future refinements.

D. MDD — Perceptual Model

The perceptual model uses language and notations (sketches or pictures) in a common format that together describe the curriculum. The perceptual model is the framework for the design. Once the perceptual model is populated with specific details, it becomes a vehicle from which the design team(s) can review, refine, and negotiate changes to the curriculum while still in the design phase.

1. Language

At the foundation of the perceptual model is a common descriptive language. This language supports the development effort and provides a clear learning environment for the students. Language needs to focus on the descriptive structural elements of each unit of the curricula as well as the instructional actions required to participate in the learning experience. The specific language selected is not as important as the consistent application of it for the entire curriculum.

For example, in one curriculum, structural elements might include program, semester, and class while another curriculum might use program, module, stream, and session. The specific taxonomy does not matter as long as one is selected or developed and applied consistently. It is this consistent application of language that develops a community-wide understanding of the new model. Similarly, instructional actions must use a consistent classification language. Instructional actions are those entities and activities that faculty and students participate in and utilize throughout the program. Instructional actions can include lecture, meeting, discussion forum, book, assignment, reading, and so on.

2. Notation

The act of sketching or modeling a design with pictures and symbols is nothing new; it has been applied to systems development and engineering for quite some time. Its use provides a visual context from which people can learn the design and develop a deeper understanding of the implied complexities of the solution. Using a set of design notations for curriculum design achieves these goals and more.

As with language, the specific notation is not nearly as important as the consistent use of a single notation across the entire project. The notation builds on the language selection by incorporating the language constructs into the pictures.

a. Example Notation — Partial Model

This partial example describes the curriculum as a series of related boxes or units. The picture is read top to bottom, left to right. The higher-level units are made up of the lower units. The width of a unit denotes a relative amount of time that the activity requires. Within a unit there are descriptors that provide details about the unit. The major units are program, module, stream, and session. In this example, a program has one or many modules, a module has one or many streams, and a stream has one or many sessions.

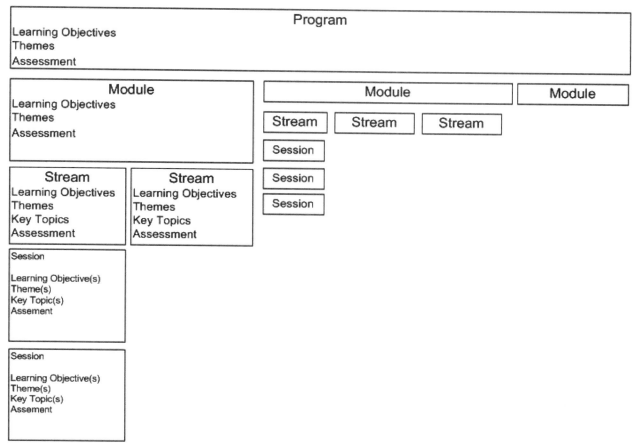

Figure 3. Partial Model

From a pedagogical perspective, the program is driven by learning objectives, themes, and assessment. This implies that the first step of the design is to identify the objectives that the learner should achieve at the completion of the program. These objectives cascade through the modules, streams, and sessions. Supporting themes and topics are developed so that the entire program of instruction supports the top-level objectives. Finally, the team needs to develop programmatic assessments that demonstrate an achievement of the learning objectives.

This model, when fully populated, provides a rich overview of what the learner will accomplish in the program (i.e., learning objectives) and the program structure. It also helps the detailed teams understand the magnitude of the detailed development activities. Content and learning experiences are created in support of each session.

E. MDD Benefits

While model-driven design requires a rigorous commitment to team, process, and the perceptual model, it creates benefits and efficiencies for the design team, the development team, and enhances the sustainability of the new curriculum.

A primary benefit is improved communication and understanding across the institutional community. A clear vision and understanding of the curriculum create the opportunity for engagement and contribution by people who might otherwise fear the change. It allows new faculty and students to learn the structure and expectations of the program faster than they otherwise would and highlights opportunities for participation. It also supports the creation of a strong, consistent marketing message and helps to clearly position the program and institution.

From a human perspective, model-driven design takes some the work out of the curriculum innovation process. Institutions committed to ongoing innovations can select a longer term model and stick to it. Energies normally spent on the how-to of innovation can be eliminated or focused on the content of model.

From a technological perspective, some of the benefits of this approach include:

- creating a learning technology platform: learning management system (LMS), assessment system, conferencing system, stream media system, directory and authentication service that support the goals and language of the perceptual model.

- establishing templates and technology frameworks to support the development of teaching and learning materials.

- developing instructional and how-to materials that enable students and faculty to learn how to use the technology platform.

- beginning the technology implementation earlier and running it in parallel with the content development.

- enhancing the ability to easily generate digital content, including modeling learning units in a reusable data store such as XML or an SQL database and generating learning unit views by learning style. These rendering engines can be developed based on the model and have the ability to serve a wide range of content.

Finally, the model makes programmatic change easier to implement in real time. Adjustments to the curriculum are easier to visualize, scope, and implement based on a model-driven approach. Interconnections and "down stream" implications can be discussed and negotiated prior to implementation. During implementation, clear lines of delineation exist, containing the change to the desired units of the curriculum.

Throughout the life of the program, the model serves as a self-documenting living map, the language allows the institution to talk about it with a common understandable meaning, and the process provides a repeatable mechanism for driving change.

IV. MODEL-DRIVEN DESIGN EXAMPLE

A. Redesigning the Intermediate Management Experience (IME)

1. Project Background

The IME is part of the Babson College undergraduate core curriculum. It is taken by all Babson undergraduate students over three semesters starting in a student's sophomore year. It is taught by a team of professors who are experts in their respective fields and conveys the interaction of each facet of business with the others. The students examine real business problems from different or combined perspectives and analyze the various factors that may affect the ability of a business to execute its strategy [3].

While this highly integrated program has been well-received over the past six years, the original design complexity created challenges on many levels, including:

- students transferring into or out of the College
- students pursuing alternative and/or advanced learning experiences while at Babson or after the completion of their degree
- faculty staffing
- overall program administration

With these issues in mind, and with the overarching goal of maintaining, if not improving the quality of the program, the College embarked on a redesign process. The IME project followed the disciplines of model-driven design and delivered a new program in less than two years.

B. IME — Team Model

The IME project was sponsored by the Babson College undergraduate decision-making body (DMB). This permanent committee is responsible for the undergraduate academic program. Among the many goals that the DMB established were:

- develop high-quality curricula
- address any weaknesses found in the original IME
- attempt to reduce delivery complexity and cost
- leverage teaching and learning technology in the delivery of the program

The DMB chartered a high-level design team composed of faculty, administrators, instructional designers, and technologists to develop a high-level design. While the high-level design team had many specific charges, among the most critical was the one to leverage learning technology in this residential program to promote learning outside of the integrated physical classroom. The DMB team believed that the quality of time spent in the classroom would increase if the students were provided with self-study experiences that:

- allow students to practice concepts and methodologies at their own pace
- refresh the student's understanding of concepts taught in previous semesters
- provide students with access to a "toolkit" for use in upper-level electives

At the conclusion of the high-level design, detailed design teams were established.

The detailed design teams were primarily faculty representatives from each academic division and instructional designers and technologists serving in a consulting capacity. The detailed design teams worked in parallel and were responsible for fleshing out the design down to the class session, assignment level of detail. Finally, key faculty were called on to find and develop the teaching materials and notes that are required to support the new IME design.

C. IME Process Model

The workflow followed a modified waterfall approach. Key documents were established for major milestones of the redesign. The documents included:

- a high-level design narrative that identified the rough structure, goals, and objectives for the program
- a model overview that set the language and conceptual model for the program design
- a completed high-level design broken down by semester

- a detailed design by class session

Each of these documents was made final before moving into the detailed development of teaching and learning content. Team meetings were structured to provide review and feedback at each development step. The process was collaborative and consensus-driven.

D. IME Perceptual Model

The IME can be thought of as a hierarchy of activities and experiences that result in an overall program of study. In a partial, highest level view, the IME is described as follows:

The IME is composed of a number of semesters and transition or summary exercises. In fact, we may want to view the transition exercise from the previous semester as a prerequisite for the current semester. During each semester, we address some number of disciplines and/or themes. From this graphic we see that the entire IME can be described at a high level as the summation of:

Semesters	A period of time that achieves a number of learning objectives.
Transitions	Reviews, exercises and assessments that demonstrate mastery of work in the prior semester and that set context for the upcoming semester.
Disciplines	A body of knowledge tied to a specific academic subject area.
Key Topics	A specific area of knowledge that supports the understanding of the discipline or theme.
Themes	A body of knowledge tied to many disciplines. Themes can be taught as independent concepts or taught as part of a discipline.

Table 1. Intermediate Management Core Experience (IME)

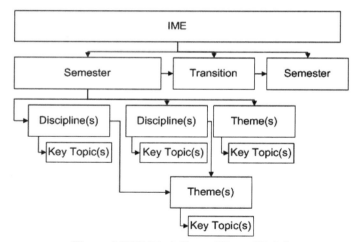

Figure 4. IME Discipline or Theme Model

If we disaggregate a discipline or theme, we expose its key components and can view their relationships.

Prerequisite disciplines or themes	Themes and disciplines that must be mastered prior to entering the current theme.
Learning objective(s)	The key objectives or outcomes that the theme will achieve.
Key topics(s)	A specific area of knowledge that supports the understanding of the discipline or theme.
Assessment(s)	Exercises and activities that, when completed to a specified level, demonstrate a mastery of the material.
Competency Connection(s)	Connections to Babson's competency model.

Table 2. Relationship Components

Finally, if we disaggregate a key topic, we see that the key components for it include:

Overview(s)	Presentation and reading materials that introduce the learning objective.
Activities(s) & Exercise(s)	Student work that reinforces the overview(s) and key topic(s) through active learning.
Assessments(s)	Exercises and activities that, when completed to a specified level, demonstrate a mastery of the material.

Table 3. Topic Components

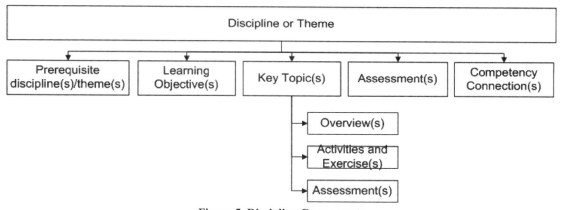

Figure 5. Discipline Components

We see from the model shell (below) that when it is fully populated, we are able adequately to describe the IME structure and flow before the creation of detailed content. We also achieve a secondary benefit of highlighting competency connections. (Competencies are key abilities that Babson students should possess at the complete of their college experience.) In essence we are now able to explicitly create themes and content that can serve a dual purpose of IME delivery and competency exploration.

This model provides the opportunity for:

- a theme to repeat over time at different levels of learning and activity

- the ability to package disciplines and themes as portable learning objects
- separate content for transition/summary activities that could be entirely supported with/by eLearning
- the ability to change components of the model over time

1. A partial overall view of the IME Structure

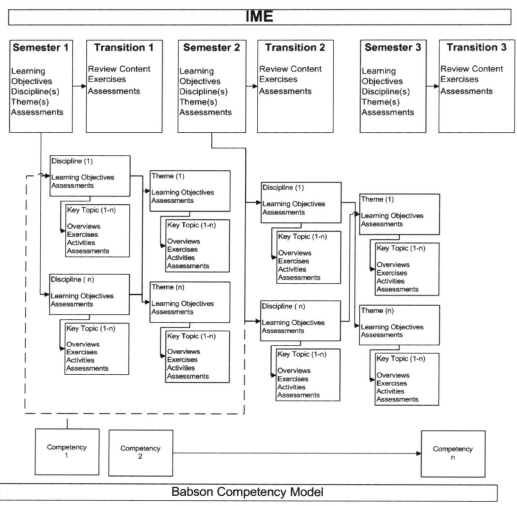

Figure 6. Competency Model

2. IME Implementation Benefits

Once the model was made final, teams were established (organized by IME semester) to develop the session content and learning units, populate the learning management system (LMS), and begin teaching the first offering of the new IME.

During the implementation phase, the teams benefited from model-driven design and the resulting model in several ways:

- a clear structure guided the development of source materials
- a clear understanding of the timing and sequencing of instruction was in place
- a faster and more flexible technology implementation (see below)
- the creation of shells or templates for the LMS, the online assessment engine, and overview Web site that follows the language structure of the model prior to content development
- the creation of reusable rendering engines, reducing the level of effort for instructional asset development

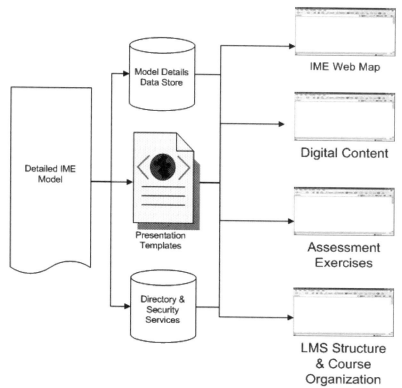

Figure 7. IME Technology Architecture

V. NEXT STEPS

As a concept and a practice, model-driven design has proved beneficial for Babson College. Our initial experience has been the ability to develop a high-quality, integrated program in a sustainable, repeatable manner. It has created the opportunity easily to introduce technology into the IME program. It has also established a methodology to support change and refinement of the IME curricula. We have begun to use this same approach for graduate and executive education programs and believe that we will derive similar benefits from the design of these programs.

From a technology perspective, we continue to purchase and develop authoring and delivery technologies that support the notion of separation of model, content, and delivery platform. We view the world as a set of templates that support the model and that free the faculty and subject matter experts to change content as warranted.

From a disaggregation, or learning unit, perspective, we have begun to see higher levels of reuse and sharing among faculty. The creation of learning units that support the model and that can stand alone in their usage allows the College to invest more resources in any given learning unit, since it will be used by a larger number of students. It also encourages faculty to develop sophisticated learning segments, since their broad adoption in the curriculum leverages the faculty time invested in the design and development.

So what comes next? For Babson, we think it is the ability to share models and learning units beyond the borders of the institution. Conceptually and practically, we support the many initiatives that are working toward open platforms for learning management systems and exchangeable content. While many are approaching this issue as a technology and packaging standards issue (which at some level it is), we believe that other hurdles include model-based thinking and a quality assurance or rating system. Additionally, the notion of the learning unit having responsibility for setting context and for covering an appropriate scope of content is a major issue with cross-institutional model-driven curriculum development.

VI. REFERENCES

1. **Bellinger, G.** http://www.outsights.com/systems/systhink/systhink.htm.
2. **McConnell, S.** *Rapid Development: Taming Wild Software Schedules*. Redmond, WA: Microsoft Press, 1996.
3. **Babson College Web Site.** http://www3.babson.edu/UG/academics/intermediate-program.cfm.

VII. ACKNOWLEDGMENTS

I am grateful to the many faculty and staff at Babson College who participated in the IME redesign and who allowed me to participate. I am also grateful to Kristin Lofblad, assistant director of Babson's curriculum innovation and technology group, who listened to my thoughts and helped me refine this paper.

VIII. ABOUT THE AUTHOR

Mr. Laster is Director of the Curriculum Innovation and Technology Group (CITG) at Babson College and an adjunct professor. His past experience includes director of product strategy, product manager, director of systems integration and director of systems development at Advanced Business Technologies, Art Technology Group, Babson College, and The Stride Rite Corporation. He also continues to consult in the areas of technology implementation and application development. Mr. Laster returns to Babson to focus on innovating with technology in the delivery of Babson's highly integrated undergraduate, graduate, and executive education curricula. This work includes the development of a blended MBA program and the formation of an internal consulting group to support faculty content development. Contact: Stephen Laster, Director, Curriculum Innovation and Technology Group, Babson College, Wellesley, MA 02457. Email: laster@babson.edu

Assessment

ASSESSMENT: CHALLENGES AND OPPORTUNITIES FOR ONLINE LEARNING

Anthony G. Picciano
Hunter College of the City University of New York

- Assessment has received attention at all levels of American education for the past two decades.

- For accreditation purposes, higher education organizations are expected to review the nature of their assessment activities.

- Online learning environments pose challenges but also provide opportunities for doing assessment.

- Higher education owes to its students formal mechanisms for assessing and improving academic programs.

- A college's or university's assessment program has evolved into a standard of excellence comparable to the quality of the faculty, the vibrancy of curricula, and the availability of financial resources.

I. INTRODUCTION

In January 2003, as part of planning for the 5th Annual Sloan Summer Research Workshop, a small committee reviewed a number of possible session topics, all of which focused on the Sloan Consortium's (Sloan-C) Five Pillars of Quality Online Education. The five pillars" have been the thematic foundation of the summer workshops since their inception in 1999 at the University of Illinois in Champagne-Urbana. It was the committee's sense that a need existed for an intensified discussion related to the national issue of assessment in higher education. The American Association of Higher Education (AAHE), the six regional accrediting agencies, and the various specialized accrediting agencies have promoted assessment of student outcomes in academic programs as a critical element of institutional effectiveness. The extent and nature of a college's or university's assessment program has evolved into a standard of excellence comparable to the quality of the faculty, the vibrancy of curricula, and the availability of financial resources. For accreditation purposes, higher education organizations are expected to review the nature of their assessment activities in institutional self-studies and in preparation for accreditation visits.

Since online learning is the underlying interest and concern of Sloan-C and all of its activities including the summer workshop series, a question for consideration might be whether online learning presents unique challenges and/or opportunities for assessment activities. In pursuing this subject, a call was sent to the Sloan-C listserv whose members include many well-informed professionals, both practitioners and researchers, in the field of online learning. The essence of the message centered on the following question:

How have you addressed the question of assessment in an online program?

The replies revealed that while assessment was indeed a topic of discussion at many institutions, there was a need for further information. For example, many of the replies sought clarification of the definition of assessment especially when compared to program evaluation. In reviewing these comments and after further consideration, our planning committee decided that a workshop session devoted to the issue of assessment and online learning would be beneficial. The purpose of this paper is to raise issues regarding assessment with regard to online learning. This paper hopes to inform faculty and administrators confronted with the need to develop or to update assessment plans as a result of the expansion of online teaching and learning in schools and programs.

II. BACKGROUND

Assessment has received attention at all levels of American education for the past two decades. Since 1983, with the publication of the National Commission on Excellence in Education Commission Report, *A Nation at Risk*, the country's priority in the primary and secondary schools has been accountability [1]. The standards movement which has swept the K–12 environment is indicative of the emphasis that federal, state, and local education policy-makers have placed on the need for accountability. Accountability and the call for standards in K–12 education are related to the push for assessment in higher education. The terms (standards and accountability in K–12 and assessment in higher education) may be different but they relate to determining whether or not academic programs are achieving their goals and objectives. In primary schools, standards attempt to determine if students have mastered basic skills such as reading, writing and arithmetic. In secondary education, emphases are placed on the mastery of content areas such as social studies, science, mathematics, and language. In higher education, programs subject to external accreditation review or state certification must now document their effectiveness in meeting established goals and objectives.

A fundamental difference exists, however, between K–12 and higher education in terms of accountability and assessment. Most K–12 schools are public and depend entirely upon government (federal, state, and local) funding. Higher education receives funding from a combination of public and private sources. While the public universities are subsidized extensively by the states, a substantial segment of higher education is privately financed through student tuition, gifts, grants, and income from endowments. Even many of the public colleges and universities derive much of their revenue from student tuition and sources other than direct state subsidy. As a result, while policies requiring the implementation of new standards and assessment have been established by governmental agencies in the K–12 environment, the same can not be implemented as easily in higher education. Instead, the responsibility for requiring or extending standards has been taken up by accrediting agencies such as the Middle States Association of Colleges and Schools, the New England Association of Schools and Colleges, the North Central Association of Colleges and Schools, the Northwest Association of Schools, Colleges and Universities, the Southern Association of Colleges and Schools, the Western Association of Schools and Colleges, and specialized accrediting associations. Nevertheless, since almost all colleges and universities participate in federally-funded programs, government policy-makers might impose requirements for standards and assessment as a condition for participating in these programs, if they chose. Academic programs that lead to professional certifications (such as nursing, health sciences, education and more) have seen an increased scrutiny by state education departments. In the past several years, many state certified programs have been required to revise and reregister their programs to include assessment components. Some states (e.g., New York) have also recently implemented proficiency examinations in public university systems that require students to demonstrate mastery of general education requirements before continuing into the junior year. Whether or not assessment is imposed by governmental agencies, an argument can be made that higher education owes to its students formal mechanisms for assessing and improving academic programs.

III. DEFINING ASSESSMENT

Assessment has been defined in a number of ways. The AAHE conducts an Assessment Forum which continually reviews the state of assessment in American higher education. In 1995, Thomas Angelo, then director of the AAHE Assessment Forum, undertook the responsibility of defining or redefining assessment. Using an inclusive process, he provided drafts of definitions and sought recommendations and clarifications from participants in the Forum. The following definition of assessment emerged:

> *Assessment* is an ongoing process aimed at understanding and improving student learning. It involves making our expectations explicit and public; setting appropriate criteria and high standards for learning quality; systematically gathering, analyzing, and interpreting evidence to determine how well performance matches those expectations and standards; and using the resulting information to document, explain, and improve performance. When it is embedded effectively within larger institutional systems, assessment can help us focus our collective attention, examine our assumptions, and create a shared academic culture dedicated to assuring and improving the quality of higher education. [2]

Other organizations and individuals have provided variations of this definition; however, fundamental to most of them are the setting of academic goals, the collection of data, and the analysis of the data to improve student learning. Serving the purposes of this discussion, these elements also serve to differentiate assessment from evaluation. Assessment concentrates on goals, objectives and student outcomes while evaluation serves a broader purpose. In the case of an academic program, evaluation frequently can include an evaluation of faculty expertise, the adequacy of curricula, the nature of the students, the availability of facilities, and student performance.

IV. WHO ASSESSES

One fundamental question associated with assessment is: Who assesses? Faculty, administrators, external consultants? This question might lead to a very long discussion but the fact is that whoever is responsible for designing or improving an academic program should also be responsible for the assessment. In many colleges and universities, this responsibility is shared by administration and faculty. While faculty can establish goals and objectives for student learning for individual programs, a college administration might be in a better position to do the same or direct the effort for the overall institution and for overarching programs such as general education which cut across the jurisdictions of a number of academic departments. Accrediting agencies generally distinguish between institutional assessment and academic program assessment. These agencies might expect to see the administration establish an overall institutional assessment plan which integrates but does not assume responsibility for individual academic department or program assessment [3]. The institutional plans set time frames for periodic assessment activities and provide resources and assistance for elements of assessment such as data collection and analysis. However, critical to these plans is the assumption by the faculty of major responsibility for assessing their own academic programs.

V. DISTANCE LEARNING

The regional accreditation agencies have been active in pursuing quality control and other issues related to distance learning. All of these agencies have established guidelines and policies for accrediting distance learning institutions and programs. The Council for Higher Education Accreditation (CHEA), which acts as the national policy center and clearinghouse on accreditation for the American higher education community including regional, national, and specialized accreditation organizations, maintains a website which contains a number of papers and monographs on the subject of accreditation and distance learning [4]. Readers wanting more detail regarding accreditation issues and distance learning are encouraged to review this material. The questions of particular interest for this paper and for the Sloan-C Summer Workshop participants are: whether online distance learning poses special challenges or provides opportunities with respect to assessment; or perhaps is not different at all. The remainder of this paper will examine these questions within the framework of individual academic programs.

VI. CHALLENGES, OPPORTUNITIES, AND NO DIFFERENCE

A. No Difference

To reiterate, the AAHE definition of assessment is a process in which academic programs determine goals and objectives, establish data collection mechanisms to analyze how well they have been achieved, and subsequently make improvements or adjustments to the academic program as need be. Part one of this definition begs the question whether goals and objectives should change because of the delivery format. This is a question being addressed by faculty and administrators especially in colleges and universities where online programs are being developed and where face-to-face programs already exist. For example, does the online MBA program offered by XYZ University have the same goals and objectives as the traditional, face-to-face MBA program? And if it does, should the assessment plan necessarily be the same? The Council for Higher Education Accreditation recommends that distance learning programs and courses achieve the same outcomes as traditional offerings. [5, p. 10] However, most academic program developers would agree that while the goals and objectives of the two programs should be the same, the overall assessment plan can and should be flexible in order to better fit and perhaps take advantage of the different delivery formats. These are important questions that have to be discussed and decided upon by those responsible for the academic program.

B. Challenges

Online distance learning may pose some problems for doing assessment depending upon the nature of the goals and objectives of an academic program. An academic program that requires student outcomes that are difficult to achieve via online distance learning coursework is an obvious starting point. For example, science programs (biology, chemistry, physics) that require hands-on experiences in doing science may have difficulty duplicating these experiences in an online environment. Many science programs pride themselves on providing quality laboratories and other facilities and expect students to develop the skills necessary to conduct laboratory experiments. These programs require laboratory classes where students are observed measuring, mixing, and handling materials. While a good deal of highly respected laboratory simulation software is available which could be used in online teaching, it has not been embraced by all science faculty. Given the current state of online technology, whether this type of learning can truly be conducted and assessed absent a physical laboratory remains an open question. The same applies to other programs such as health, nursing, engineering, physical education, and to the performing arts where dedicated facilities are generally provided for students to use to demonstrate their abilities.

Beyond those programs conducted within dedicated physical facilities, are certain subject areas such as business administration, education, public administration, nursing, and social work that require the direct observance of students by faculty. Given that these professions rely extensively on people interaction (e.g., selling, teaching, caring), an appropriate student outcome might be the development of human relations and interpersonal skills. Although interpersonal skills can be tested by traditional methods, faculty might determine that observation of students is necessary. Group dynamics activities, shared problem-solving, and mentored internships are common pedagogical techniques used to observe students applying and honing their human relations and interpersonal skills. Again, given the current state of networking technology, can this type of student outcome be assessed properly without requiring some extraordinary online learning support mechanisms?

A third challenge involves testing and other forms of summative evaluations that are frequently used to assess student learning. Many online distance learning providers require that basic written tests be conducted in proctored, face-to-face environments to ensure the identities of the students taking the tests. Certain academic programs such as communications, speech and theatre, education, and marketing may require oral presentations to audiences in order to assess student mastery of verbal skills within large group environments. Evaluating an oral presentation to a large group or class may be difficult in other than a face-to-face environment.

These challenges may not be insurmountable but certainly are problematic for online distance learning providers. In time, as the technology advances, some of these challenges may be overcome. In the interim, many online distance learning providers are relying on face-to-face activities to supplement the online component of their programs in "blended" environments. These blended environments are desirable for assessment as well as for teaching/learning activities.

C. Opportunities

Online learning also provides opportunities for enhancing and extending assessment activities. Online learning environments that rely on programmed or self-paced instruction generally have built-in assessment of student mastery of subject matter. A complete record of student progress including on-going formative testing is a common element of this type of instruction and might meet one of the needs of an assessment program. Even in more highly interactive, asynchronous online models where students are expected to communicate ideas, comments, and responses to questions via written electronic bulletin boards, instructors have a complete record of student participation in class activities. Instructors can integrate assessment into electronic group discussions that result in a complete record of the activity. Most of the popular course management software systems used in online learning allow for the entire course to be archived. An instructor can simply add comments on assessment of the students and create a complete record for future reference. This is not possible in most face-to-face class situations unless videotaping, audio taping, or some other form of recording technique is used. Electronic portfolios also can be used to provide a formal collection of student work. Class assignments, papers, student projects, and presentations can be easily collected, catalogued, and referred to in an electronic portfolio. This desirable method is referred to as "authentic assessment" by its proponents. Electronic portfolios can be used by teachers and students in face-to-face courses as well.

Certain pedagogical techniques that are used in assessment such as reflective practice can be facilitated in online courses. Critical thinking, a form of reflective practice, is a common goal in a number of subject areas. In literature, drama, and foreign language, students are expected to develop critical analysis skills by critiquing literary works. Case study analysis, another popular form of reflective practice, is a fundamental pedagogical approach used in business administration, psychology, sociology, and education that requires students to demonstrate their analytical abilities in simulated situations. All of these reflective practice techniques can be easily conducted in online courses over a period of time with all students participating through written commentary on electronic bulletin boards. It may even be argued that because the reflective activity can be extended over time (e.g., days or weeks) that it might be superior to a similar activity conducted in a typical one-hour or two-hour face-to-face class session.

Student writing constitutes a critical assessment tool. Papers, essays, and written assignments are used in most academic disciplines since writing is one of the best ways to assess what a student knows, understands, and can express. Writing is used in many ways in assessment: to demonstrate student understanding of content, to demonstrate ability to express opinions, and to critique the work of others. In a face-to-face class where oral communication is the norm, writing may be done during a class but it takes up a great deal of time. In online classes, particularly in the interactive, asynchronous learning model, writing is completely integrated into almost all class activities and can be easily used for an ongoing assessment of student learning. Furthermore, in online courses, all students are expected to participate via the written word on a regular basis. In face-to-face classes, because of time constraints, rarely are all students able to participate in even the most verbally-intense sessions.

VII. CONCLUSION

The purpose of this paper is to raise issues regarding assessment and online learning. It does not seek to answer specific questions but rather to provide food for thought for those who might be developing assessment plans for online programs or for online components added to existing face-to-face programs. The suggestions made in this paper are twofold: one, that online learning environments pose challenges but also provide opportunities for doing assessment; and two, that faculty and administrators should not change the goals and objectives of their academic programs but should provide flexibility and multiple means for doing assessment that take advantage of the different delivery formats. As college faculty and administrators make greater use of online learning, careful consideration should be given to assessment. The quality of products, services, and academic programs ultimately determine the quality of an institution. Assessment can serve to demonstrate quality and provide the mechanisms for improvement and refinement.

VIII. ACKNOWLEDGEMENTS

The author of this paper is grateful to colleagues in the Sloan Consortium who assisted in developing the workshop session on assessment especially John Bourne, Jacquie Maloney, Margie Quinlan, and Kathryn Fife. The author is also most grateful to Elaine Bowden who reviewed the manuscript and offered valuable suggestions both to its form and substance.

IX. REFERENCES

1. **National Commission on Excellence in Education**. *A Nation at Risk*. National Commission on Excellence in Education: Washington DC, 1983.
2. **Angelo, T**. Definitions of Assessment. AAHE Assessment Forum, 1995. http://www.aahe.org/assessment/assess_faq.htm#define.
3. **Middle States Commission on Higher Education.** Design for Excellence: Handbook for Institutional Self-Study, 8th Edition. Philadelphia: Middle States Commission on Higher Education, 2002.
4. **Council for Higher Education Accreditation**. Research and Information. http://www.chea.org/Research/index.cfm#qualityassurance (Last Modified, June 2003).
5. **Council for Higher Education Accreditation**. Specialized Accreditation and Assuring Quality in Distance Learning. CHEA Monograph Series No. 2. Washington, D.C.: Council for Higher Education, 2003.

X. ABOUT THE AUTHOR

Anthony Picciano is a professor in the Education Administration and Supervision Program in the School of Education at Hunter College. His teaching specializations include educational technology, organization theory, and research methods. He also currently serves on the Board of Directors for the Sloan Consortium of Colleges and Universities.

Dr. Picciano has been involved with a number of major grants from the National Science Foundation, the Alfred P. Sloan Foundation, the US Department of Education, and IBM. He has collaborated with The American Social History Project and Center for Media and Learning at CUNY on a number of instructional multimedia projects dealing with subjects such as Irish immigration in the 1850s, women's rights and labor issues at the turn of the century, and school integration in the 1950s. Currently he is a co-principal investigator of the New York City Schools Leadership Development Initiative Grant ($3.3 million) from the United States Department of Education to develop new models for preparing and supporting school leaders in New York City Public Schools, a collaborative project involving the New York City Department of Education, Hunter College Administration and Supervision Program, New Visions for New Schools, and New Leaders for New Schools, 2002–2005.

Dr. Picciano has served as a consultant for a variety of public and private organizations including the New York City Board of Education, the New York State Department of Education, Commission on Higher Education/Middle States Association of Colleges and Universities, the US Coast Guard, and CITICORP. He is the author of five books including *Educational Leadership and Planning for Technology, 3rd Edition* (Prentice-Hall, 2002) and Distance *Learning: Making Connections across Virtual Space and Time* (Prentice-Hall, 2001). His most recent book, *The Educational Research Primer* (Continuum) will be available in Spring 2004. His articles on educational technology have appeared in journals such as the *Journal of Asynchronous Learning Networks*, *Journal of Educational Multimedia and Hypermedia*, *Computers in the Schools, The Urban Review, Equity and Choice*, and *EDUCOM Review*.

Contact: Anthony G. Picciano, Professor, School of Education, Hunter College of the City University of New York, 695 Park Avenue, New York, NY 10021. E-mail: anthony.picciano@hunter.cuny.edu

MORE ART THAN SCIENCE: THE POSTSECONDARY ASSESSMENT MOVEMENT TODAY

Barbara D. Wright
Eastern Connecticut State University

- Postsecondary assessment of student learning has evolved significantly over the last 15–20 years.

- Acceptance of assessment as first and foremost a tool for improvement, a focus on student learning, the development of alternative methods, and a determination to act on findings—all have made assessment increasingly useful.

- Accreditation provides ongoing motivation for campuses to engage in assessment.

- The goal of meaningful improvement requires cultivating the art as well as the science of assessment.

- Higher education must develop more adequate ways of defining accountability.

I. INTRODUCTION

The higher education assessment movement is a young and rapidly evolving phenomenon. It looks quite different today from the way it did 15 or 20 years ago, and that has led to considerable confusion as assumptions about purpose, conceptual frameworks, instrumentation, notions of good practice, and even the definitions of basic vocabulary have shifted over time. The purpose of this paper is first to provide a reading on where the movement is today, and secondarily to place that reading in the context of assessment's past—that is, to contrast where we are now with the assumptions that marked the movement's beginnings. There are also references to the implications of these issues for online learning. The paper ends with a list of challenges the assessment movement faces, if it is to remain true to its purpose of improving student learning in the face of conflicting pressures. (For an earlier sizing up of assessment's past, present, and future based on articles that appeared in *Change Magazine* from 1969 through 1999, see [1]. The classic overviews of the early movement are Ewell [2] and Hutchings and Marchese [3]. A more recent review by Ewell [4] focuses on the contradictions of the movement).

At the outset, here is my definition of assessment. It is a process of 1) *setting goals* or asking questions about student learning and development; 2) *gathering evidence* that will show whether these goals are being met; 3) *interpreting* the evidence to see what can be discovered about students' strengths and weaknesses; and then 4) actually *using* those discoveries to change the learning environment so that student performance will be improved. Then the cycle begins again: interventions are checked to see whether they worked, and/or new questions about learning are addressed. In workshops over the last 12 years that have reached hundreds and possibly thousands of administrators and faculty, I have represented this series of steps as a cycle or loop:

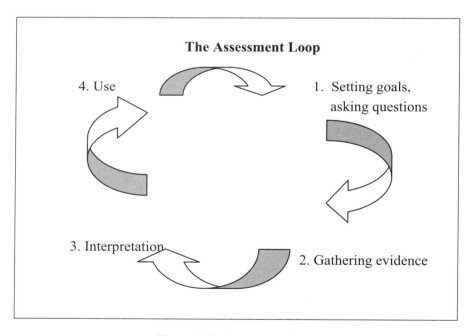

Figure 1. The Assessment Loop

In other words, assessment does not equal testing or measurement, normed scores, traditional evaluation, or program review, although it may include or overlap with those activities. Assessment done right is a thoughtful, ongoing process; it does not end with administration of a survey or reporting of results. This is a simple and robust definition, one that makes intuitive sense and has found wide acceptance. Variations on this definition can be found in most current publications on the subject [6, 7], and it has been widely adopted in campus documents. The Angelo definition, though more elaborate (quoted in Picciano, this volume, 2003), is anchored by these basic elements.

II. WHERE IS THE ASSESSMENT MOVEMENT TODAY AND HOW DID WE GET HERE?

Given that definition, what are the most important characteristics of the movement today? First and foremost, there is broad consensus in the higher education community about the reason why we are doing this: to *improve* student learning and thus strengthen programs and institutions. Second, there is consensus that the key issue is student *learning*; other information may be useful, but remains subordinate. Third, experience has shown the limitations of traditional surveys and testing, and demonstrated the benefits of more local, more authentic *alternative methods*. Fourth, *process* is as important as product if assessment is to transform the academy into a "culture of evidence." Finally, *accreditation* has made assessment a priority. While these characteristics have emerged out of traditional teaching/learning practice, they are equally relevant to assessment of e-learning.

First, there is the focus on *improvement*. This may seem utterly self-evident today. But when the assessment movement gathered momentum in the mid-80s, the dominant assumption on campuses and in statehouses was that assessment would serve evaluation and accountability. At the earliest assessment conferences organized by the American Association for Higher Education in 1985, '87, and '88, the air was thick with anxiety and the conviction that the purpose of state mandates was punitive. Nor was this a far-fetched idea, given widespread criticism of the quality of higher education from both inside the academy and beyond. High-profile reports such as *A Nation at Risk* [7], *Integrity in the College Curriculum* [8] and *Involvement in Learning* [9] all made headlines. Bennett's *To Reclaim a Legacy* [10] and Hirsch's *Cultural Legacy* [11] were widely discussed in the media and fanned popular discontent. At the same time, more and more states issued assessment mandates; by 1990, according to the *Campus Trends Survey* [12] there were some 40 of them, followed shortly by the National Governors' Association demand for "results" [2].

Below the surface of that demand for accountability, the deeper desire was to improve the quality of student learning. But insistence on accountability worked at cross purposes with the desire for improvement. It has taken nearly 20 years to reach agreement among accreditors, state departments of higher education, and the postsecondary community that improvement is priority one; however, this is still not widely accepted among legislators, and not always believed on campus. It is a nuance lost on most of the public.

An adage that accompanied early work was that assessment methods could serve either improvement or accountability, but not both; forced to choose, most institutions did assessment for accountability because of the stakes involved, then never got around to assessment for improvement. In this way, a false dichotomy was set up that has died hard. But there is a deeper dynamic at work undermining assessment when it is done for evaluation purposes.

What is the problem, exactly, in conflating assessment with evaluation, or viewing assessment as a tool that primarily serves accountability? "Evaluation" is about making value judgments and about consequences, often negative. Evaluators most often come from outside, although "outside" is a relative term; as Ewell [4] explains, "external" can mean any two steps up the administrative hierarchy. The fact that evaluators have no personal stake in the program or institution is supposed to make them "objective."

In a short visit evaluators are expected to detect strengths and especially weaknesses, write a report, and make recommendations; beyond that, they have no continuing responsibility to the program or institution. Few programs want to risk the consequences of negative findings—e.g., loss of lines, budget cuts, or even termination—so they strive to appear as strong as possible, and problems are concealed rather than confronted. Thus the process encourages damage control rather than improvement. After the visit, it is easy to dismiss evaluators' recommendations as uninformed or unrealistic, and business-as-usual continues because there is no one with real ownership of the recommendations to push for implementation. Since evaluations are episodic, they are easy to forget until the next one looms in 5 or 10 years.

"Assessment," in contrast, is a value-free process that simply looks, describes what it sees, and provides feedback on how to improve [13]. In this way assessment echoes a basic tenet of TQM: in the vast majority of cases systems, not people, are the problem. The feedback may be offered to students with the goal of improving their individual performance, or it may provide insight for a faculty on the strengths and weaknesses of a program as a whole. Assessment is carried out by insiders who care deeply about their discipline, their students, and their program. The process does not stop with reporting of data midway through the cycle—that is, after step 2—but continues through the difficult interpretive conversations to arrive at implementation. Instead of gaming the evaluation process, educators engaged in assessment are candid about the problems that demand attention, attend to them with integrity, and make a difference. This assumes a prevailing climate not of fear and coercion but of trust and support, one in which candor and risk-taking are rewarded, not punished.

Of course, the distinction between evaluation and assessment is not as stark as I have just drawn it. In a program review or a self-study for accreditation, assessment may be one element within a larger process of evaluation. In practice, evaluation and assessment have borrowed one another's methods: evaluators, for example, have involved "insiders" to help construct the meaning of the evaluation; and assessment practitioners may invite external examiners—employers, internship supervisors, neighboring faculty—to help in the assessment of student work. There is also some overlap of purpose: evaluation and assessment alike care about both quality assurance *and* quality improvement; the difference lies in the relative emphasis. And finally, as noted, the notion of who is "internal" or "external" is elastic. Still, there is a crucial difference between assessment and evaluation, and the common practice of using the two words interchangeably is most unfortunate. Particularly when there is strong faculty resistance to assessment, maintaining the distinction can help allay fears and make the point to faculty that they are being asked to do this for themselves and their students, not to satisfy some distant bureaucracy.

Even today, programs and institutions frequently assume that assessment is for purposes of quality *assurance*, that is., to satisfy external audiences or some external standard of quality, rather than for their own quality *improvement*. In the online learning community, this is particularly evident in the quest to establish "no significant difference." Higher education should certainly strive to meet high standards, and accountability demands are legitimate. But accountability can be served while keeping improvement as the main focus, whereas an exclusive focus on accountability is to sabotage improvement. Currently, most accountability demands are satisfied by a report at the halfway mark through the loop, when data are collected and submitted. To achieve improvement, however—that is, not only to ask questions about learning and get some data but also to create information out of data and *use* it—it is essential to trace the entire loop and actually *close* it, not just with feedback but with action. An institution that closes the loop *also* has an impressive story to tell, for purposes of accountability, about progress and improvement, a story that emerges naturally as a by-product of improvement efforts. Will this approach satisfy the audiences demanding accountability? Higher education cannot ignore the issue of audience expectations, and just as traditional educators need to educate those holding them accountable, so too will programs of e-learning.

Another achievement of the last 15 years has been the realization that to improve learning, the focus needs to be on *learning*. This, too, seems utterly self-evident. Yet the descriptive data that institutions traditionally have collected for assessment purposes have to do primarily with resources or reputation, inputs and outputs: SAT scores, numbers of valedictorians, availability of study abroad or writing across the curriculum, retention and graduation rates, time to completion, GRE scores, salaries of graduates, and so on. Such information can be useful, but it does not achieve the salience of the questions: Just what do our students know? What can they do? At what level of skill? How much do they grow from entry to exit? Is this good enough? How can we improve? Today these surrogates are still collected, but they are viewed more skeptically: as necessary, perhaps, but not sufficient. Online learning programs, too, need to ask themselves what kind of data they are collecting, and how salient it is to student learning.

Besides making us more wary of the value of descriptive data, the sharper focus on learning has led to another important distinction, that between direct and indirect evidence of learning. Indirect evidence comes from surveys, interviews, questionnaires, focus groups, and the like. The responses reveal what students *think* they learned, or how employers perceive their recent hires' training, but they cannot show directly what students know and are able to do. That can only be revealed through examination of direct evidence, that is, actual samples of student work and performances.

Traditionally, testing and grading have been cited as direct evidence, but assessment has moved beyond both. Alternative methods that provide more complex insight into students' learning are gaining favor, and the usefulness of passing grades has been questioned: apart from the national phenomenon of grade inflation, for example, grades are often awarded for reasons other than amount and quality of learning; there is great variability from instructor to instructor; and grades are too global to provide the detailed feedback on strengths and weaknesses that is required for improvement at either the individual or program level. Particularly in this area, online programs need to re-examine their current practice. A brief review of assessment literature citations on the "No Significant Difference" web site over the past 5 years reveals overwhelming reliance on grades and satisfaction surveys, both of which measures have serious drawbacks.

The analysis of learning based on high-quality, direct evidence has forced the development of new methods. Fifteen years ago, when postsecondary administrators heard the word assessment, they assumed they should buy a standardized test from ETS or ACT and report the normed scores; some still respond this way. However, since the dawn of the movement there has been a steady stream of criticism of standardized testing, its formats, underlying assumptions, and effects. Critics have included eminent educators such as Mentkowski and Astin [14], Darling-Hammond [15], Heffernan and colleagues [16], and Wiggins [13] among others. With its *Assessment Standards for School Mathematics* [17] the National Council of Teachers of Mathematics provided both a powerful critique and alternatives—in a discipline where standardized testing always seemed particularly unproblematic. The limitations of the standardized test format, lack of content validity, and failure of generic tests to generate information useful for local improvement, caused many institutions to abandon such efforts after a few years; others, like Truman State University, continue to use them but have adopted a policy of multiple methods and triangulation of results.

The other automatic reflex institutions had when told to assess was to cite survey results. Surveys and related approaches can be helpful in two ways. First, they can offer insight into what lies "behind outcomes" [18]. Useful information may be generated if the questionnaire is constructed to ask not just what students think they learned, but what helped or hindered them in learning it. Second, if survey results consistently show that students are dissatisfied with some aspect of their learning—development of writing skills, say, or ability to work with diverse individuals—then that is a clear signal that direct evidence in those areas needs to be examined.

As traditional methods such as surveys and standardized tests have been abandoned or scaled back, approaches more adequate to assessing complex outcomes have been developed. Early on, many faculty expressed a fear, not unfounded, that assessment would lead to reductive, behaviorist notions of learning and trivialize the mission of higher education. But what exactly is "higher education," and why are traditional methods such as commercial tests unequal to the task? There are many ways to define higher learning. They include Benjamin Bloom's well-known taxonomy of cognitive processes, which begins with "knowledge" and "comprehension," then moves up to more demanding intellectual activities such as "application," "analysis," "synthesis," and "evaluation" [19]. More recently, Bloom's taxonomy has been revised [20] so that analysis no longer appears as a lower-level cognitive process in relation to synthesis and evaluation. Constructivist approaches to learning suggest that students will zigzag up and down the hierarchy, rather than progressing up it in linear fashion.

Another approach is Entwhistle's distinction between "surface" and "deep" learning [21]. For Entwistle, surface learning remains at the level of unrelated bits of knowledge mastered through memorization and rote application of formulas, whereas deep learning involves seeing relationships and patterns, recognizing the logic behind the organization of material, and achieving a sense of understanding. There is the Perry Scheme of Intellectual Development [22], which maps students' progress from a dualistic right/wrong view of learning through multiplicity and relativism to commitment based on a fully developed and internalized value structure. Most provocative in my view, however, is Lauren Resnick's list of the characteristics of "higher order thinking" (Figure 2). Her list reflects the complexity and open-endedness, the contingency, of real-world dilemmas, whether in the workplace, civic or private life. The list also makes considerable demands on individuals, who must not only exercise their knowledge and skills but also qualities such as self-discipline, initiative, and an ability to tolerate ambiguity. *All* educators, I believe, whether in traditional or online environments, want their students to develop abilities such as these.

Higher order thinking . . .
• is nonalgorithmic. That is, the path of action is not fully specified in advance.
• is complex, i.e., the total path is not "visible" from any single vantage point.
• often yields multiple solutions, each with costs and benefits.
• requires nuanced judgment and interpretation.
• involves application of multiple criteria, which may conflict with one another.
• often involves uncertainty; not everything about the task is known or can be.
• requires self-regulation; someone else is not giving directions.
• involves making meaning, discerning patterns in apparent disorder.
• is effortful: the elaborations and judgments required entail considerable mental work and are likely to take time.
(adapted from L. Resnick, Education and Learning to Think, 1987) [23]

When we compare Bloom or Entwistle, Perry or particularly Resnick with the demands placed on students by a typical multiple-choice or true-false test, the shortcomings of such tests become obvious. The format is highly structured, and the items provide bits of information with no context. Students make a forced choice among possible answers, one of which is correct, and the tests essentially reward speed, recall, and test-taking savvy. Such tests do not tap students' problem-solving or thinking skills or ability to discriminate among "good" and "better" answers. They give students no opportunity to construct their own answers or demonstrate important traits such as persistence, creativity, or open-mindedness. Indeed,

190

such qualities may actually impair performance if they cause students to think too long about a single item or see multiple sides of what is supposed to be a straightforward question.

In her discussion of what she calls "epistemic development," Marra [24] argues that online educators need to become much more sensitive to the limitations as well as the potential of online learning environments to support sophisticated cognitive growth. Working from the Perry model, Marra asserts that "current online learning environments simply replicate the worst of face-to-face methodology" (p.18) when they follow traditional "teach-and-test" practices and reward students for employing "naïve beliefs" (p.19). Marra criticizes heavy reliance on quizzes and tests supplied by software makers that reinforce dualistic belief structures (such as, answers are either right or wrong), and discussions lacking evaluative support from the instructor. Her alternative is to create assignments that involve modeling, designing, decision making, problem solving, and other open-ended tasks that require high-level, integrative thinking and meaning making; she also recommends structured discussions that develop students' metacognitive awareness of argument, including such elements as hypothesis, data, conclusions, and counter-indications. Finally, Marra calls for more instructor awareness both of cognitive development and the activities that can be used to promote or assess it, along with more sophisticated online assessment tools and course management packages. In a similar vein, Dees argues that technology may afford even better opportunities than the traditional classroom for students to develop knowledge-construction skills or appreciation for the arts, but this is not a foregone conclusion [25]. See also Merisotis' call for more attention to critical thinking [26].

Marra's views are entirely consonant with the approaches to assessment emerging in the conventional classroom. These alternatives include capstone projects, portfolios, performances, and a wide variety of tasks embedded in everyday classroom procedure. The products that become evidence of learning may range from computer programs, research papers, business plans, actuarial projections, and engineering designs to a brochure written during an internship, or a diary of cultural observations kept during study abroad. Evidence can also include performances, live or recorded, e.g., responding to an in-box exercise, carrying out a laboratory procedure, giving a recital, teaching a class, critiquing a piece of art, or taking a medical history. Such products and performances may be generated in response to special "assessment" assignments, but it is more efficient and elicits a more representative level of student effort to simply embed them in the normal business of a course, as Alverno and Kings College have done [27]. (See Appendix 1 for a more detailed look at the advantages and disadvantages of alternative methods as well as locally developed and commercial tests.).

To make sense of student work and performance, it is necessary to develop criteria for *what* we are looking for. That is, general goal statements must be broken down into subgoals that specify various facets of the overarching goal, and rubrics must be created that describe *skill levels* for the criteria. The use of criteria and rubrics has exploded in the last five years, and many examples are now available on the web, at assessment conferences, or on request. With criteria and rubrics it becomes possible, for example, to look at the masses of material in a portfolio, and in a focused, efficient way find the characteristics that answer specific questions about students' achievement of learning goals. "The Rubric Processor" [24] is a particularly promising tool for creating rubrics, managing the information generated, and sharing it with students in both face-to-face and online courses.

Simply having evidence, however, is not the same as knowing what to do with it. In addition to the evidence, a *process* for interpreting and using it is needed. Interpretation, the third step on the assessment loop, is critical if tangible change is to come out of the previous two steps, yet it has frequently been minimized or left out altogether. The interpretive conversation needs to include the full range of voices that can provide insight into what the data may mean: faculty, of course, but also students, professional

191

staff, perhaps graduates or employers or faculty from neighboring institutions. Through inclusive dialogue, a campus can achieve a consensus; create campus-wide buy-in; facilitate communication about assessment; and educate faculty and staff. The interpretation step can also provide the bridge from assessment findings to academic planning and budgeting—a connection that must be made if assessment is to have any structural or systemic basis. The transformation of campus culture is impossible without interpretation.

Thus the "Nine Principles of Good Practice for Assessing Student Learning" [28] refer to the importance of broad representation at the assessment table in order to cross traditional boundaries (e.g., those between administrators and faculty, or individual departments and programs, or academic and student affairs, internal and external communities, or staff and students) and take a holistic look at student learning. In this respect the online environment offers both opportunities and challenges. Clearly electronic communication should make it easier to link and create virtual communities of interpretation. However, online learning and particularly ALN has an atomistic quality—isolated individuals, students and instructors alike, attending primarily to a single course with a unique community of learners who may never see each other—that may work at cross purposes with collective interpretation. Merisotis [26] in fact identifies the lack of studies of academic programs *in toto* as a major gap in research on e-learning.

Accreditation, finally, has played a key role in supporting assessment. In 1988, as the momentum for assessment was building, the US Department of Education promulgated new criteria for the recognition of all accrediting bodies. Commissions were to focus on "educational effectiveness" and determine whether institutions or programs could document students' educational achievement. In other words, a review of inputs and processes would no longer suffice. Accreditors responded by embracing these new expectations, which offered a means for accreditation to prove itself in the face of widespread criticism [29]. In the last 12 years, all 6 regional and most professional agencies (including AACSB and ABET) have revised their standards, sometimes radically, to emphasize student learning outcomes as the core of institutional review. Most institutions care deeply about accreditation, so linking assessment with accreditation meant a huge gain in status for assessment. Campuses invested in training for faculty and staff, assessment offices were created, coordinators hired, and mini-grants offered for assessment projects. The synergy between assessment and accreditation has thus contributed enormously to the development of human capital and structures to sustain assessment.

As assessment approaches its 20th birthday, it is a movement of considerable vitality. It has defined itself in a way that makes intuitive sense to educators, offers a powerful tool for improvement, and has helped in the task of reorienting campuses from teaching to learning, from teacher-centeredness to student-centeredness, as Barr and Tagg called upon the profession to do nearly a decade ago [30, 31]. Attendance at the last 3 AAHE assessment conferences has ranged between 1500 and 1800, and demand for other development opportunities such as the annual assessment institute at IUPUI, the workshops at Alverno College, and those offered by regional accreditors remains very strong. Disciplinary societies have begun to offer sessions and publish materials on assessment in their fields. There are countless pockets of good work, supported by countless faculty and staff. A web search for assessment plans, instruments, and the like will result in thousands of references. It is almost impossible to find an institution in the US today that has not been touched by the assessment movement in some way.

III. WHAT ARE THE CHALLENGES TO GOOD ASSESSMENT?

Despite its longevity and success, the assessment movement faces serious challenges. This section reviews some of the most important ones, beginning with practical problems and ending with more theoretical concerns.

First, despite nearly two decades of effort, we are still struggling to make assessment truly influential on campus, something more than isolated pockets of activity, more than a phenomenon a mile wide and one molecule deep. Of course there are exceptions, but consistent *use* of assessment findings—at classroom and program levels but even more at the level of planning, budgeting, and decision making—remains elusive. Accreditors (e.g., [32]) and national surveys as well as anecdotal evidence suggest that while virtually every institution is doing assessment in some form, it has had relatively little effect, particularly in the realm of higher order intellectual skills. The National Center for Postsecondary Improvement's survey of postsecondary institutions [33], for example, revealed that while the overwhelming majority reported collecting assessment data, only about one third assess higher-order learning or complex outcomes, and such data reportedly are seldom used for program improvement or decision making. In other words, there is compliance for accountability purposes, but little more. More recently, Ewell [4] has acknowledged with some chagrin that when pressed to cite studies of the difference assessment has made, he and other leaders in the field have little to point to beyond a handful of model institutions.

Another phenomenon, possibly related to the problem of modest impact, also bears watching. For years, a bimodal distribution of participants has characterized the attendance at assessment conferences: some attendees who know a great deal about assessment, and many more who come as novices and know little or nothing. The perennial problem for conference organizers has been how to serve both audiences and get them talking to each other. Now that pattern may be replicating itself on campus. The vast majority of faculty and administrators were not trained in assessment, they know little about it; many are suspicious; and even when intrigued, they generally believe they are too busy to take the time to learn. This is probably as true for online instructors as for those in the conventional classroom. The assessment movement thus faces a monumental re-education project. Meanwhile, a cadre of sophisticated assessment professionals is emerging, with a tendency to focus on the technical aspects (as opposed to the human process) of collecting data, generating reports, developing new software, managing information, and so on. While technical expertise is essential and very welcome, the movement cannot afford to become fixated on it. We need to keep the art in assessment and remember that ultimately it is human judgment, not science.

As a corollary of this caution, it is essential to keep focused on the real prize: understanding and improving student learning. Conference presentations and publications must focus not merely on how the assessment committee was chosen or why electronic portfolios were introduced, but on tangible *findings*: what, exactly, have campuses discovered about their students' quantitative skills or information literacy, their learning styles or ethical development, the more fine-grained differences between face-to-face and online learning, and what steps have led to improved outcomes. Only in this way can local discoveries have wider impact and support the scholarship of teaching and learning in specific disciplines.

Related to that small-bore focus on technical issues is the danger that we may lose sight of the bigger picture. In the early years of the movement, external pressures and non-academic actors were much in evidence, reminding us that higher education exists to serve the larger society. This reminder wasn't always welcome, but it was bracing and salutary, helping academics out of a dangerous isolation and false sense of autonomy. Of course, we may soon be forcibly reminded of that larger context. Indications are growing [34–39] that postsecondary education can expect sharper scrutiny at federal and state levels, most likely in a second Bush administration and possibly even earlier, as a campaign issue. We can anticipate a renewed emphasis on accountability with punitive overtones, and a renewed focus on standardized testing. The operative assumptions seem to be, first, that standardized testing is an effective model; and second, that higher education should have its equivalent of the No Child Left Behind Act. While online instruction may be cut a little more slack because of its innovativeness, such steps are likely to damage the improvement agenda and result in neglect of higher-order thinking, authenticity, and curricular or pedagogical reform for all programs, e-based or conventional. The challenge for educators will be to form a united front and deal responsibly with calls for accountability while protecting higher education

The next challenge is to maintain our honesty and humility. Whether online or in the classroom, we need to formulate goals that capture our most complex, demanding ambitions for students; we need to assess what *matters*, not just what is readily measurable. But at the same time, we need to be honest about the limitations of our current assessment technology. The fact is that at present, our technology is petty primitive. We are just beginning to explore what can be done with alternative, non-traditional methods such as portfolios, capstones or performances. We have barely begun to tap the potential of course management programs. We do not have a good single assessment method for complex outcomes today, and we may never have one. The point is that we need to raise our assessment technology to match the level of our educational ambitions for students. What we should *not* do, under any circumstances, is lower our educational ambitions for students to the level of current assessment technology.

Given those limitations, we must do no harm. We need to be conservative in drawing conclusions or taking actions that could have disastrous consequences. Of course it is legitimate to raise standards. But then it is essential to also provide the support and the setting in which it is possible to take risks, investigate real concerns, and exercise honesty, humility, self-reflection, and improvement. We cannot afford an environment in which these qualities are suicidal for individuals or institutions. Otherwise, there will be gamesmanship in the interests of raising the score, but no improvement in real learning. And we cannot afford to be silent about these concerns when the debate goes public.

The greatest challenge of all is to our courage in the face of a needed paradigm shift. Higher education and policymakers alike need to entertain a new notion of accountability, one able to capture complexity and ambiguity instead of dealing in 2-digit data points and deceptive clarity. We need a new notion of accountability, one that does not rely exclusively on quantitative data or comparisons among institutions but rather is *also* qualitative, descriptive, seeks understanding of the issues and improvement, respects institutional differences and acknowledges, as Albert Einstein phrased it, that not everything that can be counted counts, and not everything that counts can be counted.

Within the assessment community and especially beyond it, we need a notion of accountability that *serves* improvement instead of undermining it. The contemporary notion of accountability relies heavily on the positivistic assumptions of quantitative research, with its reliance on a natural science worldview, its biases in favor of "objective," "outsider" measurements, its attempts to control variables and capture "the truth," its ambition to achieve generalizability. A qualitative approach to accountability will be more phenomenological and descriptive, it will value the "insider" perspective, and it will be as interested in process, discovery, and explanation as it is in outcomes or confirmation of predictions. It will have a place for what is unique or of limited generalizability, and seek "truthfulness" in a given context rather than "the truth." We need a kind of accountability that includes measurement, but also makes use of demonstrations, documentation, evidence of *all* kinds, and relies in the end on human judgment to make meaning.

This is a daunting list of challenges, but with persistence, intelligence, and "pragmatic idealism," in Peter Senge's words, we can succeed.

IV. REFERENCES

1. **Wright, B.** Assessing Student Learning. *Learning from Change: Landmarks in Teaching and Learning in Higher Education from Change Magazine, 1969–1999*, DeZure, D., ed., 299–304. Sterling, VA: Stylus Publishing, 2000.

2. **Ewell, P. T.** To Capture the Ineffable: New Forms of Assessment in Higher Education. *Reprise 1991: Reprints of Two Papers Treating Assessment's History and Implementation*. Washington, DC: AAHE, 1991.

3. **Alexander, L., Clinton, B., and Kean, T. H.** A Time for Results. *The Governors' 1991 Report on Education*. Washington, DC: National Governors' Association, 1991.

4. **Hutchings, P. and Marchese, T. J.** Watching Assessment: Questions, Stories, Prospects. *Reprise 1991: Reprints of Two Papers Treating Assessment's History and Implementation*, 47–71. Washington, DC: AAHE Assessment Forum, 1991.

5. **Ewell, P. T.** Perpetual Movement: Assessment After Twenty Years. Unpublished paper. Boston: AAHE Assessment Conference, 2002.

6. **Maki, P. L.** Developing an Assessment Plan to Learn About Student Learning. AAHE, 2002. http://www.aahe.org/assessmentplan.htm.

7. **Palomba, C.A. and Banta, T. W.** *Assessment Essentials. Planning, Implementing and Improving Assessment in Higher Education*. San Francisco: Jossey-Bass, 1999.

8. **US Department of Education.** A Nation At Risk: The Imperative for Educational Reform. A Report to the Nation and the Secretary of Education. Washington, DC: US Government Printing Office, 1983.

9. **Association of American Colleges.** Integrity in the College Curriculum. A Report to the Academic Community. Washington, DC: Association of American Colleges, 1985.

10. **National Institute of Education.** Involvement in Learning: Realizing the Potential of American Higher Education. Report of the Study Group on the Conditions of Excellence in American Higher Education. Washington, DC: US Government Printing Office, 1984.

11. **Bennett, W.** To Reclaim a Legacy. Washington, DC: National Endowment for the Humanities, 1984.

12. **Hirsch, E. D.** *Cultural Literacy: What Every American Needs to Know*. New York: Houghton Mifflin, 1989.

13. **El-Khawas, E.** Campus Trends Survey. Washington, DC: American Council on Education, 1990.

14. **Wiggins, G.** Feedback—How Learning Occurs. *AAHE Bulletin* 50(3): 7–8, 1997.

15. **Mentkowski, M., Astin, A. W., Ewell, P. T. and Moran, E.T.** Catching Theory Up With Practice: Conceptual Frameworks for Assessment with a Foreword by K. Patricia Cross. Washington, DC: AAHE Assessment Forum, 1991.

16. **Darling-Hammond, L.** Assessment and Incentives: The Medium Is the Message. Three Presentations: From the Third National Conference on Assessment in Higher Education, Hutchings, P. ed., 1–14. Washington, DC: AAHE, 1988.

17. **Heffernan, J. M., Hutchings, P., and Marchese, T. J.** Standardized Tests and the Purposes of Assessment. Washington, DC: AAHE Assessment Forum, 1988.

18. **National Council of Teachers of Mathematics.** Assessment Standards for School Mathematics. Washington, DC: National Council of Teachers of Mathematics, 1995.

19. **Hutchings, P.** Behind Outcomes: Contexts and Questions for Assessment. Washington, DC: AAHE Assessment Forum, 1989.

20. **Bloom. B. S., ed.** *A Taxonomy of Educational Objective: The Classification of Educational Goals*. New York: D. McKay Co., 1956.

21. **Anderson, L. W. and Krathwohl, D., eds.** *A Taxonomy for Learning, Teaching and Assessing: A Revision of Bloom's Taxonomy of Educational Objectives*. New York: Longman, 2001.

22. **Entwistle, N.** Promoting Deep Learning through Teaching and Assessment. Assessment to Promote Deep Learning. Insight from AAHE's 2000 and 1999 Assessment Conferences, Suskie, L., ed., 9–20. Washington, DC: American Association for Higher Education, 2001.

23. **Perry, W. G.** *Forms of Intellectual and Ethical Development in the College Years.* New York: Holt, Rinehart and Winston, 1970.

24. **Resnick, L. B.** *Education and Learning to Think.* Washington, DC: National Academy Press, 1987.

25. **Marra, R. M.** The Ideal Online Learning Environment for Supporting Epistemic Development. *Quarterly Review of Distance Education* 3(1): 27, 2002.

26. **Dees, S.** Measuring Success in the Virtual University. *Journal of Academic Librarianship* 28(1–2): 47–53, 2002.

27. **Merisotis, J. P., Phipps, R. A.** What's the Difference? Outcomes of Distance vs. Traditional Classroom-Based Learning. *Change Magazine* 31(3): 12–17, 1999.

28. **Farmer, D. W.** Course-Embedded Assessment: A Catalyst for Realizing the Paradigm Shift from Teaching to Learning. *Journal of Staff, Program and Organization Development* 16(4): 199–211, 1999.

29. **American Association for Higher Education**, Nine Principles of Good Practice for Assessing Student Learning. Washington, DC: AAHE, 1992. http://www.aahe.org/assessment/principl.htm.

30. **Wright, B.** Accreditation and the Scholarship of Assessment. In *Building a Scholarship of Assessment*, Banta, T.W. and Associates, 240–258. San Francisco: Jossey-Bass, 2002.

31. **Barr, R. B., and Tagg, J.** From Teaching to Learning: A New Paradigm for Undergraduate Education. *Change Magazine* November/December:12–25, 1995.

32. **Tagg, J.** *The Learning Paradigm College.* Bolton, MA: Anker Publishing, 2003.

33. **Burd, S.** Accountability or Meddling? *Chronicle of Higher Education* 49(4): 9/20/02.

34. **López, C. L.** *A Decade of Assessing Student Learning: What We Have Learned; What's Next?* Chicago, IL: North Central Association, 1999.

35. **National Center for Postsecondary Improvement.** Revolution or Evolution? Gauging the Impact of Institutional Student Assessment Strategies. *Change Magazine* 31(5): 53–56, 1999.

36. **Burd, S.** Bush's Next Target? *Chronicle of Higher Education* 49(44): 7/11/03.

37. **Burd, S.** Colleges Catch a Glimpse of Bush Policy on Higher Education and Aren't Pleased. *Chronicle of Higher Education* 48(26): 3/8/02.

38. **Burd, S.** Education Department Hears Appeals to Make Colleges More Accountable for Student Performance. *Chronicle of Higher Education* 49(26): 3/10/03.

39. **Burd, S.** Will Congress Require Colleges to Grade Themselves? *Chronicle of Higher Education* 49(30): 4/4/03.

40. **López, C. L.** Assessment of Student Learning: Challenges and Strategies. *Journal of Academic Librarianship* 28(6): 356–67, 2002.

41. **Morgan, R.** Report Calls for Major Research Effort Into How to Improve Higher Education. *Chronicle of Higher Education*: 11/26/02.

V. ABOUT THE AUTHOR

Barbara Wright currently coordinates assessment efforts at Eastern Connecticut State University. Prior to that, she served for over 25 years as a faculty member in German at the University of Connecticut. Although her graduate training was in German language and literature of the 16th, 17th, and early 20th centuries, her interests have expanded over the years to include language acquisition and communicative language methods, women's studies, curricular reform, general education, and assessment. From 1988 to 1990 she directed a FIPSE-funded project to assess a new general education curriculum at the University of Connecticut, and from 1990 to 1992 she served as director of the American Association for Higher Education's Assessment Forum. From 1995 to 2001 she was a member of the New England Association of Schools and Colleges' Commission on Institutions of Higher Education, and she has participated in team visits for several regional accreditors. She has published on assessment and is frequently invited to campuses to speak and conduct workshops. She is especially interested in qualitative approaches to the assessment of general education's more challenging, seemingly ineffable goals. Contact: Barbara D. Wright, Assessment Coordinator, Eastern Connecticut State University, Willimantic, CT 06226. E-mail: wrightb@easternct.edu

ACHIEVING QUALITY AND SCALE IN ONLINE EDUCATION THROUGH TRANSFORMATIVE ASSESSMENT: A CASE STUDY

Jacqueline Moloney
Steven Tello
Continuing, Corporate and Distance Education
University of Massachusetts Lowell

- Assessment is an iterative process that leads to continuous improvement of teaching and learning.

- Assessment should be guided by a purpose that reflects institutional mission, goals and objectives.

- Assessment engages an expanding circle of participants, including faculty, students, administrators and community members.

- Assessment collects, analyzes, and applies data in a manner that contributes to improvements in student learning.

- Assessment of online education presents unique challenges and unique opportunities that offer a powerful potential to transform student learning, programs and institutions.

I. INTRODUCTION

Assessment of higher education is rapidly changing as faculty, administrators and other stakeholders grapple with the public's demand for accountability and the academy's own desire to improve. Best practices in assessment strategies continue to evolve in a field that is no longer focused on evaluation of students, programs and institutions, but rather on the continuous improvement or transformation of the same. At the same time, alternatives to traditional higher education, such as online education, have emerged that present unique challenges and exciting opportunities in assessment. One way to discover and unlock the powerful potential of those innovations is through transformative assessment that focuses on the use of systematic inquiry of student learning to build program and institutional quality. In this article, we present a case study that:

- Demonstrates how current theories of transformative assessment, coupled with research on online education, may be used to create a framework for transformative assessment of online programs;

- Demonstrates the potential of transformative assessment for contributing to the development of scalability and quality of online education programs;

- Provides examples of how the powerful combination of transformative assessment and online education can transform mainstream student learning, programs, and institutions;

- Identifies future challenges and opportunities with transformative assessment and online education.

II. BACKGROUND ON ASSESSMENT

Much of the current thinking on assessment in higher education can be traced to the nine principles set forth by the American Association of Higher Education and its Assessment Forum [1](AAHE, 2003). The principles, captured in *Assessment Essentials* [2] stress the importance of planning, a focus on student learning, engagement of key stakeholders and a process for bringing about continuous improvement by applying assessment findings (p.15). Throughout their work, Palomba, Banta and others stress the importance of "viewing the assessment process itself as dynamic rather than fixed" [2, p. 17], [3].

Building on the AAHE work, The North Central Association of Schools and Colleges' Higher Learning Commission (NCA) created a tool to assist institutions in their region to study institutional assessment programs. The tool, called *Levels of Implementation*, provides a ranking system that characterizes assessment programs along a continuum from Beginning, to Making Progress, to Maturing Stages of Assessment [4]. Suggested qualities and characteristics at each level are defined around institutional culture, shared responsibility, institutional support and efficacy of the assessment program. Institutions are encouraged to move from Level I-Beginning, where there is 'no shared understanding of the purpose of assessment,' to Level III-Maturing, where 'assessment has become a way of life'. Common to both of the above models is a focus on student learning and continuous improvement of teaching, programs and institutions.

While much of this work has focused on traditional student populations, there are emerging national initiatives such as the National Learning Infrastructure Initiative (NLII) committed to the assessment of the use of technology to improve teaching and learning [5]. In collaboration with the AAHE, the Flashlight Project of the Teaching and Learning with Technology Group and the Coalition for Networked Information, the NLII is mid-way through a three-year study, called the Transformative Assessment Project (TAP), which examines how systematic assessment of teaching with technology initiatives can result in institutional transformation [5]. The TAP has developed a useful rubric for examining the *purpose of the assessment*, the *type and method of data collection, application of assessment results*, and *dissemination activities* along a continuum from Administrative, to Progressive, to Transformative outcomes. The TAP continuum parallels the NCA's Levels of Implementation ranking and again emphasizes that assessment should be conducted to continuously improve student learning and ensure programmatic and institutional growth.

The opportunity to pair transformative assessment with online education is significant and increasingly critical as student participation in this learning environment continues to outpace growth in all other sectors of higher education. Asynchronous learning networks (ALNs) currently represent the most popular form of online education in this country, with 90% of 2 and 4-year institutions offering distance education courses asynchronously [6]. Sloan-C, a consortium of over 500 colleges and universities and the leading online education organization, has developed a framework for assessing the quality of online education programs based on access, learning effectiveness, cost effectiveness, faculty satisfaction and student satisfaction [7]. By integrating a transformative assessment framework with the Sloan-C pillars, programs may realize the full potential for online education to transform their institutions.

A synthesis of the above scholarship reveals five principles underlying transformative assessment that can help institutions realize the potential of online education to improve student learning and transform their institutions.

1. Assessment is an iterative process that leads to continuous improvement of teaching and learning.
2. Assessment should be guided by a purpose that reflects institutional mission, goals and objectives.
3. Assessment engages an expanding circle of participants, including faculty, students, administrators and community members.
4. Assessment collects, analyzes, and applies data in a manner that contributes to improvements in student learning.
5. Assessment of online education presents unique challenges and unique opportunities that offer a powerful potential to transform student learning, programs and institutions.

Figure 1 depicts our vision of how these principles may be operationalized.

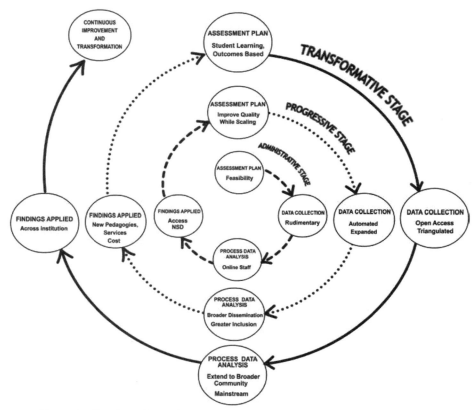

Figure 1: The Transformative Assessment Process, © Moloney and Tello, 2003

Using the terminology presented in the TAP rubric, an institution or program begins at the Administrative Stage (center of Fig. 1) where data is collected and studied by a limited number of stakeholders. Findings are applied to make improvements and adjustments in the assessment process itself so that the institution can evolve to the Progressive Stage. At the Progressive Stage, the purpose and process are informed by a much broader constituency which helps to lead to a deeper questioning of the assessment of quality and of teaching and learning. Application of the findings leads to improvements in access, learning effectiveness and cost effectiveness and, when shared with an even broader community, evolves the institution to the Transformative Assessment Stage. At the Transformative Stage, assessment is integrated into the culture of the institution where all goals and objectives are uniformly assessed and the results are applied to achieve continuous improvement.

III. BACKGROUND ON THE CASE

The case study presented to illustrate an online program's evolution in the Transformative Assessment process is based on the authors' seven years experience as founders and directors of the online program at the University of Massachusetts Lowell (UMass Lowell, or UML). UMass Lowell's online education program started small with the hope of identifying new markets to expand access and bring needed revenues to the campus. The Division of Continuing, Corporate and Distance Education (CCDE) was charged with developing Lowell's online program to achieve those goals. The online program at UMass Lowell now offers 6 full degree programs with approximately 6400 enrollments per year, is one of the largest in New England and is a major contributor to UMassOnline (UMOL), UMass' system-wide portal for online education. The UMass Lowell online program is entirely self-supporting and returns significant revenues to the campus and UMOL to seed continuous growth [8].

The study is a retrospective of the transformation of the program as a result of ongoing assessment that increasingly focused on student learning. The organizing principles outlined above served as a guide for forming the assessment plan and the Sloan-C pillars emerged as essential considerations in designing the program. The case will be presented along the continuum suggested by TAP: Administrative, Progressive and Transformative. We will outline the purpose, method, findings, and application of the findings for each stage of the assessment process based on a format proposed by Banta, Lund, Black, and Oblander [9]. The findings will be summarized according to 3 of the 5 pillars: Access, Learning Effectiveness, and Cost Effectiveness and discussion of the final two pillars, Faculty Satisfaction and Student Satisfaction, will be woven throughout the study as essential metrics for our assessment program.

IV. STAGES OF ASSESSMENT

A. Administrative Assessment Stage: Feasibility

A plan to continuously assess the quality of the online education program at UMass Lowell was set in place from the outset in 1996. The focus of this initial plan was evaluative in nature and could be characterized in the TAP/NCA categories of Administrative or Beginning. A shared institutional understanding of the assessment program was not in place; there was no focus on meaningful assessment of student learning outcomes, or a process for engaging a broader community. There was however, an intent to apply the findings to expand the program and to improve the quality of student learning. This last characteristic is what enabled our assessment plan to evolve from the administrative stage to a more progressive approach that will be discussed in Section B below.

1. Assessment Purpose

At this stage, the purpose of the assessment plan was to conduct comparative research examining the feasibility of using online education to provide quality access and learning to students equal to on-campus face to face programs. Like many institutions experimenting with online education, the 'no significant difference' benchmark for comparing distance education with face to face education had to be established to achieve credibility with the faculty and administration [10, 11]. Only then, could plans for scaling the program to increase access, improve quality of learning and enhance revenues for the campus be considered.

2. Data Collection

To address the feasibility question for online education, we had to collect a great deal of data around the technical competency of students and faculty, the adequacy of their hardware and software and of our technical support services. Data was collected from a review of student technical support requests, student administrative communications and a review of student petitions for refunds.

To assess learning effectiveness, the data collected at this stage paralleled what we were using to evaluate student performance in our face to face courses. To establish the 'no significant difference' benchmark, faculty administered the same kinds of tests, projects and writing assignments as they did with their face to face courses to assess student learning. Grade distribution and retention data were examined to ensure that online students were achieving at the same level as their face to face counterparts. Overall student satisfaction was assessed through course evaluations created for face to face courses and simply posted online at the end of the semester. Course enrollment trends were also collected and studied for indications of student satisfaction and market analysis.

During this start-up phase, we were aware of the need to collect data around cost effectiveness, yet we had no pre-existing mechanisms in place to examine course development costs (including intellectual property), infrastructure development or staff expansion. Therefore, cost assessment that "integrates learning impact with cost efficiencies" (a TAP characteristic) was delayed until the Progressive Assessment Stage.

3. Data Analysis

Only the professionals responsible for developing the online program conducted the data collection and analysis. Summarized data was then shared with the online faculty who had an opportunity to respond to the analysis, but were not involved in the formation of initial research questions or the interpretation of the data. The NCA Level I of Implementation characterizes this pattern where "…faculty are not engaged in assessment activities that get to the core of measuring student-learning outcomes." [4, p. 19].

4. Findings and Application of the Findings

In this section we present our Administrative Stage findings and how they were applied to make improvements, and highlight discoveries unique to online education. Using the Sloan-C pillars as the organizing framework, we will present our analysis of the impact of our assessment activities around learning effectiveness, access and cost effectiveness, again, student satisfaction and faculty satisfaction are woven throughout the discussion.

a. Improvements in Access

According to Sloan-C, the access pillar ensures that *"all learners who wish to learn online have the opportunity and can achieve success."* This pillar focuses on technical access as well as access to courses and programs and student services [12]. Assessment findings on technology access indicated that although students were satisfied in general with the program (75% indicated they would take another online course), they were frustrated by the technology including lost dial-up connections, access to chat and their own limited understanding of browser and email software. These findings resulted in the expansion of online technical support hours, the addition of a toll-free support telephone, an online technical support Webboard and online "Help" tutorials, and the development of an online orientation that addressed frequently asked questions and outlined hardware and software requirements.

In terms of access to courses and programs, scans of enrollment data showed that student demand exceeded course availability in volume and content. Students also expressed a need for fully online degrees. As a result, we launched our first online certificates and degree, the Bachelor of Science in Information Technology (IT) and developed a plan to migrate only courses and certificates in this degree program. This decision helped support the large-scale growth of the UMass Lowell online program.

b. Improvements in Learning Effectiveness

The Learning Effectiveness pillar maintains that *"learners who complete an online program receive educations that represent the distinctive quality of the institution"*. Not surprisingly, our studies proved that we achieved the "no significant difference" benchmark in grades and final course evaluations between students in face-to-face and online/distance education courses, consistent with the literature on this topic [10, 11, 13, 14, 15]. What was surprising was given our "novice" status as online providers in the 1996 – 1997 period, both online students and faculty expressed such high levels of satisfaction with our online program. Despite the limitations of the technology and our crude learning management system, on average, 77% of online students indicated a high to very high degree of satisfaction with their courses and 95% of the online faculty, asked to continue to teach online in future semesters. These findings exceeded our expectations, and we began to wonder why.

While flexibility and convenience were obvious explanations, we were also hearing faculty and students talk about increased interaction in their online courses; and faculty began questioning traditional assumptions about seat-time, their roles as instructors (lecturer versus facilitator) and the evaluation of student learning. For example, knowing that online multiple choice exams could be taken by anyone at the other end of the computer terminal, some faculty began to wonder about their true value in assessing student performance. While faculty were reportedly pleasantly surprised by the amount of interaction in their online courses, they wondered how much of it was improving their students' learning and expressed concerns about the limitations of the learning management system. We knew we had access to a wealth of data to assist in the study of these dynamics such as online lecture notes, PowerPoint presentations and student communication archives, yet we needed faculty input to frame the questions and guide the process in a meaningful way. As a result, consistent with the TAP/NCA recommendations, we greatly expanded faculty participation in the assessment process.

c. Cost Effectiveness

Course enrollment trends and student satisfaction data offered ample evidence of the potential of the online education program to expand access and generate new revenues. At the same time, the costs for implementing these findings to improve learning effectiveness and access were daunting. As a result, an assessment plan was implemented in the Progressive Stage to collect data regarding the cost of course development, faculty development, infrastructure and human resources.

B. Progressive Assessment Stage: Quality and Scalability

The realization that students and faculty were satisfied with their online experience, combined with our access to new kinds of data, ignited our assessment activities as new questions about learning effectiveness, access and cost effectiveness emerged.

1. Redefining the Purpose for Progressive Assessment

The purpose of assessment during the Progressive Stage became more focused on *how to improve the quality of student learning while expanding the program and the return on investment to the campus.* Based on Administrative Stage findings, a strategic plan for the expansion of the online program was created with program objectives and targeted benchmarks to help assess our progress toward the goals of the plan. The objectives were similar to the pillars and included: a) expanded access to online course offerings, certificates and degrees, and support services (both technical and academic); b) improved instructional design to enhance student learning or learning effectiveness and c) standardized cost analysis for developing courses, programs and delivery of the same.

2. Data Collection

Each objective outlined above was mapped to a set of data to measure our progress under each benchmark. Student surveys were revised to aid data collection on access issues as well as learning effectiveness. For example, we revised the course evaluation to assess the effectiveness of communication tools to achieve interaction and build learning communities. Data collection was automated by developing protocols for querying course communications and online surveys to parse data directly into spreadsheets. These enhancements facilitated a more scholarly approach to assessment and made possible a number of important studies. For example a doctoral study, conducted by co-author Steven Tello [16], examined the relationship between interaction in online courses, student satisfaction and student retention—a study that could not have happened without the archived data which was triangulated with telephone interviews and other qualitative methods.

To better assess faculty needs for support and development, surveys of faculty satisfaction with both their online teaching and course development experience were initiated. In particular, we were interested in examining data on the time it took to develop and teach online courses as well as technical and learning effectiveness challenges encountered by online faculty.

Cost effectiveness data was collected from several sources, including course enrollment and tuition records, faculty teaching and development stipends, faculty development and support staff, technology infrastructure costs and division overhead analysis. This analysis laid the groundwork for a strategy to track the return on investment in the online program.

3. Process for Data Analysis

The process for analyzing the data was greatly expanded and formal procedures were established to share the information with a much broader audience. Faculty participation in the assessment of data increased significantly and over 70% of the online faculty reviewed evidence of student satisfaction, grade distribution, retention and course enrollment trend data.

In addition to open meetings with online faculty, we invited our learning management system vendor and other administrators to explore how to improve the quality of our online program. Faculty, online professionals and our LMS vendor discussed assessment findings as a team and examined programmatic and pedagogical challenges, alternative interpretations of the findings, and then collectively defined the next set of questions. This public discussion of the teaching learning dynamic was transformational as faculty examined data in a public forum, for many a first in their teaching careers.

4. Findings and Application of the Findings:

By expanding the kind of data collected and the process for engaging the faculty in particular, our program began to yield the powerful impact of assessment as an educational tool. The more that faculty worked with technical support staff, administrators and the learning management vendor, the more significant our improvements turned out to be and the improvements began to focus more and more on improvements in student learning.

a. Improvements in Access

The data on access to technology and student services indicated that though we had made great strides in creating stability in the infrastructure and technical support, we needed a more efficient, user-friendly, electronic approach to academic services such as advising, registration and library services. A cross-functional team composed of faculty, staff and administrators was created and all student applications, forms and services were moved online. Support staff were retrained to deliver services electronically and within a year we noted an improvement in student satisfaction with these services. This cross-functional approach to improving student access for online students began a process for mainstreaming these changes and enhancing services to face-to-face students as well.

Student demand for online degrees continued to rise so we launched a second degree, the Bachelor of Liberal Arts (BLA) and several related certificates. All faculty and course development resources were applied to migrating these two degree programs (75 courses) online which was accomplished within two years. Based on faculty and student surveys that revealed dissatisfaction with student technical preparedness for taking online courses, our face-to-face student orientation was redesigned for online students and expanded to include detailed technical and pedagogical considerations for students taking online courses.

The findings from the doctoral research study described above showed that students' family and work commitments and the student's enrollment in a certificate or degree program were all factors contributing to a student's decision to persist or withdraw from a course. The study also found that despite the online orientation program, students' expectations for their online learning experience didn't match their actual experience. Based on these findings a brief online quiz was developed to enable students to assess their own readiness for online education (available online at http://continuinged.uml.edu/online/123.htm). The quiz examines a student's technical knowledge, learning style and ability to manage time—all factors that appear to contribute to student success in online education.

b. Improvements in Cost Effectiveness

During this stage, considerations of access, learning effectiveness, faculty satisfaction and student satisfaction were considered in the context of costs, bringing a much needed business discipline to our planning. As we moved to a full cost-accounting of the online program and broke out costs for instruction, faculty development, course development, technology, marketing and other division overhead, we were able to make informed decisions about which programs to develop and what staff, faculty and technology resources were needed to support it. In addition to guiding investments, the cost effectiveness data assisted in establishing guidelines for faculty compensation, royalty fees, course minimum and maximum enrollments, and related policies.

The creation of a budget template that aggregated expenses and revenues provided evidence that the program was exceeding the targeted return on investment and enabled the program to grow at a rate of nearly 75% for two consecutive years while generating new revenues for the campus. These findings, shared with departmental faculty, academic deans and the Chancellor, brought new enthusiasm for the program and a commitment to seed new development. However, the fiscal discipline that this process imposed on the process drew some faculty resistance and we realized that we needed mechanisms to engage the faculty deeper in the assessment of cost effectiveness as suggested in the TAP and NCA assessment rubrics.

C. Transformative Assessment Stage: Continuous Improvement

Over the past three years we have made tremendous gains in maturing our assessment program and are now poised to enter the Transformative Assessment Stage. This stage is challenging to enter and even more challenging to sustain as it requires an institution-wide commitment to the development and growth of a learning community while maintaining an ultimate focus on the assessment of student learning.

1. Purpose

While we continue to study how we can improve the quality of learning and expand enrollments, we now continuously explore new ways of applying what we are learning from assessment to bring about institutional improvements in access, learning effectiveness, and cost effectiveness. As such, the purpose of our assessment program has evolved from establishing the feasibility of online education in the Administrative Stage to transforming the institution by mainstreaming the best of what we have learned from our online education program.

2. Data Collection

At each stage of the assessment process, we have built on the data collection efforts in the previous stages. As such, student surveys continue to be a reliable and efficient method of collecting data and are heavily utilized to study access, learning effectiveness and cost effectiveness. Similarly, technical access data continue to be collected through online technical support forms, a technical support discussion forum, and monthly usage reports.

Input from the faculty in previous stages resulted in dramatic changes in our capacity to assess learning effectiveness and holds tremendous promise for improving student learning. For example, technical changes to our course management system now enable us to customize surveys based on specific course and discipline needs. Faculty are taking advantage of automated reports on student discussion and chat participation to assess student learning. Additionally, more instructors have introduced formative assessment strategies, building on assignments, rather than administering one multiple-choice exam at the mid-term and conclusion of their courses.

To strengthen our ability to assess student learning, we have begun to collect data on the content of course syllabi to determine what percent conform to Division standards for statements of course goals, learning outcomes, course requirements and detailed grading criteria. This effort is integrated with a faculty development effort to encourage more faculty to incorporate formative assessment strategies into their courses to reinforce our commitment to developing learning through assessment. An expanded faculty survey now enables us to collect data on the progress the division has made in these areas as well as to assess the carry over of effective online teaching strategies to face to face courses. The survey continues to query faculty on satisfaction with course migration, training and other development services and needs. Data on faculty satisfaction are also collected through interviews, at open meetings and other important qualitative venues.

To expand student participation in the assessment process, a recommendation by NCA and TAP, the student graduation interview process, previously designed for face-to-face students, is being redesigned to collect more pertinent and qualitative data from online students. Data regarding community and corporate educational needs are now routinely collected as part of our program development process and include needs assessment of students at companies and educational organizations.

In addition to the full-cost accounting data collected in the Progressive Stage, a new template to assess cost effectiveness at the program level has been implemented. These data along with enrollment trends, are factored into Division and University budgetary data to determine revenue, expense and net ratio targets in the 5 year strategic plan.

3. Process for Data Analysis

Our process for analyzing data has evolved from a closed, limited review in the Administrative Stage to an open, inclusive process in this Transformative Stage. Faculty are now actively involved in setting the assessment agenda, conducting studies and influencing the development of the online program. This high level engagement of the faculty has significantly enhanced the impact of assessment on continuous improvements in course design, instruction and program development.

The process for engaging the faculty has been encouraged in two ways. First, by enabling the faculty to conduct scholarly research related to the assessment process, several of the faculty have published their findings in professional publications and enhanced their professional portfolios while contributing to the developing literature on this topic. Second, we have provided additional compensation to several faculty to expand and formalize data collection, analysis and dissemination. This has helped to institutionalize assessment by cultivating a pipeline of assessment experts who are able to advance our assessment program continuously.

4. Findings and Application of the Findings

a. Improvements in Access

As our online program and institution transitions into the Transformative Stage, we have found that online students and faculty are much better prepared in terms of Internet connectivity, hardware and software skills than they were two years ago. Over 63% of our online students have high speed Internet access, suggesting the possibility of increasing the use of bandwidth intensive media and communications tools in our online courses. However, any decision regarding changes in technology platforms or media must now be assessed for its potential impact on access, learning, and cost effectiveness, an example of the integration of assessment activities.

The changes brought about as a result of earlier assessment stages have dramatically increased online student and faculty satisfaction with both technical access and technical support. In AY 2003, 98% of students and 98% of faculty indicated that the course website was available when they needed to engage in course related activities. Approximately 16% of online students have made use of technical support services over the past year and 90% of these have indicated the services helped to promptly resolve their technical issues. An AY2003 survey of all online faculty indicates that 100% of faculty agree that technical support staff quickly helped to resolve their technical issues.

Application of the Progressive Stage findings on student services has resulted in increasing demands from face to face students and faculty for the kind of user-friendly, automated services now provided to our online populations. As a result, all of CCDE faculty and student services have been redesigned, and now online and face to face students have integrated access to quality academic services. Further, findings on access needs are now being integrated into the campus' migration to its new student records system, again an example of the transformative impact of the assessment program on the institution.

Student survey data also revealed an increasing need for accelerated semesters and for expanded access to programs at the graduate level. Since many faculty had already discovered that the 14 week semester was no longer necessary in the online environment, they, the academic deans and the Chancellor agreed to pilot a 10 week semester in Fall 2003. Additionally, several face-to-face courses will be offered in the same timeline with blended online supplemental instructional activities. To respond to the need for online graduate level programs, the faculty initiated three online graduate certificates followed by three online masters degrees, and finally, in 2003, our first online doctoral program. Drawing on our assessment findings, we developed a comprehensive business plan in collaboration with the sponsoring departments to launch each of these degrees while sponsoring departments received grants to launch the degrees that enabled them to add staff and faculty support.

b. Improvements in Learning Effectiveness

Characteristic of the Transformative Assessment Stage, we continue to deepen the focus of assessment on student learning and continuous improvement. Toward these ends, the first degree launched under the seed grant program described above is our first truly outcomes-based program which is described below. Best practices in online education, as defined by the faculty and professionals at UML, are making their way into the mainstream of the institution, transforming the way we think about teaching, learning and assessment.

Outcomes-based Program Development

The Masters of Education in Educational Administration represents the first online graduate degree developed at the University, designed around student learning outcomes and based on community and student needs. Partially funded with a grant from the Sloan Foundation, the Graduate School of Education developed the program to address a shortage of school administrators and prepare students for K–12 Principal certification in the state of Massachusetts. Each course is designed to prepare students to be transformational leaders in their school systems and to pass a state certification exam. The first graduates of this program are just entering their final semester, which includes a year long, field-based practicum in School Leadership that will result in a portfolio of the student's achievements in the program. In addition to all of the assessment activities outlined above, the success of this program will be measured by our students' ability to meet state certification requirements. This program has also been customized for the Lawrence Public Schools, an inner-city school system challenged to improve student test scores and ranking by the state Department of Education. Ultimately, the true assessment of the effectiveness of this online program will be the improvement of student learning in the school system. Again, this program characterizes the TAP and NCA definitions for transformational assessment.

The Online Teaching Institute

The UMass Lowell Online Teaching Institute is another example of how a training project initially introduced to support online courses in CCDE has expanded its role and services to support effective online teaching across the institution, UMass system and region. The Institute emphasizes the development of effective teaching strategies for online courses through a sequence of online workshops, face-to-face trainings, and ongoing pedagogical and technical support. This cost effective approach has resulted in the development of over 300 online courses at UMass Lowell, and an annual online enrollment of 6400 students. Table 1 summarizes the impact of Institute training and development activities at UMass Lowell.

Table 1. Impact of Online Teaching Institute

	AY2000	AY 2001	AY 2002	AY 2003
Faculty Trained	55	101	126	108
New Courses Developed	26	37	44	34
Total Online Courses	115	210	264	293
Total Online Enrollments	2564	4371	5428	6374

Though the Institute was launched to migrate online courses for CCDE, demand from traditional face to face faculty grew as word of the Institutes successes spread among faculty. To respond to this demand, the Institute, in collaboration with the UML Faculty Teaching Center, now provides on-going seminars open to all UMass Lowell faculty. As a result, approximately 150 web-enhanced courses in the undergraduate and graduate day programs have been developed at little cost to the institution. Perhaps more importantly, 84% of faculty participating in Institute training activities in AY 2003 indicate their face-to-face teaching was enhanced by this training. These joint training programs helped move Institute offerings beyond technical discussions of chat tools and course management systems to workshops which explore deeper issues regarding the development of online course objectives, student assessment across disciplines and the facilitation of deep learning with online communication tools.

The Institute opened their faculty development services to colleges and universities across New England, and with help from a grant from the Sloan Foundation, the Institute was expanded to include online development courses. The Online Teaching Institute has introduced over 400 faculty from across New England to online teaching and course development and has provided training and development services to all five UMass campuses as well as faculty and staff from the region's community, state and private colleges.

In 2003, 93% of faculty participating in the training program indicated the program provided them with the skills and understanding needed to develop and teach online. Over 90% of the UMass Lowell faculty who participated in the Institute training program went on to develop and teach at least one online course, 97% of these faculty also indicated they will develop and teach another online course at UMass Lowell. A review of online course teaching assignments confirms that 95% of online faculty continue to teach in subsequent semesters.

Cost effectiveness

Currently, online student enrollments and revenues account for approximately 30% of the Division's enrollments and income. Several templates to assess cost effectiveness in relationship to access and learning effectiveness have been offered in various Sloan C publications [17]. Similarly, UML now has a robust system for monitoring and assessing our capacity to generate new income for the campus and this year exceeded the campus FY 2006 targets three years ahead of schedule. As a side benefit, the program has also contributed approximately $500,000 per year in faculty development in online education, positioning the faculty to keep pace with cutting edge technologies and constantly to seek the best of online education. In addition, the online education program has paid for the development of the technical infrastructure that allows faculty to integrate the web, discussion forums and chat into their online or face to face course.

V. SUMMARY

The explosive growth of online education over the past decade has presented higher education with challenging questions regarding its feasibility as an educational medium. As a result, online education had to enter the assessment arena earlier and more intensely than its traditional, face to face counterpart. As can be seen from the study above, online education has greatly benefited from the imposition of this rigorous assessment requirement, leading to significant improvements in both the process of developing online courses, faculty and programs as well as the overall quality of online courses and programs. True to the Transformative Assessment Process, those practices which have been established as best practices in online education after several years of assessment are now being mainstreamed into our institution and higher education in general. If this trend continues, all students may benefit from the rigorous assessment initially focused on online education.

We hope that the framework created by using the TAP Assessment Rubric with the Sloan-C pillars provides others with a map of how to proceed in what can appear to be a daunting undertaking. Still, significant challenges lie ahead in this important work. This assessment effort will have to put greater emphasis on assessment of student learning outcomes if we are to achieve a truly transformative assessment program. Also, as we delve deeper into assessment of student learning, we will undoubtedly encounter challenges and limitations with the technology and our ability to maximize its potential. As outlined above, we have initiated several projects this year that will move this agenda forward for the online education program; however, our capacity to mainstream these efforts is yet untested.

Despite these challenges, we are excited about the wealth of information about student learning that online education brings. New opportunities exist within emerging technologies and evolving pedagogies to improve the teaching and learning dynamic in higher education significantly. Already we have yielded tremendous evidence that online learners invest more time interacting with faculty, each other and course content than in face to face courses. We know that faculty can shift their roles from lecturers to facilitators in the online classroom and improve student learning as a result. Most importantly, we now have access to more data on student learning than ever before; our challenge is to identify what questions are important to bring about continuous improvement in programs and student learning.

Clearly, achieving a high quality, transformative assessment program takes time, patience and diligence on the part of faculty and administrators. As Angelo suggests in his article, *Doing Assessment As if Learning Matters Most,* institutions that foster a shared trust, shared motivation, shared language and shared guidelines have the optimum conditions for moving into transformative assessment [3]. We hope that this case study motivates other academics to take a new look at assessment as an opportunity to build a learning community characterized by trust and a capacity to continuously improve the way in which faculty teach and students learn.

VI. REFERENCES

1. **American Association for Higher Education Assessment Forum.** 9 Principles of Good Practice for Assessing Student Learning, http://www.aahe.org/assessment/principl.htm. Available online 8/28/03.
2. **Palomba, C. and Banta T.** *Assessment Essentials*, San Francisco: Jossey-Bass, 1999.
3. **Angelo, T.** Doing Assessment as if Learning Matters Most, *AAHE Bulletin*, May 1999, http://www.aahebulletin.com/public/archive/angelomay99.asp?.pf=1.
4. **North Central Association of Colleges and Schools, Higher Learning Commission.** *Levels of Implementation*, http://www.ncahigherlearningcommission.org/resources/assessment/index.html. Available online 8/28/03.
5. **National Learning Infrastructure Initiative.** Transformative Assessment Systems, http://www.educause.edu/nlii/keythemes/transformative.asp. Available online 8/28/03.
6. **U.S. Department of Education.** National Center for Education Statistics. *Distance Education at Degree-Granting Postsecondary Institutions: 2000–2001,* NCES 2003-017, by Tiffany Waits and Laurie Lewis. Project Officer: Bernard Greene. Washington, DC: 2003.
7. **Mayadas, F., Bourne, J. and Moore, J. C.,** Introduction. In: Bourne, J. and Moore, J. C. (Eds.). *Elements of Quality Online Education, Vol. 3,* 7–12. Needham, MA: Sloan-C, 2002.
8. **Moloney, J. and Tello, S.** Principles for Building Success in Online Education. *Syllabus* 16(7): 15–17, Feb. 2003.
9. **Banta, T., Lund J., Black, K. and Oblander, F.** *Assessment in Practice.* San Francisco: Jossey-Bass Publishers, 1996.
10. **Russell, T.** The "No Significant Difference Phenomena" website. http://teleeducation.nb.ca/nosignificantdifference. Available online 8/28/03.
11. **Swan, K.** Learning Effectiveness: What the Research Tells Us. In: Bourne, J. and Moore, J. C. (Eds.). *Elements of Quality Online Education: Practice and Direction, Vol. 4,* 13–45. Needham, MA: Sloan-C, 2003.
12. **Moore, J. C.** *Elements of Quality: The Sloan-C Framework.* Needham, MA: Sloan-C, 2002.
13. **Spooner, F., Jordan, L., Agozzine, B. and Spooner, M.** Student Ratings of Instruction in Distance Learning and On-Campus Classes. *Journal of Educational Research* 92(3): 132–141, 1999.
14. **Verduin, J. R. and Clark, T.** *Distance Education: The Foundations of Effective Practice.* San Franciso: Jossey-Bass Publishers, 1991.
15. **Wideman, H. and Owston, R. D.** Internet-Based Courses at Atkinson College: An Initial Assessment. *Technical Report 99-1*, York University, 1991. http://www.edu.yorku.ca/csce/tech99-1.html. Available online 8/28/03.
16. **Tello, S.** An Analysis of the Relationship between Instructional Interaction and Student Persistence In Online Education. Doctoral Dissertation: Graduate School of Education, University of Massachusetts Lowell, 2002.
17. **Bishop, T. and Schweber, C.** Linking Quality and Cost, In: Bourne, J. and Moore, J. C. (Eds.), *Elements of Quality Online Education, Vol. 3,* 45–58. Needham, MA: Sloan-C, 2002.

VII. ABOUT THE AUTHORS

Jacqueline Moloney has been actively involved in curriculum and instructional innovation in higher education for the past fifteen years. In addition to spearheading the development of a comprehensive student learning center and faculty development center, Dr. Moloney led the successful redesign of Lowell's Division of Continuing Studies, Corporate and Distance Education. Under her leadership, the Division developed one of the region's largest online education programs which has received national acknowledgement and three Sloan Grants for program and faculty development. In addition, she has crafted numerous innovative partnerships with business and industry that have yielded impressive results for the Lowell campus.

As an active member of the Sloan Consortium for of Asynchronous Learning Networks, Dr. Moloney has served as a contributor to the national dialogue on the emergence of online learning programs. In addition to consulting with numerous private and public institutions on faculty and student development, Dr. Moloney assisted in the creation of UMassOnline, a system-wide effort to expand its online programs. Dr. Moloney has authored articles on the use of technologies in the classroom; cross-disciplinary approaches to curriculum reform; and the organizational reform of higher education.

Steve Tello received his Doctorate of Education in Leadership in Schooling from the Graduate School of Education, University of Massachusetts Lowell in 2002 and is Associate Director of Continuing Studies, Corporate and Distance Education at UML. Dr. Tello oversees the operation and development of the campus' online program. Dr. Tello has extensive experience in the development and delivery of technology training and education for both college and K–12 faculty. Dr. Tello has taught as an adjunct for the University's Multimedia Certificate program and recently developed the UML Online Teaching Institute to provide higher education faculty with an online training on teaching online.

Dr. Tello is affiliated with the University Continuing Education Association, Association for the Advancement of Computers in Education, and Association for Supervision and Curriculum Development and with Sloan-C. He has authored numerous articles on online education, and served as a consultant to several colleges and educational organizations seeking to develop online education and faculty development programs.

Contact: Jacqueline Moloney

Steven Tello

Continuing, Corporate and Distance Education

University of Massachusetts Lowell

One University Ave.

Lowell, MA 01854

978-934-2262

978-934-4064

Jacqueline_Moloney@uml.edu

Steven_Tello@uml.edu

ASSESSMENT, ONLINE LEARNING AND A FACULTY PERSPECTIVE: A COURSE CASE STUDY

Anthony G. Picciano
Hunter College of the City University of New York

- Assessment is an ongoing process aimed at understanding and improving student learning.

- Assessment involves making our expectations explicit and public; setting appropriate criteria and high standards for learning quality.

- Assessment uses the information to document, explain, and improve performance.

- Assessment can help us focus our collective attention, examine our assumptions, and create a shared academic culture dedicated to assuring and improving the quality of higher education.

- Techniques that encourage community building and promote social presence are being more extensively integrated into the pedagogy.

I. INTRODUCTION

In 2000–2001, the faculty in the graduate program in education administration and supervision at Hunter College undertook a review of the program in order to comply with anticipated New York State Education Department re-certification requirements. As part of this review, the faculty examined all aspects of the program including admission requirements, curriculum and course offerings, and exit criteria. The review also included an attempt to formalize the assessment of the program components with each faculty member taking responsibility for a course(s). This case study describes the assessment of one online course, Contemporary Issues in Education Administration, in the program.

Assessment has been defined in a number of ways. The AAHE conducts an Assessment Forum which continually reviews the state of assessment in American higher education. In 1995, Thomas Angelo, then director of the AAHE Assessment Forum, undertook the responsibility for defining or redefining the definition of assessment. Using an inclusive process, he provided drafts of definitions and sought recommendations and clarifications from participants in the Forum. The following definition of assessment emerged:

> *Assessment* is an ongoing process aimed at understanding and improving student learning. It involves making our expectations explicit and public; setting appropriate criteria and high standards for learning quality; systematically gathering, analyzing, and interpreting evidence to determine how well performance matches those expectations and standards; and using the resulting information to document, explain, and improve performance. When it is embedded effectively within larger institutional systems, assessment can help us focus our collective attention, examine our assumptions, and create a shared academic culture dedicated to assuring and improving the quality of higher education. [1]

Other organizations and individuals have provided variations of this definition, however, fundamental to most of them, is the setting of academic goals, the collection of data, and the analysis of the data to improve student learning. These elements of the definition serve as an appropriate framework for this case study.

II. THE PROGRAM AND COURSE

The education administration and supervision program at Hunter College is a thirty-credit graduate program leading to New York State certification as a school administrator. New York State requires a minimum of eighteen graduate credits plus an internship. The program at Hunter requires twenty-four credits (eight courses) plus a six-credit internship. Web-based courses have been offered in this program since 1997, and students can complete a majority of the coursework for the program online. Almost all students take one or more online courses. A small number take a majority of their courses online. For the past ten years, the program has maintained an enrollment of 100 to 125 students, almost all of whom are part-time. Because of funding and a desire to ensure academic quality, enrollment in the program has been limited.

As a result of the review of the program which commenced in 2000–2001, a number of changes were made which were designed to improve its overall quality. For example, admission criteria were changed and expanded.

Prior to the review, the admission criteria were:

- satisfactory completion of a master's degree;
- achievement of a 3.00 grade point average or higher in undergraduate and graduate coursework;
- three years of experience as a teacher, counselor, social worker, or other professional education
- position in a K–12 setting;
- three letters of reference; and
- a writing sample.

After the review, the admission criteria included all of the above plus:

- an in-person simulation activity designed to determine how applicants can function/behave in group decision making;
- the viewing of a video of lesson during which applicants write recommendations/suggestions for improving the lesson; and
- a one-on-one interview with a faculty member and/or practicing school administrator.

Faculty members as well as practicing school administrators participate in and score each of the new activities. An average of the scores is taken and an applicant must achieve a 65 or higher to be admitted into the program. Since implementing the new admissions criteria, approximately 50 percent of the applicants are accepted into the program compared to 80 percent using the previous criteria.

The program also adopted national standards prepared by the Interstate School Leaders Licensure Consortium (ISLLC) as the framework for the curriculum. Individual course objectives were aligned to meet these standards. In addition, students are required to prepare a contract specifying performance-based activities that they will complete within each of six specified standards. Students are required to maintain a portfolio of the activities and present it before a panel of faculty and New York City practicing administrators as part of an oral exit interview

For individual courses, faculty shared the responsibility of defining objectives and methods for assessment. The course, Administration and Supervision (ADSUP) 722—Issues in Contemporary Education Administration, is the subject of this case study. This course is designed to provide a forum for the presentation and discussion of issues in contemporary education administration. Thirteen contemporary issues in education such as charter schools, teacher unionization, bilingual education, and special education form the content of the course. The course is structured around readings and a weekly discussion which aims to engage the students in active discourse on the issues. In addition, written assignments designed to put the student in the position of an administrator making a decision or recommending a course of action are required.

In Fall 2001, a completely asynchronous model (ALN) was used for delivering this course via a course Web site utilizing the BlackBoard course management system (CMS). To connect to the course Web site, most students used a commercial Internet and e-mail provider such as America Online or Compuserve in their homes. Students also used Internet facilities available in their schools. The Web site for the course included a syllabus, reading assignments, weekly discussion topics and questions, supplementary reading material, and related links. These materials were always available and served as the organizational anchors for the course. Each topic was organized for an asynchronous discussion on an electronic discussion board during a specific week and was based on assigned readings and case studies. Four students were selected each week to work with the instructor as discussion facilitators. The use of students as facilitators was designed to encourage them to be contributors to and not simply receivers of learning activities. Once the discussion of a topic commenced on Sunday morning, any student could contribute to the discussion, ask a question of another student or of the instructor. At the end of the week's discussion, on the following Saturday, the instructor summarized the topic, added additional notes and comments, and posted these to the Web site for access by the entire class.

The major learning objectives of this course were:

- to develop and/or add to the student's knowledge base regarding contemporary issues in education administration;
- to provide future administrators with an appreciation of differences in points of view and an ability to approach and resolve issues that can be divisive in a school or community.

In addition, a pedagogical objective was to develop an active, participatory, high-quality online learning environment.

To determine the achievement of these objectives, multiple assessment techniques were used:

1. Data on student perceptions of interaction and learning were collected through a student satisfaction survey conducted at the end of the course.
2. Student participation in the course as well as participation as discussion facilitators was graded.
3. A written examination was designed to assess knowledge of the course content based on the thirteen issues explored during the semester. An objective, multiple choice question and answer format was used.
4. Three written assignments were designed to assess students' ability to formulate and to express their opinions on issues which they might face as school administrators. One of these assignments (see Appendix) was a simulation that required the students to put themselves in the position of a newly appointed principal considering implementation of a new, controversial academic program. To grade this assignment, a rubric was develop to identify phrases and concepts to determine student abilities to integrate multiple perspectives and differing points of view in deciding whether and how to implement the academic program.

III. COURSE ASSESSMENT

A. Basic Assessments

While grades and their derivatives such as grade point averages are common student performance measures, they can be problematic particularly in light of the homogeneity of the student body and concerns about issues such as grade inflation. At Harvard University, for example, the Boston Globe reported that "48.5 percent of the grades last year [2000] were A's and A-minuses, B grades were 45 percent...Grades in the three C categories [were] 4.9 percent... D's and failing grades accounted for less than 1 percent each" [2]. Susan Pedersen, Harvard's dean of undergraduate education, commented that with such a narrow range of effective grades available [essentially, B, B+, A-, and A], faculty find it difficult to distinguish adequately work of differing quality [2]. All of the students in the Hunter College's education administration and supervision program are full-time teachers, who write well, do well on tests, and are highly motivated. Of twenty three students enrolled in ADSUP 722 in Fall 2001, twenty students received grades of A, and three received grades of B. There were no course withdrawals or drop-outs.

To assess better the learning outcomes in this course, a combination of assessment indicators concentrating on student interaction and participation, student perception of learning mastery of content (the written examination), and ability to integrate multiple perspectives into resolution of an issue (written assignments) were used. Additional analyses were also performed in order to examine relationships of these indicators to each other in an online learning environment.

Questions 9E and 9F (see Appendix) on the student satisfaction survey referred to the quality and quantity of their learning experiences compared to traditional courses. Responses were formatted in a Likert scale with values ranging from 1–5 (Decreased - Somewhat Decreased - No Change - Somewhat Increased - Increased). The responses to these questions were scored and combined into an overall perception of student learning that ranged from 1 to 5. The mean for all students on this perception of learning was 4.32 (Somewhat Increased plus).

Questions 9A through 9D (see Appendix) compared the amount and quality of interactions with students and with the instructor compared to traditional courses. Responses were formatted in a Likert scale with values ranging from 1–5 (Decreased - Somewhat Decreased - No Change - Somewhat Increased - Increased). The responses to these questions were scored and combined into an overall perception of student interaction that ranged from 1 to 5. The mean for all students on this perception of interaction was 4.00 (Somewhat Increased).

In addition to student perceptions of interaction, data were collected on actual interaction through the number of student postings to the discussion board (see Figure 1). The postings included in this count were substantive comments or questions made to the discussion board and excluded one line "me too" type of postings and social messages. The number of total student weekly postings for the semester ranged from a low of 21 to a high of 101 with a mean of 42.26 or approximately 3 postings per student per week (42.26 / 14 weeks). Students were not required to make a particular number of postings to the discussion board each week. However, students were informed that part of the grade for the course would be based on participation in these discussions.

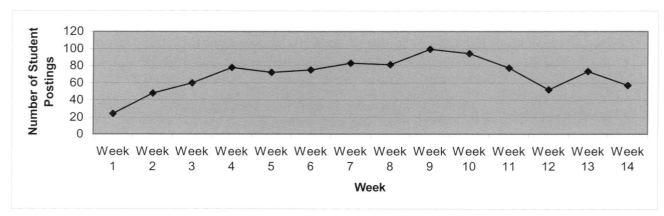

Figure 1. Total Student Postings per Week

The examination was administered at the end of the semester and consisted of multiple choice questions designed to assess mastery of content. An example of a question on the examination is:

16S. What is perhaps the greatest appeal of charter schools?
  a. more funding for all schools
  b. vehicles to use statewide curriculum
  c. freedom from most bureaucratic procedures and oversight
  d. children-centered learning
  e. none of the above

For this class, the mean score on this examination was 85.4. This assessment is straight forward and uses a standard technique (testing) to examine student's mastery of the content.

The written assignment (see Appendix) was a case study simulation that placed students in the position of a newly appointed principal considering the implementation of a controversial inclusion (special education) program. In addition to a conventional grade for this assignment, a rubric was developed to determine student willingness and ability to integrate multiple perspectives and differing points of view into the decision making process. The scoring rubric was developed as follows:

  5   Points for Each Perspective (Society, General Education Teachers, Special Education Teachers, Parents, Students) Mentioned.
  10 Points for Mentioning Pros AND Cons
  3   Points for Each Pro and
  3   Points for Each Con

The scoring for the rubric was open-ended and not based on a 100 point system. For this class, the mean score on the rubric portion of the written assignment was a 70.0. A passing score would be the equivalent of 53 and an outstanding score would be 80 or above. 19 of the 23 students in the class scored 53 or higher; 9 scored 80 or higher, and 4 scored less than 53. In examining these scores, the vast majority of the students were willing and able to integrate multiple perspectives into their decision making processes.

B. Relating Assessment Indicators to Each Other

While each of the indicators provided valuable information regarding student learning in this course, integrating them and looking at their relationships to each other can provide further insight into student outcomes.

In performing a simple correlation on two variables (perception of learning and perception of interaction), the resulting coefficient was positive (.6732) and statistically significant (.05 level).

These results indicated that there was a strong, positive relationship between student perceptions of their interaction in the course and their perceptions of the quality and quantity of their learning. These results are similar to studies conducted on larger populations [3, 4].

In performing a correlation on actual student postings and actual student performance scores on the examination and the score of the written assignment, the results were positive at .1318 and .4577 but not statistically significant (.05 level). While positive, these correlations especially on the exam were somewhat weaker than the coefficient (.6732) for student perceptions of their interaction and their learning.

In pursuing this relationship, the data on interaction were sorted by the number of student postings and divided into thirds representing low interaction, moderate interaction, and high interaction student groups. Mean scores on the exam and on the written assignment were then calculated for each group (see Table 1).

	Mean	Mean (Rubric/Multiple Perspective)
Interaction Group	**Exam Score**	**Written Assignment Score**
Low	85.0	63.7
Moderate	85.7	64.4
High	85.6	81.1

Table 1. Mean Student Scores on Exam and Written Assignment Controlling for Interaction Group (N=23)

The data in Table 1 indicate that there were no differences among the three interaction groups in terms of actual performance on the examination. On the written assignment, the high interaction group scored significantly higher than the low and moderate interaction groups. These data indicate that actual student interaction as measured by the number of postings on the discussion board had no relationship to performance on the examination but did have a relationship to performance on the written assignment.

VI. DISCUSSION AND CONCLUSIONS

As indicated earlier in this paper, assessment should be used to improve programs and courses. For the course (ADSUP 722 — Contemporary Issues in Education Administration), the assessment data are being used to refine course delivery and assignments. The key word here is "refine." Assessment of a course provides insights into taking small steps or refinements for improving student learning. Rare is the case that a major overhaul or change to a course is made because of a semester's assessment. Assessment indicators are collected over time and are used to smooth out a course more so than to tear it down and rebuild it. Furthermore, assessment indicators may not always provide conclusive evidence for making changes but suggest possible directions that faculty must weigh and consider in developing course syllabi and pedagogical techniques.

The data in Table 1 indicated that there were not differences among the three (low, moderate, high) interaction groups in terms of actual performance on the examination. Speculation regarding this phenomenon was in order. For instance, it was likely that all students including the low interaction group, studied for the examination. The questions on the examination were derived mostly from the readings, the weekly discussions and instructor notes which were available online. The low interaction students may have read much of the material posted during the weekly discussion but simply chose not to post a comment. This is not unlike the student in a regular face-to-face class who listens attentively but does not raise his or her hand and still does well on a test or exam.

On the written assignment, the high interaction group scored significantly higher than the low and moderate interaction groups which scored about the same. The written assignment was based on a case study/simulation designed to determine students' ability to integrate multiple perspectives and differing points of view into decision making and was similar to situations presented on the weekly discussion board. Students posted their comments and opinions by building upon and taking into consideration what already had been posted by their colleagues in the class. Hence, a relationship, perhaps causal, might exist between extensive interaction on a discussion board and a positive outcome on the case study/simulation. On the other hand, students in the high interaction group might naturally be sensitive to differing points of view. Whether these students already possessed these abilities and they were honed as part of the weekly discussion board activities is difficult to determine. The results of the assessment were nevertheless encouraging.

As a result of these findings, faculty planning the online components of this course will make provisions to ensure that student interaction remains high. Techniques that encourage community building and promote social presence are being more extensively integrated into the pedagogy. Faculty are also looking more carefully at the examination and the written assignments. The objective examination (mastery of content) may not be the most appropriate technique for assessment. Another form of examination (e.g., essay) designed to integrate course objectives (mastery of content and appreciation for differing points of view) is being considered.

At the time of this writing, the New York State Education had just issued (July 2003) its guidelines for re-certification of all education administration and supervision programs. All programs must resubmit their program requirements including assessment plans and criteria in order to be re-certified by May 2004. The guidelines specifically include language that indicates that program performance must be assessed and subject to a programmatic review by a professional education accrediting organization and/or by the New York State Board of Regents. A new statewide test will also be developed within the next year which all candidates for certification as school administrators must pass. The faculty in the administration and supervision program at Hunter College are less anxious than they might have been had they not begun reviewing their program including assessment several years ago. It is hoped that this case study provides insights to faculty facing similar situations.

VII. APPENDICES

A. Student Evaluation of ADSUP 722 — Fall 2001

Name: _____   Date: _____

1. Number of Credits Completed in this Program: _____

2. Age: _____

3. Gender:
   Female___ Male___

4. I would rate my level of computer expertise as:
   Novice_____ Intermediate_____ Expert_____

5. Where did you most frequently use a computer for this course?
   Home___ Work___ Other ___ If other, specify: _____

6. How easy/difficult was it for you to use technology to participate in this course?
   Easy___ Somewhat Easy ___ Somewhat Difficult ___ Difficult___

7. How would you rate your overall educational experience in taking this course?
   Poor___ Satisfactory___ Good___ Very Good___ Excellent___

8. Would you take another Internet (asynchronous learning) course if offered?
   No___ Maybe___ Definitely ____

For questions 9A through 9H, in comparison to traditional classroom instruction, in this course

	Somewhat Increased	Increased	No Change	Somewhat Decreased	Decreased
9A. The amount of interaction with other students					
9B. The quality of interaction with other students					
9C. The amount of interaction with the instructor					
9D. The quality of interaction with the instructor					
9E. The quantity of your learning experience					
9F. The quality of your learning experience					
9G. The motivation to participate in class activities					
9H. Your familiarity with computer technology					

10A. On average, regardless of whether you posted a message or not, how often did you access the course Web site each week?
   a. once a week
   b. twice a week

c. three times a week
d. four times a week
e. five or more times a week

10B. On average, how often did you post a message to the Discussion Board each week?
   a. once a week
   b. twice a week
   c. three times a week
   d. four times a week
   e. five or more times a week

11. Would you rate your experiences to date with this course as
   Successful____ Not Successful____

   If successful, what aspect of the course most contributed to its success:

   _____
   _____
   _____
   _____

   If not successful, what aspect of the course was most problematic:

   _____
   _____
   _____
   _____

12. Should the Hunter College ADSUP Program offer more Internet (asynchronous learning) courses?
   Yes___ No____

   If yes, because:

   _____
   _____
   _____
   _____

   If no, because:

   _____
   _____
   _____
   _____

13. I have the following suggestions for improving this course:

_____

_____

_____

_____

14. To provide materials and to communicate online, software system called BlackBoard was used. Can you please rate how easy/difficult it was for you to use the BlackBoard software?

Easy____ Somewhat Easy ____ Somewhat Difficult ____ Difficult____

15. During this course, you had several tools available to you at the Course Web site for accessing information and for communicating with colleagues and the instructor. Please rate the following:

	Not Used	Somewhat Important	Important	Very Important	Critically Important
15A. Course Information					
15B. Course Documents					
15C. Weekly Summaries					
15D. Discussion Board					
15E. Online Library Resources					
15F. Digital Drop Box					
15G. Other					

B. Written Assignment

You have just been appointed principal of P.S. 123. You have been requested by the superintendent in your district to consider adopting an inclusion program that would mainstream into regular classes most special education students currently housed at P.S. 123. Inclusion programs are broadly defined as combining special and regular education students in the same classes. Class size is currently 30 students for regular classes and 15 students for special education; classes will be established and carefully monitored not to exceed 23 students. Each class will be team-taught with a regular teacher and a special education teacher. In discussions with the teaching staff, there is ambivalence at best and possibly hostility to the proposal. Regular teachers have indicated that the special education students will be too disruptive. Special education teachers are concerned that the needs of the special education students will be compromised in larger integrated (regular and special education students) classes.

Prepare a three-page memorandum outlining your position on this matter for the superintendent. Identify the strengths and weaknesses of the inclusion program based on the information provided above and any other information that you deem helpful. Conclude your paper with a well-developed argument/decision for accepting or rejecting the proposal.

VIII. ACKNOWLEDGEMENTS

The author is grateful to Elaine Bowden who reviewed the manuscript and offered valuable suggestions both to its form and substance.

IX. REFERENCES

1. **Angelo, T**. Definitions of Assessment. AAHE Assessment Forum, 1995. http://www.aahe.org/assessment/assess_faq.htm#define.
2. **Healy, P.** Harvard Figures Show Most of its Grades are A's or B's. *The Boston Globe*, p. B6, November 21, 2001.
3. **Shea, P., Fredericksen, E., Pickett, A., Pelz, W., and Swan., K.** Measures of Learning Effectiveness in the SUNY Learning Network. Paper presented at the 2000 Sloan Summer Workshop on Asynchronous Learning Networks in *Online Education Volume 2, Proceedings of the 2000 Sloan Summer Workshop on Asynchronous Learning Networks*, J. Bourne and J. C. Moore, Eds. Needham, MA: Sloan-C, 2000.
4. **Dziuban, C. and Moskal, P.** Emerging Research Issues in Distributed Learning. Orlando, FL: Paper delivered at the 7th Sloan-C International Conference on Asynchronous Learning Networks, 2001.

X. ABOUT THE AUTHOR

Anthony Picciano is a professor in the Education Administration and Supervision Program in the School of Education at Hunter College. His teaching specializations include educational technology, organization theory, and research methods. He also currently serves on the Board of Directors for the Sloan Consortium of Colleges and Universities.

He has been involved with a number of major grants from the National Science Foundation, the Alfred P. Sloan Foundation, the US Department of Education, and IBM. He has collaborated with The American Social History Project and Center for Media and Learning at CUNY on a number of instructional multimedia projects dealing with subjects such as Irish immigration in the 1850s, women's rights and labor issues at the turn of the century, and school integration in the 1950s. Currently he is a co-principal investigator of the New York City Schools Leadership Development Initiative Grant ($3.3 million) from the United States Department of Education to develop new models for preparing and supporting school leaders in New York City Public Schools. This is a collaborative project involving the New York City Department of Education, Hunter College Administration and Supervision Program, New Visions for New Schools, and New Leaders for New Schools, 2002–2005.

Dr. Picciano has served as a consultant for a variety of public and private organizations including the New York City Board of Education, the New York State Department of Education, Commission on Higher Education/Middle States Association of Colleges and Universities, the US Coast Guard, and CITICORP. He is the author of five books including *Educational Leadership and Planning for Technology, 3rd Edition* (Prentice-Hall, 2002) and Distance *Learning: Making Connections across Virtual Space and Time* (Prentice-Hall, 2001). His most recent book, *The Educational Research Primer* (Continuum) will be available in Spring 2004. His articles on educational technology have appeared in journals such as the *Journal of Asynchronous Learning Networks, Journal of Educational Multimedia and Hypermedia, Computers in the Schools, The Urban Review, Equity and Choice*, and *EDUCOM Review*.

Contact: Anthony G. Picciano, Professor, School of Education, Hunter College of the City University of New York, 695 Park Avenue, New York, NY 10021. E-mail: anthony.picciano@hunter.cuny.edu